History Maker

John Roberts

*The man with 30 grandsons
in the Great War*

Paul Roberts

Published 2018

© Paul Roberts 2018

ISBN 978-1-5272-1546-7

Cover illustration

An original illustration of John Roberts by Devon-based Illustrator Tor Allen. Inspired by pictures of John and my father, the rustic style of this portrait captures the character of John and the contrasting landscapes which helped shape his life. It shows how John was filled with pride as his grandsons – many of whom worked on the land before volunteering to fight for King and country – went to war. The background to the portrait provides a glimpse of the stark contrast in landscapes they faced at home and on the Western Front. It features ploughed fields to represent Devon, and a silhouette of the blackened, lifeless trees found destroyed on the Great War battlefields in France and Belgium. The back cover includes a silhouette of John walking through a ploughed field. The brilliant illustration helps to bring John, a humble agricultural worker, to public attention for the first time – almost a century after his death in 1919. Tor, who was born and raised in Devon, enjoys working as an illustrator in the south of the county. She produces a wide range of work and appreciates the variety of commissions that she's asked to undertake. They often include the countryside or wildlife in some way. www.torallen.com

Typeset, printed and bound by
Short Run Press, Exeter, Devon

'They were men of Devon ... nourished among their own hills and vales, lovers of their streams and meadows and rugged shores, who died ... with a vision before their eyes of the old fields of home far away'

Words spoken by the Dean of Exeter, the Very Rev Henry Reginald Gamble, at a memorial service for Devon's war dead, held at Exeter Cathedral in June 1919

For my beautiful wife Jenny, my inspiration and eternal love

For my much-loved son David and daughter Harriet

For my grandson Conrad, who has brought
so much joy to so many

For my grandfather George Burnett Roberts, one of the 30

And for my great-great-grandfather John Roberts,
forever out of the shadows of history

CONTENTS

Part one: John, his family and astonishing happenings at home

1	An extraordinary find – a remarkable man	3
2	The magnificent seven	7
3	Patriotism – and great sacrifices	13
4	Humble life of a history maker	23
5	Three brothers marry three sisters	34
6	Devon farmers in recruitment 'war of words'	38

Part two: The grandsons who did not come home

7	The day death visited John and his family	51
8	Jack – baptism of fire on the Western Front ends in tragedy	55
9	Albert – cut down at Battle of Loos	67
10	Sam – killed on first day of Battle of the Somme	81
11	John Francis 'Frank' – shelled while enjoying a cup of tea	96
12	William Henry – struck down by heart disease in Mesopotamian desert	109
13	Walter – killed just 52 days before the war ends	124
14	Sidney – fatally wounded in Battle of Langemarck	135

Part three: The grandsons who survived

15   Archie – survivor of two of the greatest ever cavalry charges   153

16   Frank – shot in the head in fierce fighting in Palestine   171

17   John Francis Bryant – how he faced 70 days of hell on the Somme   185

18   George – artillery veteran of two wars   197

19   William John – naval stoker who survived torpedo attack   207

20   Thomas – twice saved from fighting in the war   214

21   George Burnett – one of the great unsung heroes of the war   223

22   Ben – the only one of three brothers to come home   232

23   Samuel and Sidney – new tragedy strikes 20 years after the war   237

24   Archie, Harry and Walter – the Sandford survivors   241

Part four: The grandsons-in-law who survived – and a great nephew killed in action

25   Wilfred Banting – wounded in courageous attack near Kut   249

26   William Western – a blacksmith in huge ASC 'tin town'   254

27   William James – killed in First Battle of Ypres   260

Part five: Devon's tributes to its fallen heroes

28   Memorial to thousands who died in the war   269

29   How cities, towns and villages honoured their war dead   273

Acknowledgements   279

Sources   285

Part One

JOHN, HIS FAMILY AND ASTONISHING HAPPENINGS AT HOME

1

AN EXTRAORDINARY FIND —
A REMARKABLE MAN

It was an extraordinary family sacrifice – told in just 11 words. As a tidal wave of patriotism swept the country during the Great War, a picture of a proud grandfather, sporting majestic bushy sideburns and a beard, and wearing a bowler hat, was published in a local newspaper with the understated caption: 'Mr John Roberts, of Witheridge, has 30 grandsons on active service.'

I was astonished and curious. It seemed almost impossible to believe that one man living in the heart of rural Devonshire could have so many grandchildren 'fighting for King and country'. I was eager to know more about him and his family, and to find out as much as I could about the grandsons who had gone to war.

The truth could not have been more remarkable.

I had discovered the grainy old picture of John by pure chance, on an unidentified newspaper cutting on the Witheridge Historical Archive. I was hugely impressed by his family's wartime service. But I was also intrigued because he shared my surname, and his distinctive eyes, bushy eyebrows and impressive whiskers reminded me so much of my father.

I visited John's home village in Devon but could find no trace of him or his family. I walked through the streets, talked to residents and checked the gravestones in the churchyard. But there were no memorials to John. I discovered just one possible connection – an A Roberts, named on the local war memorial as one of 17 men from the parish who had given their lives in the Great War.

Birth, wedding and death certificates, and checks of numerous Census returns, village, school and parish records confirmed that John, a humble agricultural worker, who had 15 children, almost 100 grandchildren and who lived to the grand old age of 90, was a direct ancestor of mine. He was my great-great grandfather.

The A Roberts on the war memorial turned out to be one of his grandsons, Albert, who was just 19 when he died on October 3, 1915 from wounds sustained in the Battle of Loos, one of the bloodiest offensives in a war that would impact so shockingly and dramatically on every community across the country.

In just a few days, a link beyond my imagination had been established between that old picture of a smiling pensioner and a name on a war memorial. More importantly, the connection provided the inspiration to unearthing, as far as possible, the truth about John and his family's incredible and selfless contribution to the war.

In the past ten years, I have researched John's life and attempted to track down as many, if not all, of those Devon-born grandsons and to tell their stories of life, and death, at war. Seven never made it home – six being killed in action or dying from wounds in France and Flanders, and one dying from heart disease in Mesopotamia.

Those that did survive included my grandfather, George Burnett Roberts, a young farm worker who went to war in 1915. As a young man, I was given a picture of him and the shiny buttons from his uniform. I was both amazed and thrilled that he turned out to be one of John's 30 grandsons in active service.

John Roberts had one of the largest families in Devon. He had at least 96 grandchildren, all bar one born while he was alive. Some did not survive infancy. He had more than 50 grandsons, 36 of whom were believed to have been eligible to serve in the war. Many shared the same Christian name – John, Frank and Sidney, in particular – and the vast majority were farm labourers.

The losses suffered by John and his family would have been devastating. The grief they endured was experienced by countless others who had husbands, sons, sons-in-law, grandsons, nephews, cousins, friends and neighbours fighting in the war. Of the 956,000 British servicemen who died between 1914 and 1918, more than 11,600 were from Devon.

The losses in many local communities were devastating, none more so than in the small village of Zeal Monachorum in Mid-Devon. Of its 200 inhabitants, more than a third of its population – 75 in all – served in the war. All were volunteers, and at least 19 never made it home. 'Probably no other parish in the United Kingdom had more of its young men serving in proportion to its size,' *The Devon and Exeter Gazette* reported in December 1923.

More than 160 families in the county had four or more sons serving in the war. Many were personally congratulated by King George V for their patriotism. Newspapers regularly carried pictures and reports of proud fathers and sons on the front line, of multiple brothers and other relatives serving in the Army or Navy.

On March 12, 1915, *The Western Times* reported that John Roberts, 'an old-age pensioner' living at Newland Farm, Witheridge, had at that stage 'no less than 21 grandsons serving their King and country', and added: 'Surely this is good enough to be a record.' I was certainly unable to find anyone else in Devon who could match this number.

With John's serving grandsons increasing to 30 later in the war, I looked further afield to see if this number had been surpassed. I found an 84-year-old Elizabeth Spratt, of Erdington, Birmingham, who had 27 grandsons and grandsons-in-law serving in the Army, principally with the Royal Warwickshire Regiment. But none with 30 or more.

Though no stranger to tragedy in his life or experiencing family members going off to war, nothing could or would prepare John Roberts for the horrors to come in the Great War.

He, along with millions of others in Britain, would experience new depths of despair as the 'war to end all wars' unfolded across Europe and beyond.

His undoubted pride at seeing his young grandsons march off to France and other theatres of war would soon be replaced by the agony of losing them one by one, and seeing others return home injured and battle-weary, their lives changed forever. When he died on May 21, 1919 from bronchitis and 'old age', he was a broken man.

In the days after the war and up to the time of his death, he spent many long hours in all weathers on an old, ramshackle wooden bench outside his family's farmhouse at Newland Farm, remembering the grandsons who had lost their lives so gallantly, and wondering why he had been spared to live such a long life.

The picture of him published in a local newspaper heralding the 30 grandsons he had in active service came back to haunt John as the war raged on and finally ended. His smile in that photograph now seemed so inappropriate. Delight in his family's bravery had given way to a deep sense of sorrow that so many lives had been sacrificed. 'What was it all for?' he must have asked himself.

John's only joy in his last days was in spending more time with his surviving children, grandchildren and great-grandchildren. They knew him as a kind, often jolly and generous man with a warm smile. But they were aware that his demeanour frequently masked the immense sadness that blighted his final years.

When his funeral took place on May 26, 1919, a special card produced for mourners, carrying the following verse, indicated the esteem in which he was held.

Day after day we saw him fade,
And quietly sink away;
Yet often in our hearts we prayed
That he might longer stay.
He's gone, the one we loved so well,
To his eternal rest;
He's gone to Heaven we need not fear,
To be forever blessed.

2

THE MAGNIFICENT SEVEN

They were Devon's magnificent seven. The youngest was just 19. The oldest, 28. All grandsons of farm worker John Roberts, they left the green hills of home to fight in some of the bloodiest battles of the Great War.

Many of them witnessed unimaginable horrors on the Western Front in France and Belgium as they took part in major offensives at Neuve Chapelle, Aubers Ridge, Loos, the Somme and in the shadow of Germany's formidable fortress, the Hindenburg Line.

They included two sets of brothers – Sam and John Francis Roberts, of Rackenford, who went to France together in 1914, and William Henry and Walter Kingdom, of Tiverton, who served thousands of miles apart.

None of the seven made it home.

Three were killed on the battlefields of France, three died from wounds sustained in action, and one succumbed to heart disease. Their lives were lost in 1,210 days – or a period of three years, three months and 22 days – between May 1915 and September 1918.

The first to lose his life was former cattle boy John 'Jack' Roberts, of Cruwys Morchard, who died from wounds sustained at, or in the aftermath of the Battle of Aubers Ridge in northern France, on May 30, 1915, just two days before his 21st birthday.

A private in the 2nd Devons, he had been in France for just

111 days, and fought in two major British Army offensives. Jack died at Boulogne Hospital. He was buried at the Boulogne Eastern Cemetery, and is remembered on the war memorial at the Church of the Holy Cross in his home village.

Teenager Albert Roberts, who had worked on his father's farm in Witheridge and at two local rectories before going to war, died from wounds sustained in his first battle, at Loos, on October 3, 1915, just three days before his 20th birthday.

The battle was heralded as one of the most remarkable of the war. Albert, a private in the 8th Devons, had been in France for 71 days when he died at Wimereux Hospital. Buried in the town's communal cemetery, he is remembered on Witheridge War Memorial.

Sam Roberts, aged 21, was killed in action on the first day of the Battle of the Somme. He was among more than 19,200 British soldiers to die in the battle on July 1, 1916, the heaviest losses ever suffered in one day by the British Army.

He had returned to the front line after miraculously surviving being shot in the chest just before Christmas 1914. He lived to fight again because the bullet first hit a small book he kept in his breast pocket.

Sam was buried in the Devonshire Cemetery on the Somme where a defiant and poignant ten-word message *'The Devonshires held this trench, the Devonshires hold it still'* – originally carved into a wooden cross – is inscribed on a permanent memorial.

Perhaps the most famous of all cemeteries on the Western Front, it is unique in being almost exclusively devoted to a single regiment and its dead from one day of battle. A corporal in the 8th Devons, Sam is remembered on two war memorials in Rackenford.

His brother, John Francis, was killed by a shrapnel shell 71 days later, on September 9, 1916, aged 25. He too had narrowly escaped death in the previous year when shrapnel grazed his shoulder as he charged enemy lines at the Battle of Neuve Chapelle.

John Francis, a lance-corporal in the 2nd Devons, took part in one of the most extraordinary events of the war, the 'Christmas Truce' of 1914 when British and German troops stepped out of their trenches, shook hands, exchanged cigarettes and gifts ... and buried their dead.

The Western Times reported that he was 'killed instantly when having tea in the trenches'. Described by his commanding officer as 'one of the very best' soldiers, he is commemorated at Vermelles British Cemetery, near Lens, and remembered on the Rackenford War Memorials.

William Henry Kingdom died from heart disease in Sheikh Sa'ad, Mesopotamia on May 27, 1916, aged 26. A gardener before joining the Army, he was the only one of the seven to serve in the country, which today is known as Iraq.

A corporal in the 1/4th Devons, a husband, and father of two young children, he is remembered on the Basra Memorial, which honours more than 40,000 members of the Commonwealth forces who died in the war in Mesopotamia.

His brother, Walter Kingdom, was killed on September 20, 1918, in the aftermath of the Battle of Epehy, close to the Hindenburg Line – some 52 days before the Great War ended. He was just 20-years-old.

A private in the 1st Battalion of the Loyal North Lancashire Regiment, Walter is remembered on the Vis-en-Artois Memorial, near Arras, in France. It bears the names of more than 9,000 soldiers who fell between August and November 1918 and have no known grave.

Sidney Roberts, born in Cruwys Morchard and brought up on a dairy farm in the village of Washfield, died from wounds sustained in the Battle of Langemarck, part of the Third Ypres offensive, on August 17, 1917, aged 28.

A rifleman in the Queen's Westminster Rifles, he was buried at the Brandhoek New Military Cemetery (No 3) in Belgium, and is remembered on two war memorials – at Oakford, in Devon, and at nearby Dulverton, in West Somerset.

Of the 20-plus grandsons of John Roberts to survive the war, many were lucky to escape the battlefields of Europe, Gallipoli and the Middle East. At least one missed death by a whisker. Another was involved in two of the greatest cavalry charges in history.

Frank Roberts, of the 16th Devons, was shot in the head in

fierce fighting at a hilltop village close to Jerusalem in early December 1917. The eldest brother of Albert, who died in 1915, Frank recovered sufficiently from his 'serious wound' to continue service in the Army.

Archibald Roberts took part in a cavalry charge in a dust storm in Mesopotamia in 1917 – a death ride matching the bravery of the soldiers who took part in the legendary Charge of the Light Brigade in the Crimean War more than 60 years earlier.

A private in the 13th Hussars, he also took part in a heroic attack at Hadraniya in October 1918 when his regiment not only charged their enemy in the face of heavy gun fire across open sands, but climbed a steep cliff to fight on foot with rifles and bayonets.

Archibald, or 'Archie' as he was known, was a brother of Sidney, who died in 1917. Another brother, infantryman John Francis Bryant Roberts fought in some of the bloodiest battles on the Somme in 1916, including the attacks on Mametz and Delville Wood and a remarkably bold and courageous assault on the village of Ginchy.

George Henry Roberts had the rare distinction of serving in two wars – the second Boer War in South Africa and the 1914–18 War. The veteran soldier, who joined the Royal Artillery in 1899, survived one of the greatest bombardments of the war, at Vimy Ridge in France in 1916, when German gunners fired 70,000 shells deep into British defences, killing and maiming hundreds of soldiers.

William John Roberts, a stoker on *HMS King Alfred*, survived a torpedo attack on the ship in April 1918 as she was close to completing a journey across the Atlantic, convoying food ships from Halifax in Nova Scotia, Canada to Glasgow.

Born in Bolham, near Tiverton, he may well have been the only one of John Roberts' grandsons to have served in the Royal Navy during the Great War. He joined eight days after his 18th birthday, in 1917.

George Burnett Roberts – my grandfather – was in the Army Service Corps, the unsung heroes of the Great War. He was just 17 when he left his farm job in Devon to become a horse transport driver on the Western Front.

Also among John Roberts's grandsons to serve King and country were:

- Thomas Roberts – brother of Albert and Frank, of Witheridge – who missed the war not once, but twice.

- Samuel and Sidney Roberts – brothers of Jack, who died in 1915.

- William Ben Roberts – brother of Sam and John Francis (known as Frank), who both died in 1916.

- Archibald 'Archie' Roberts – a local preacher in Sandford, near Crediton – and his brothers Henry 'Harry' and Walter.

The stories of those who died and survived are told here for the first time. They reveal how ordinary men, born and raised in rural Devonshire, went on to achieve extraordinary things in exceptional times.

In all, after more than ten years of painstaking research, I have traced 20 of John's grandsons who went to war. Sadly, the others may never be identified because of a lack of information about their service.

Two of John's grandsons-in-law also served in the war – blacksmith William Western, who served in the Army Service Corps, and gardener Wilfred Banting, of the 1/4th Devons, who survived an attack on Turkish trenches in Mesopotamia in February 1917.

John's great nephew, Sergeant William James Roberts, of the Coldstream Guards, was killed in the First Battle of Ypres in October 1914. His family lived at the farm where I grew up – Farthing Park, in Morchard Bishop, Devon.

Their stories are also revealed here.

The losses endured by John and his family were among the greatest of the war. But this book also includes an account of many other Devon families who had up to nine sons as well as multiple grandsons and other relatives serving their King and country.

The controversy that raged as farmers and their sons became

caught up in a bitter and divisive war of words at home over recruitment to the Armed Forces – and exemption from war service when conscription was introduced in 1916 – is examined.

How Devon paid a magnificent tribute to its fallen, with hundreds of city, town and village memorials, ranging from imposing granite crosses to stained glass windows, clock towers, village halls and institutes, completes the narrative.

3

PATRIOTISM — AND GREAT SACRIFICES

Was John Roberts a record breaker? Did he have more grandsons in the war than anyone else in Devon, or in Great Britain? Perhaps we can never be certain. What I can be sure of is that in all my researches in the past ten years, I have not found anyone else who had 30 or more grandsons serving King and country.

His family's contribution to the war effort was phenomenal to say the least, a remarkable example of the patriotism sweeping across the nation. But the years of fighting on the Western Front and in the Middle East would come at a terrible price for John – and for thousands of families in his home county.

Extraordinary instances of unwavering flag-waving loyalty emerged across Devon in the early years of the war. Over a number of weeks in February and March 1915, *The Devon and Exeter Gazette* published a series of lists of patriotic families who had four or more sons, and other relatives, serving in the Army and Navy.

The Western Times in November 1915, reporting on the death of Mrs Susan Alford, of Bondleigh, near North Tawton, revealed that she had had 16 grandsons in the Armed Forces, one of whom had been killed. Eight were the sons of one daughter, with many serving in the Navy or as bombardiers in the Royal Field Artillery.

In 1917, the same newspaper carried a picture of, and report on, Private and Mrs W Heard, of Cheriton Bishop who, between them, had 15 brothers serving in the war. The couple's two families had nearly 50 relatives 'doing their bit' said the newspaper which described their contribution to the war campaign as 'splendid' and 'remarkable'.

In 1915, Arthur Cotton, of Brookdale Cottage, Dawlish had 24 relatives, including four sons, in the forces. Mr and Mrs John Shaddick, of Green Lane, Barnstaple, had 24 relatives, six sons, three sons-in-law and 15 nephews, serving. And the Hewett family, of Ivy Cottage, Chelston, Torquay, had 17 relatives, including five sons and ten nephews, in the Navy and other Armed Forces.

The entire Anderson-Morshead family from Salcombe Regis, near Sidmouth dedicated their lives to the war effort. The father was in the Home Defence Brigade, the mother and daughter were working in temporary hospitals in Topsham and Exeter and four officer sons were serving on the front line, in India or at home.

Mrs B Bourne, of George Nympton, a small village near South Molton, had 19 relatives, including four sons – Bertie, who served with the Devonshire and Royal Warwickshire Regiments, and who was awarded the Military Medal in 1918, Charles, Frederick and John – and five nephews serving King and country.

Under the provocative headline 'There are no "conscience cranks" in this family', *The Western Times* in March 1916 reported that Mrs W Burton, of Beer Down, Uplowman, near Tiverton, the wife of a rural postman, was justly proud that she had 15 relatives, including two sons, two brothers and seven nephews, in the Army and Army Service Corps.

Many fathers and sons throughout Devon volunteered for service. Mr W H Carpenter, an 'old soldier', of Summerland Street, Exeter and his six sons, Ernest, Montague, Alfred, Sidney, Frederick and Loyal, all volunteered. 'The father ... when his sons, one after the other, went off to the colours, four to the Army, one to the Marines and one to the Navy, could not resist the temptation to follow suit,' reported The *Western*

Times in June 1916. Mr Carpenter, with the Labour Battalion in France, was in the Coldstream Guards between 1878 and 1884 and then spent ten years in the Army Reserve.

The Rodd family of Ilfracombe had a father and five sons in the Army. George Pike, of Uffculme, served with the Royal Engineers in France while his four sons, Henry, Sydney, Arthur and George, were in the Army in France and India. John Newbery, of Membury was in the Army Service Corps while his sons, Robert and Simon served in the Army and Royal Marine Light Infantry.

James Gilbert, of Barnstaple, was in the Army as his three sons, William, Albert and Walter fought at sea in the Royal Navy and with the Army in France, Egypt and Mesopotamia. Albert, who went on to serve in the Australian forces, was a noted wrestler, having held heavyweight championships for the west of England, Ireland, Scotland, Gibraltar and the Armed Forces.

At least four families in Devon each had nine sons serving, mainly in the Army or Navy – including the Sealeys, of Alexandra Terrace, Teignmouth. The Mole family of Shaldon, near Teignmouth had nine sons and three sons-in-law serving. Mr R J Davey, senior choirman at St Paul's Church, Torquay had nine sons serving by the end of 1915. And William Bartlett, of Heavitree, near Exeter, had eight sons in the Army and one in the Navy.

A Thorverton widow, Mrs W Rawle, who later lived in Exeter, had eight sons in the Armed Forces. The Stentiford family of Morchard Bishop, my home village, and the Turner family of North Tawton each had eight sons serving. At least a dozen or more families had seven sons serving, the vast majority of whom were in the Army or Navy. Another 50 or more families had five or six sons involved in the war.

The enormous pride and patriotism fuelled by these great family sacrifices was sorely tested in communities across Devon as the war dragged on year after year, and the names of thousands of young men who had been killed or wounded on the battlefields of Europe and beyond or lost at sea were published in local newspapers.

Publican Richard Ellis, of the Three Horse Shoes, Upton Pyne, Exeter received a letter of sympathy from the King and Queen after losing four of his six sons – Walter, a private in the 1/4th Devons, who died in Mesopotamia on June 17, 1916; Richard Henry, a private in the South African Infantry, who died from wounds received in action in France on July 27, 1916; Ben, a private in the London Regiment, who was killed in France on September 16, 1916; and Percival, an acting corporal in the Cheshire Regiment, who died of wounds in France on April 6, 1918.

'While grieved to hear that so heavy a toll has been taken from one family, the King and Queen trust that the knowledge that your four sons gallantly gave their lives in the service of their sovereign and country, fighting for the honour of the British Empire, will lighten your burden and will prove a sustaining thought and solace to you in years to come,' said the letter, sent by Sir Frederick Ponsonby, Keeper of the Privy Purse.

William Henry and Thirza Gratton, of Landkey, near Barnstaple lost four of eight sons serving in the British, Australian and Canadian Armies – William Lewis, a private in the 2nd Devons, who was killed in action on March 13, 1915, aged 41; Alfred Frank, a lance-corporal in the same battalion, who was killed in France on October 6, 1916, aged 22; Sydney James, a private in the Australian infantry, who died on December 14, 1916; and Thomas John, a private in the Canadian infantry, and holder of the Military Medal for gallantry, who died in France on August 21, 1917, aged 37.

A number of the Gratton brothers emigrated to Australia before the war. At the outbreak of hostilities, Alfred enlisted in the Australian Commonwealth Forces and, on arriving in England, was transferred to the Devonshire Regiment in which he had served before emigrating. On the day before he was killed, he informed his parents that he was 'quite safe and in the best of health', *The North Devon Journal* reported in October 1916. Just a few days later, his parents received a letter from the Devonshire Regiment chaplain, the Rev H B Burnaby, expressing his 'deep sympathy' at their loss. 'One knows how hard it is for you poor mourners at home, I think, perhaps, harder than for us out here. May God give you strength to bear your terrible sorrow,' he wrote.

Three sons of the Bishop of Exeter, Lord Rupert Ernest William Gascoyne Cecil, were killed in action between 1915 and 1918 – Rupert Edward, aged 20, Randle William, 28, and Jack, 25. The Bishop of Crediton, the Right Rev Robert Edward Trefusis, lost two sons in July and November 1916 – Captain Arthur Owen Trefusis, of the Loyal North Lancashire Regiment, and Captain Haworth Walter Trefusis, of the Northamptonshire Regiment.

As many as 20, or more, families across Devon, from Thorverton to Uplyme, Chulmleigh to Bideford, Dartmouth to Filleigh, Teignmouth to Bampton and Exeter to Barnstaple, lost three sons – on the battlefields of France, Belgium and the Middle East, in battles at sea, or from sickness which claimed so many lives in the Great War.

They included:

Richard Henry and Emma Knapman, of Cann's Cottage, Little Raddon, Thorverton, who lost: Herbert Knapman, a private in the 1st Devons, who was killed in action at Festubert in France on October 30, 1914; James, aged 22, of the Royal Marine Light Infantry, who was killed when his ship, *HMS Goliath*, was sunk in the Dardanelles by the Turkish destroyer *Muavenet-i Milliye* on May 13, 1915. James was among 570 crewmen to lose their lives after *Goliath* was hit by two torpedoes and his body was never recovered; William John, aged 25, a private in the 2nd Devons, who died of wounds in France on October 30, 1916. All three brothers were born in Zeal Monachorum and are remembered on Thorverton War Memorial. Herbert was buried at Canadian Cemetery (No 2) Neuville-Saint Vaast, near Arras, and William was buried at Grove Town Cemetery, Meaulte, on the Somme.

Albert and Elizabeth Stephenson, of 2 Victoria Lawn, Barnstaple, who had three sons killed in action on the Western Front in just over a year: John Albert, a lance-corporal in the 1/6th Battalion of the Gloucester Regiment, who died on November 3, 1916, aged 28; William Henry, a private in the 8th Battalion of the Somerset Light Infantry, who died 11 days later, aged 22;

17

David Thomas, a private in the 13th Battalion of the East Surrey Regiment, who died on November 26, 1917, aged 27. John and William are remembered on the Thiepval Memorial and David on the Cambrai Memorial. All three are commemorated on Barnstaple War Memorial.

Albert James and Selina Clow, of 30 Codrington Street, Newtown, Exeter, who lost three sons in less than 12 months: Henry Floyd, a private in the Royal Marine Light Infantry, who was killed in action in France on July 31, 1917, aged 19; Ernest Alfred, a private in the 9th Devons, and holder of the Military Medal for gallantry, who died from wounds sustained in action at Passchendaele on October 10, 1917, aged 31; Bertram George, a private in the Royal Scots Fusiliers, who was killed in action on the Marne on July 20, 1918, aged 30. All three were buried in France and are listed in Marquis De Ruvigny's celebrated Roll of Honour.

Samuel and Dinah Bater, of South Molton Street, Chulmleigh, who lost: Samuel, or 'Sammy' Bater, a private in the 8th Devons, who died of wounds on September 6, 1916, aged 20. Awarded the Military Medal for keeping the enemy at bay while serving with the battalion's machine gun section, he was buried at the Dartmoor Cemetery in Becordel-Becourt; John, a private in the 7th Battalion of the East Yorkshire Regiment, who was killed in action on March 25, 1918, aged 29, and is remembered on the Arras Memorial; Richard, a private in the Canadian Medical Corps, who was killed in action on August 16, 1918, aged 27. A holder of the Military Medal, he emigrated to Canada before the war. He is remembered on the Warvillers Churchyard Extension, near Bouchoir.

Frederick and Caroline Blight, of Filleigh, near South Molton, who lost: Frederick, a private in the 8th Devons, who was killed in action at Loos on September 25, 1915, aged 24, and is remembered on the Loos Memorial; William Heal, a lance-corporal in the 9th Devons, who was killed in action on April 2, 1917, aged 28, and buried at H. A. C. Cemetery, Ecoust-St. Mein, near Arras; Walter, a private in the 1/6th Devons, who died from dysentery in Basra, Mesopotamia on July 18, 1917, and was buried at Basra War Cemetery. In early 1915, the Blight brothers were among 17 old boys of Castle Hill School, Filleigh in active service in the Army or Navy. All three brothers are remembered on Filleigh War Memorial.

James (a former soldier) and Hannah Woodman, of Kilmington, near Axminster, who lost: Eli White, a corporal in the 1st Battalion of the Royal Berkshire Regiment, who was killed in action on January 10, 1915, aged 32. He had a wife, Rose, and one child. He is remembered on the Le Touret Memorial, near Bethune; John Henry, a private in the 8th Devons, who was killed in action at Loos on September 25, 1915, aged 22, and is remembered on the Loos Memorial; Fred, a private in the 1/4th Devons, who was killed in action in Mesopotamia on February 3, 1917, aged 19, and was buried at Amara War Cemetery. All three are remembered on Kilmington War Memorial.

Thomas and Emma Greenslade, of Bampton and Tiverton, who lost: Reginald James, a corporal in the 1st Battalion of the Somerset Light Infantry, who was killed in action in France on August 23, 1915, aged 21, and buried at Mesnil Ridge Cemetery, Mesnil-Martinsart, on the Somme; John Thomas, a private in the 1/4th Devons, who was killed in action in Mesopotamia on December 3, 1915, aged 25, and buried at Kut War Cemetery; William Charles, a corporal in the 7th Battalion of the Somerset Light Infantry, who was killed in action in France on November 30, 1917, aged 23, and is remembered on the Cambrai Memorial. All three are remembered on Bampton War Memorial.

John and Elizabeth Ann Greenslade, of Newport, Barnstaple, who lost: Owen, a corporal in the 10th Battalion of the Durham Light Infantry, who was killed in action on August 19, 1915, and is remembered on the Ypres (Menin Gate) Memorial; Conrad, a private in the 6th Battalion of the Bedfordshire Regiment, who died of wounds at the Military Hospital, Chatham, Kent, on October 11, 1916, aged 24, and was buried at Fort Pitt Military Cemetery, Chatham; Herbert, a lance-corporal in the 1st Battalion of the Worcestershire Regiment, who was killed in action on May 2, 1917, aged 30, and is remembered on the Thiepval Memorial. All three are commemorated on Barnstaple War Memorial.

Charlotte (and the late James) Couldridge, of Queen Anne's,

High Street, Bideford, who lost: Leslie, a private in the 12th Battalion of the Middlesex Regiment, who was killed in action on September 26, 1916, aged 19, and is remembered on the Thiepval Memorial; Jack Oswald, a 2nd lieutenant in the same regiment, who was killed in action on November 6, 1916, aged 22, and is remembered on the Thiepval Memorial; Claude Lavin, a sergeant in the 8th Devons, who died (from wounds received in Italy) at the Orthopaedic Hospital in Shepherd's Bush, London on June 24, 1918, aged 27. He was buried in Bideford Church Cemetery. All three are remembered on Bideford War Memorial.

Thomas and Emma Hamlyn, of Teignmouth, who lost: Henry Thomas, a private in the 2nd Devons, who was killed in action on July 1, 1916, the first day of the Battle of the Somme, aged 23. He is remembered on the Thiepval Memorial; Holroyd Edward, a lance-corporal in the 7th Battalion of the Somerset Light Infantry, who was killed in action on September 16, 1917, aged 22. His widow, Caroline, received a letter from an officer which said that Holroyd had been occupying a 'small post in the front line and his death, which was instantaneous, was caused by a German shell'. The letter, published in *The Western Times* in September 1917, said he was 'buried behind the post which he had held, and a cross was erected to mark the grave'. The officer said he 'always found him to be a brave soldier'; Thomas William, a private in the 12th Battalion of the Suffolk Regiment, who was killed in action on April 9, 1918, and is remembered on the Ploegsteert Memorial in Belgium. All three are remembered on Teignmouth War Memorial.

Frederick and Emma Paskey, of Summerland Street, Barnstaple, who lost: Francis Albert ('Bertie'), of the 8th Battalion of the Royal Fusiliers, who was killed in action on August 6, 1916, aged 27, and is remembered on the Thiepval Memorial; Leonard Montague, of the 16th Devons, who was killed in action on September 2, 1918, aged 24, and was buried at the Peronne Communal Cemetery Extension, on the Somme; Gunner Reginald James, of the Royal Garrison Artillery, who died from tuberculosis at Reading War Hospital, after serving in Mesopotamia, on October 5, 1918, aged 32, and was buried in

Barnstaple Cemetery. All three are remembered on Barnstaple War Memorial.

Harry and Henrietta (Hettie) Stocker of Loom Cottage, Uplyme, near Lyme Regis, who lost: George, a petty officer (gunner) in the Royal Navy, who drowned off Malta on June 9, 1917, and was buried in Capuccini Naval Cemetery, near Rinella in Malta; Harry, a private in the 19th Battalion of the Manchester Regiment, who was killed in action at Passchendaele on July 31, 1917, aged 29, and is commemorated on the Ypres (Menin Gate) Memorial; Frank, a sergeant in the 1st Battalion of the Coldstream Guards, who died in Hainaut, Belgium on October 27, 1918, and was buried at St Symphortien Military Cemetery, near Mons. All three are remembered on the Uplyme War Memorial.

William and Mary Burnell, of Dartmouth Post Office, who lost: George, a private in the 8th Devons, who was killed in action on February 10, 1916, aged 27, and buried at Dartmoor Cemetery, Becordel-Becourt in France; William Robert, a lance-corporal in the 10th Battalion of the Rifle Brigade, who was killed in action on August 14, 1917, aged 35, and is remembered on the Ypres (Menin Gate) Memorial; Edwin, a lance-corporal in the 1st Devons, who was killed in action on October 4, 1917, and is remembered on the Tyne Cot Memorial, Belgium. All three are commemorated on memorials in Dartmouth.

At least a dozen families in Britain each lost five sons. They included Amy Beechey, widow of the Vicar of Friesthorpe, Lincolnshire, who had eight sons serving in the war, five of whom were killed in action or died of wounds in France and East Africa, with a sixth being maimed for life. Elizabeth Davies, of Parr, St Helens, who lost five sons, assisted the local mayor in unveiling the St Helens Cenotaph in front of 30,000 people in 1926 – having played a key role in raising money for the memorial.

In October 1915, The *Western Times* reported on a recruitment speech given in Reading by Lieutenant-General Sir Edward Cecil Bethune. He referred to 'an old Cornish lady who had had six sons serving in the Army, five of whom have been killed'. She wrote to him, asking: 'Do give me back the 6th.' In his reply, he pointed out the need of every man at the present time and she promptly replied: 'Please keep him then.' Lt-Gen Bethune said that that was the kind of spirit they wanted throughout the whole country.

A month later, the extraordinary story of a father and five sons killed in action in 1914 and 1915 was reported in the *Coventry Evening Telegraph*. It told how a Corporal E Parish, of the Queen's Regiment, had lost a brother in the Great Retreat from Mons, with three others killed at Dixmude and Ypres in Belgium. His father was killed at Neuve Chapelle and a fifth brother, wounded in the same battle, later died from wounds. The sacrifice made by the Parish family, originally from Croydon in Surrey, was probably the greatest made in the war, said the newspaper.

4

HUMBLE LIFE OF A HISTORY MAKER

The sweat was pouring down his face and back as he shouted 'hold' to the two shire horses ahead of him. It was a day to remember for young farm worker John Roberts as he helped to plough a large field at Stickeridge Farm, Cruwys Morchard.

Leaves and small twigs drifted across the broken soil as he rested in the cool autumn breeze while hundreds of rooks and small birds trailed in his wake, feeding on the worms and insects exposed in his toil.

Exhausted, he patted the horses and fed them oats, thanking them for staying 'true' and not letting him down as he 'worked the land' under the watchful eye of farmer Thomas Badcock, who had been impressed at what he had seen.

John was just 12-years-old. He had finished school two years earlier and was employed as a 'farm boy', earning a shilling or two each week to give to his mother, who was raising a growing family at a cottage near Stickeridge.

He worked long hours, from dawn to dusk during planting and harvesting. He helped feed livestock and the horses, sowed potatoes and wheat, assisted with milking cows and spent many long hours brushing dirt and dust from the farmyard.

John was exhilarated that he had successfully ploughed part of a field for the first time, working two 12-hour days to get the job done after assisting his employer to attach the wooden plough and harnesses to the shires.

He had got up at 5am on both of those days, had bread and treacle for breakfast and had just a 20-minute break for lunch, gobbling down a cheese and pickle sandwich and an apple. A warm broth awaited him at the farmhouse for supper.

He was following in the footsteps of his father, his grandfather and his ancestors before him who had all eked out a living as farm labourers in Mid-Devon. It would be John's way of life for the next 70 years or so.

He was born in Cruwys Morchard on September 13, 1829 when King George IV ruled over a huge British Empire and the Duke of Wellington, who defeated Bonaparte at the Battle of Waterloo in 1815, was Britain's Prime Minister.

John was born in the same year as Geronimo, the great American Apache leader, William Booth, founder of the Salvation Army, and Chester A Arthur, the man who would become the 21st President of the United States of America.

1829 was an extraordinary year for transport in Britain with Robert Stephenson designing his famous 'Rocket' for use on the Liverpool and Manchester Railway, and the first public horse-drawn bus services being introduced in London.

Robert Peel established the Metropolitan Police Service in that year. The infamous body-selling murderer William Burke was hanged in Edinburgh. The last of the Bounty Mutineers died on Pitcairn Island. And the first Oxford and Cambridge University Boat Race was held.

The 1800s, particularly during the Victorian era, were a time of extraordinary change for agriculture, with increased mechanisation on farms putting many jobs at risk and the lure of a 'better life' abroad leading to thousands of working men and women leaving Devon.

Many farm labourers worked long hours for just a few shillings each week and lived in poorly maintained and over-crowded cottages. Large families, with children as young as six working the land, often lived in cramped one or two-room hovels.

When Queen Victoria came to the throne in 1837, agriculture had unrivalled influence and status in Great Britain, with more than half the population of England, Wales, Scotland and Ireland working in the countryside.

Almost 1.8 million men, women and children worked the land in 1851. Census returns for that year showed that Britain had 1,460,896 agricultural labourers, farm servants and shepherds. By 1871, this number had plummeted by almost half a million to 980,178.

The National Labourers Union led a campaign to improve farm workers' pay and conditions in the 1870s, holding meetings across the country, including one at the village school room in Broadclyst, near Exeter in the autumn of 1874.

The Western Times in October that year, said it looked 'like the whole population' of the village had turned up for the meeting, with farmers mustering in force and the room filled with men, women and children of the 'labouring class'.

'Few villagers have enjoyed the novelty and excitement of seeing squire, parsons and farmers brought face to face with union delegates to hear all the hard things which are said of them,' reported the newspaper.

The five-hour meeting was chaired by George Mitchell, proprietor of a marble works in London, who told the gathering that he began his life at the 'tail-end' of a plough, often with 'nothing in his belly but raw turnips'.

He said he knew that if a man was well fed, he worked well and, as a rule, good pay ensured good service. When he asked the labourers what they were paid in Devon, one man said he got 2s 6d a day and two quarts of cider.

One replied that he was paid 11s a week and 'my house is like a pig's house'. Many said they were not paid when poor weather stopped them from working and women working the fields told Mr Mitchell they got as little as 8d a day for their toils.

A letter from a 'working man' published in *The Western Times* in September 1886, said if a 'poor labourer' took a day's holiday he would lose pay. If he did take a day off, his wife and family would probably 'have to starve'.

A well-paid farm worker was paid 12s a week, or just over £31 a year. Out of that sum, he had to pay £5 a year rent for his home, leaving the 'poor fellow', his wife and children a meagre £26 to survive on for a whole 12 months.

With low pay remaining a problem for many, and fewer jobs to go around, young men and women planned a future away from Devon and Britain, in America and the then British colonies of Canada, Australia and New Zealand.

Many were attracted by the offer of assisted or, in some cases, free passages to the 'New World' and the opportunity of starting their own farm with the help of 'free grants' of – or the chance to obtain under deferred payments – up to 160 acres of land.

Concerns about the fate of the emigrants were repeatedly raised in newspapers in Devon and further afield amid allegations that speculators were tempting people abroad under schemes that made the rich richer and the poor poorer.

At a conference held in London in 1886, two men told how assisted emigrants were 'miserably accommodated on their passage out' and 'still more wretchedly provided for' on arriving on the other side of the world.

Working men arrived desperately seeking employment but, in many cases, were unable to secure jobs of any kind. Young women, arriving with hopes of bettering their lives, were frequently driven into prostitution.

However, a clergyman told the conference that the number of failures was far exceeded by the success stories. He considered that, all too often, people arriving in the New World were 'quite unfit for colonial life'.

Claims made in 1891 that there was 'plenty of work' available in Queensland, Australia and 'great demand' for farm labourers and female servants, were challenged in a strongly-worded letter published in *The North Devon Journal*.

Arguing that the assertions were 'altogether false', Mr J Dendle, who himself emigrated from England to Queensland seven years earlier, painted a grim picture of the situation facing many of those who had emigrated there.

'I hear that an agent is again being sent to England, going from one town to another, lecturing, in order to get more people to emigrate out here. Such an agent was in Devonshire lecturing when I came away from there,' he wrote.

'There is many a man here that curses them and wished that they had never listened to them, men that had always got work at home though small pay; but when they came out here, they could not get work to do, so could not get any pay, big or small.'

He claimed there were 'no farms here' – only cattle and sheep 'stations' which were all 'grazing land' – so 'there cannot be any labourers wanted. The land here is not fit for tillage. There are some little spots of which you might make a small garden, but they are few and far between.'

There was, alleged Mr Dendle, 'no demand' for female servants. 'There is many a young girl that has left England respectable and coming here, having no home and getting no situation, has gone to the bad,' he wrote.

Twenty-six years earlier, Henry Jordan, Agent General for Emigration to Queensland, defended the colony's record in attracting tens of thousands of farm and other workers from Britain, in a controversial letter in *The North Devon Journal*.

He wrote of a group of people who had not succeeded in Britain being 'among the first to rush to any new country, in the absurd expectation of getting on without patient, persevering industry', and had the idea they would do well if they got to the other side of the world.

'They forget that the reason of their want of success at home, is simply that they don't like to work; and they are perhaps ignorant that this is a disqualification which makes their failure in a new country even more complete than in Britain.'

He dismissed claims made in the 1860s that land in Queensland was not fit for cultivation. Farmers were growing wheat and other European cereals and fruits and scrubland had been successfully planted with maize, sugar cane and sweet potatoes.

Of the 30,000 people he had seen move to Queensland, many of them graziers, farmers, labourers and domestic servants, the vast majority had 'done well' having grasped the mantra that hard work and patient, persevering industry were 'absolutely necessary to prosperity'.

Worries over the loss of thousands of workers from rural Devon were voiced over many decades and spilled into the 20th Century. 'There is growing anxiety in Devonshire respecting the constant stream of emigrants from our rural districts to places abroad,' *The Western Times* reported in March 1913.

The county was losing 'much of its best blood' to Canada, Australia and New Zealand with towns and villages seeing an increasing number of young men seeking their fortunes overseas, particularly in Canada.

In the year leading up to March 1913, an estimated 8,500 men, women and children emigrated from Devon, with Cullompton and villages like Bradninch losing 10% of their inhabitants. The newspaper described the figures as 'disquieting'.

Many of those leaving were farm workers. Great concerns had been voiced about the poor state of housing in rural Devon. 'Even if a labourer is housed in a hovel, he has no security of tenure of that hovel. It goes with his job, and if for any reason he loses his job, he loses his home as well.'

Emigration offered to the farmer's son and to the labourer, the great opportunity of securing a farm. 'In this country, he can scarce hope to acquire a smallholding, sometimes not even an allotment,' said *The Western Times*.

John Roberts and his family were tempted by a new life overseas, but they stayed in Devon. They were successful in finding work on a series of farms in villages in Mid-Devon and John enjoyed being surrounded by his children and grandchildren.

One of eight children, John was the second eldest son of Thomas and Lucy (nee Hedgeman) Roberts who married in Cruwys Morchard on March 30, 1827. He had three brothers and four sisters, at least one of whom died in infancy. Baptised in his local parish church in the year of his birth, he started work at the age of eight while still at school, and never learned to read or write.

He was just ten when he had his first paid work away from his family – at Stickeridge Farm. The first Census return of 1841 shows that he lived at the farm with farmer Thomas Badcock, his wife Elizabeth and three members of their family.

John was one of two young workers at Stickeridge, the second being 18-year-old John Thorne.

In 1851, John Roberts, at the age of 21, was a servant at a 55-acre farm at Yeadbury Mill, Cruwys Morchard. He was working for farmer John Thorne, who had a 41-year-old wife, Honor and an 18-year-old daughter, Elizabeth. Also working there were two teenage farm boys, John Collard and Thomas Crocker.

At the age of 26, John married Mary Couch, a former house servant, at Thelbridge Parish Church on May 2, 1855. Twenty-three-year-old Mary was the daughter of William and Elizabeth Couch who lived at Stretchdown Farm, Thelbridge after previously residing in the villages of Creacombe and Meshaw.

By April 1861, John and Mary had five children, all boys aged between six years and two months, and were living at Backstone in the parish of Witheridge, where John was employed as an agricultural labourer.

Ten years later, John and Mary were living in Moor Cottage, Cruwys Morchard with seven of the 15 children they would go on to have. John was then working on the 180-acre Moor Farm, run by John Hill and his family.

He and Mary were still at Moor Cottage at the time of the 1891 Census, then living with a daughter and a grandson. John, aged 61, was working at Moor Farm, still run by John Hill but now enlarged to almost 300 acres.

Mary, who also never learned to read or write, died from 'senile decay' at Moor Cottage on April 21, 1900, aged 67. John was with her at the time. A special card produced for her funeral by one of her sons indicated that she had been unwell for some time.

It read: *'Oh, do not weep for me, or wish me back again. But only think how sweet 'twill be to suffer no more pain.'*

In 1901, John was working as an agricultural labourer for his son Thomas at Newland Farm in Witheridge and continued living there in retirement until his death in 1919, six months after the end of the Great War.

In a newspaper tribute to John after his death, Witheridge village correspondent Ganymede described him as a 'well-known working agriculturist … experienced in all the phases of his important calling of farm work'.

A man 'full of years, and respected by all', he had lived through many difficult eras for agriculture and knew of times when 'the farm hand was of no reputation', the correspondent wrote in *The Western Times* in May 1919.

On the same day, *The Devon and Exeter Gazette* reported that John's funeral had taken place in Witheridge parish churchyard, with the service conducted by the Vicar, the Rev Prebendary John Peter Benson.

John lived to see some of the greatest changes ever witnessed, from the invention of the motor car to the aeroplane, the birth of railways in Britain and the aftermath of the industrial revolution that brought radical changes to agricultural employment.

John lived in rural Devon under four monarchies – that of George IV, Victoria, Edward VII and George V – and in the eras of some of the bloodiest conflicts in history, including the American Indian Wars, the American Civil War, and two Boer Wars.

He and Mary had 12 sons and three daughters. They had nine sons between 1855 and 1867 before their first daughter, Lucy, was born. Their youngest children were twins, Sidney and Leah, born in 1876. John not only outlived his wife but also four of his sons, one of whom James, was just seven when he died in 1875.

Many years before the Great War, he had seen two of his sons, Walter and John Jnr, join the Army and spend 12 or more years in service. Walter enlisted in the Royal Horse Artillery in 1878 when he was 19. A driver, he spent seven years in India and was discharged in 1890. John Jnr was 20 when he joined the Army in 1879. A gunner with the Royal Horse Artillery, he spent six years in the East Indies and was discharged in 1891.

At one stage, John Jnr acted as orderly – or batman – to Field Marshall Frederick Roberts (the 1st Earl Roberts) in the Khyber Pass in Afghanistan. The Field Marshall later successfully led British forces in the Second Boer War.

Three of John and Mary Roberts' sons – Daniel, Thomas and Benjamin, my grandfather – were farmers and the other sons worked on the land, as cattlemen, carters, stockmen, shepherds, waggoners and general agricultural labourers. John and Mary's children were all born in Mid-Devon, in Cruwys Morchard, Puddington, Thelbridge, or Witheridge.

Their sons and daughters were born over a period of 21 years. Of their – known – 96 grandchildren, at least 12 died very young. Thirty-six of their grandsons were believed to have been eligible to fight in the war.

Their children were:

- **William** – who married Elizabeth Eliza Sage. They had 11 children by 1911.
- **Daniel** – who married Leah Ann Stevens. They had 14 children, 11 of whom were still living in 1911.
- **John** – who married Elizabeth Morrish. They had seven children.
- **Walter** – who married Helena Cook. They had at least three children.
- **Henry** – who married Mary Ann Kerslake. They had ten children, only five of whom were living in 1911.
- **Charles** – who married Eliza Bryant. They had eight children.
- **Samuel** – who married Maria Morrish. They had three sons.
- **Benjamin** – who married Elizabeth Burnett in 1893. They had four children.
- **James** – who died aged seven.
- **Lucy** – who married George Kingdom. They had 11 children, nine of whom were still living in 1911.
- **Thomas** – who married Mary Ann Morrish. They had ten children, eight of whom were living in 1911.
- **Caroline** – whose whereabouts after 1891 are unknown.
- **Frank** – who married Sarah Maslin. They had one child.
- **Sidney** – who first married Edith Tapp, and then Bertha Cockram. Sidney and Bertha had eight children.
- **Leah** – who married Frederick Sharland. They had six children.

The grandsons believed to have been eligible for war service in 1914–1918 were:

1. **George Henry Roberts** (son of William and Eliza), who served in the Royal Artillery.
2. **James Ernest Roberts** (son of William and Eliza).
3. **William Wallace Roberts** (son of William and Eliza).
4. **Frederick Roberts** (son of Daniel and Leah).
5. **Walter Roberts** (son of Daniel and Leah).
6. **John Roberts** (son of Daniel and Leah).
7. **Daniel Roberts** (son of Daniel and Leah).
8. **Tom Roberts** (son of Daniel and Leah).
9. **John Francis 'Frank' Roberts** (son of John and Elizabeth), who served in the 2nd Devons and was killed in the trenches on September 9, 1916.
10. **William Ben Roberts** (son of John and Elizabeth), who served in the Royal Engineers.
11. **Samuel 'Sam' Roberts** (son of John and Elizabeth), who served in the 8th Devons and was killed in action on July 1, 1916.
12. **Sidney Roberts** (son of Walter and Helena).
13. **William John Roberts** (son of Walter and Helena), who served as a stoker in the Royal Navy.
14. **John Roberts** (son of Henry and Mary Ann).
15. **Henry 'Harry' Roberts** (son of Henry and Mary Ann), a soldier, regiment unknown.
16. **Walter Roberts** (son of Henry and Mary Ann), a soldier, regiment unknown.
17. **Archibald 'Archie' Roberts** (son of Henry and Mary Ann), who joined the Armed Forces in June 1917. Regiment unknown.
18. **John Francis Bryant Roberts** (son of Charles and Eliza), who served in the 9th Devons.
19. **Bertie Roberts** (son of Charles and Eliza).
20. **Ernest Roberts** (son of Charles and Eliza).
21. **Sidney Roberts** (son of Charles and Eliza), who served in the Queen's Westminster Rifles and died from wounds on August 17, 1917.
22. **Archibald 'Archie' Roberts** (son of Charles and Eliza), who served in the 13th Hussars.
23. **Charles Roberts** (son of Charles and Eliza).

24. **Sidney Roberts** (son of Samuel and Maria), who is believed to have served in the Royal Engineers.

25. **John 'Jack' Roberts** (son of Samuel and Maria), who served in the 2nd Devons and died of wounds on May 30, 1915.

26. **Samuel Roberts** (son of Samuel and Maria), a soldier, regiment unknown.

27. **George Burnett Roberts** (son of Benjamin and Elizabeth), who served as a horse transport driver in the Army Service Corps.

28. **William Henry Kingdom** (son of Lucy and George), who served in the 1/4th Devons and died from heart disease on May 27, 1916.

29. **George Kingdom** (son of Lucy and George).

30. **Frank Kingdom** (son of Lucy and George).

31. **Ernest Kingdom** (son of Lucy and George).

32. **Walter Kingdom** (son of Lucy and George), who served in the Loyal North Lancashire Regiment and was killed in action on September 20, 1918.

33. **Frank Roberts** (son of Thomas and Mary Ann), who served in the Royal 1st Devon Yeomanry and 16th Devons.

34. **Thomas Roberts** (son of Thomas and Mary Ann), who served in the Royal 1st Devon Yeomanry, the Warwickshire Regiment and 8th Devons.

35. **Albert Roberts** (son of Thomas and Mary Ann), who served in the 8th Devons and died of wounds on October 3, 1915.

36. **John Roberts** (son of Thomas and Mary Ann).

5

THREE BROTHERS MARRY
THREE SISTERS

They were undoubtedly momentous, happy days for three of John Roberts' sons. They created history within their family by marrying three sisters in the same village parish church in rural Devon.

The sons – John Jnr, a gunner in the Royal Artillery, and agricultural labourers Samuel and Thomas – wed their sweethearts, the Morrish sisters, of Knowstone, at All Saints Church, Rackenford within two years.

They were halcyon days indeed for the three couples, for the parents, John and Mary Roberts and William and Mary Morrish – and for the community of Rackenford who were amazed and thrilled by the rare 'hat-trick' of weddings.

John Roberts Jnr married Elizabeth Morrish on March 20, 1889. Samuel Roberts wed Maria Morrish on March 26, 1890. And Thomas Roberts and Mary Ann Morrish were joined in marriage on March 6, 1891. The three couples had 20 children between them, 15 of them sons.

Just over 25 years later, they would be united in grief.

Remarkably, each of the three couples had three sons serving in the Army in the Great War. Four of the nine would not make it home.

Two of John Jnr and Elizabeth's boys, Samuel and John Francis (Frank), were killed within weeks of each other in 1916

– after they both had near-miraculous escapes from death, from rifle fire and shrapnel, earlier in the war.

Samuel and Maria lost their second son, Jack in the aftermath of the Battle of Aubers Ridge in France in 1915. And Thomas and Mary Ann's third son, Albert, died from wounds after the Battle of Loos in France in 1915.

The devastation of the Great War is starkly demonstrated in statistics that almost defy belief. Eighteen million soldiers and civilians died in four years of fighting and more than 20 million were wounded. More than 950,000 British soldiers were killed in action, died of wounds or from disease.

However, the tragic losses suffered by the Roberts and Morrish families provide a more personal and chilling account of the devastating impact of the war on ordinary men and women and their communities.

Official documentation produced three years before the bloodshed began – from the population counts taken in the 1911 Census – also present an emotional insight into how lives would be so dramatically changed in the years ahead.

The Census return for Newland Farm, Witheridge reveals that John Roberts, then an 81-year-old widower, and described as a 'boarder' and 'old-age pensioner', was living with his son, Thomas and daughter-in-law Mary Ann Roberts in a household of 12.

Thomas, aged 41, was 'head' of the household, the farmer. He and Mary Ann, aged 42, had by then been married 20 years and had living with them their eight surviving children. Also residing at Newland was farm labourer, William Snow.

Thomas and Mary Ann's eldest son Frank, aged 18, was a farrier on the farm. Sons Thomas Jnr, 17 and Albert, 15, were working there as a carter and cattleman. The youngest children were John, 13, Ivy, aged nine, Reuben, aged seven, Beatrice Mary, aged four, and Courtney, aged two.

Three generations of one family were living and working together on the farm in a small village in the heart of Mid-Devon. It was a way of rural life shared by many and it was shattered by the outbreak of war that would change all their lives.

Young Albert lost his life three days before his 20th birthday – and just 71 days after he had sailed to France with the 8th (Service) Battalion of the Devonshire Regiment, hoping for a 'great adventure' in Europe.

Frank, who had joined the Royal 1st Devon Yeomanry in 1912, sailed with them to Gallipoli, just before his brother's death in 1915. In December 1917, he was shot in the head, near Jerusalem. He survived – and later married and had his own family.

Thomas Jnr followed in his brother Frank's footsteps in joining the Royal 1st Devon Yeomanry, in 1913. He was discharged as medically unfit on August 5, 1914, a year and 169 days after he had joined, and before he had an opportunity to see active duty in the war.

Almost four years later, on June 26, 1918, he joined the Devonshire Regiment. At that stage, he was regarded as 'fit for despatching overseas', and was posted to Italy in November 1918, serving with the Devonshire and Warwickshire Regiments, before arriving home in April 1919. He married in 1923.

Thomas Snr and Mary's son John almost certainly served in the Yeomanry. However, there are no records to confirm this. Reuben and Courtney were too young to fight, although Courtney went on to serve as a Royal Artillery gunner in the 1939–45 War.

The 1911 Census return for Howden Cottage, Tiverton, is another study in the lives of a family later to be torn apart by the war. The cottage was the home of John Roberts' eldest daughter, Lucy, her husband, George Kingdom, and six of the 11 children they had had in 22 years of marriage.

George, aged 48, and born in the Devon village of Woolfardisworthy, was a domestic gardener. Living with him and Lucy were 20-year-old William Henry, their eldest son, and also a gardener, and their daughter Kate, aged 17, a dressmaker.

Also residing in the cottage were son Ernest, aged 14, a grocer's errand boy, Walter, 13, who was still at school, and daughters, Gladys and Elsie, aged five and two respectively.

Their world was turned upside down in May 1916 when

William Henry, then a corporal in the 1/4th Battalion of the Devonshire Regiment, died from heart disease thousands of miles away in the arid desert of Mesopotamia. He was 26.

More than two years later, with the end of the war just 52 days away, Walter was killed in action in the aftermath of a battle in the shadow of Germany's last great defensive line in France. A private in the 1st Battalion of the Loyal North Lancashire Regiment, he was just 20.

Lucy, who had comforted her brother and sister-in-law, John and Elizabeth Roberts, after the death of their two sons on the front line in France, thus became the second member of her family to lose two sons in the war.

It is believed that Ernest – and another son, Frank – also served in the war, but I have been unable to confirm this.

On April 11, 1939, as Britain was just months away from the start of the Second World War, George and Lucy Kingdom celebrated 50 years of marriage at their then home, 5 Prospect Place, West-exe North, Tiverton.

I have often wondered how they coped with the tragedy they had faced – and how difficult it must have been for them facing another war and wondering if their grandsons would be fighting for their lives on the front line.

6

DEVON FARMERS IN RECRUITMENT 'WAR OF WORDS'

A different kind of war raged at home as tens of thousands of young men left our shores to fight in France and Flanders, the Balkans and the Middle East. A bitter and divisive war of words erupted over enlistment in the Army and Navy – and farmers and their sons were at the centre of the uproar.

In an acrimonious debate that lasted almost as long as the Great War itself, many farmers were accused of being unpatriotic, of putting their interests above those of King and country. Their sons who stayed at home to help work the land were frequently condemned as 'duty dodgers' in failing to join the Armed Forces.

The farmers hit back, warning that food production could grind to a halt if too many of their sons and other agricultural workers went to war. They said they faced a huge dilemma, for while being urged to grow more crops to help feed men on the front line, they were losing more and more of their best horsemen, waggoners and other labourers to the military.

Tens of thousands of young men from Devon fought overseas with the Devonshire Regiment between 1914 and 1918. Many more from the county served with the Household Cavalry, Royal Engineers, Coldstream Guards, Yeomanry, Army Service Corps, and with Somerset, London, Midlands and Northern-based regiments.

Many of those men volunteered to fight – including John Roberts' grandsons. With Devon being a predominantly rural county, large numbers of young men signing up in 1914 and 1915 worked on the land. Hundreds responded to the 'Your country needs you' recruitment campaign led by the Secretary of State for War, Lord Horatio Herbert Kitchener.

As British forces suffered devastating losses in France and Flanders, Army recruitment marches were organised throughout Devon. These flag-waving processions stirred the emotions, with crowds wildly cheering those signing-up and denouncing men who failed to turn up at, or enlist during, a series of town and village rallies.

Much of the stinging criticism was levelled at local farmers and their sons attending, or absent from, the rallies. An article in *The Western Times* in February 1915, headlined Farmers' sons: stumbling block to recruiting in North Devon, provided a flavour of the kind of excoriating attacks targeted at the men of the land.

The farmers' sons are the trouble. That is a fact that has been realised all along, but the Devons, in their recruiting march, in North Devon, had the fact forced home more plainly yesterday than ever before. There are men quite ready to enlist but they say, and say very determinedly they will not go until the farmers' sons enlist.

And what say the farmers' sons? Some of them would probably blush to read their utterances in cold print. When one fine strapping fellow at Parkham (a small village on the North Devon coast) was asked whether he would enlist, he replied: 'No, I'm gwain to stay home and make money.' And he grinned in a stupid sort of way, adding that he farmed 100 acres.

'Aren't you ashamed to talk like that when men have been at the front fighting for you?' he was asked. Again, he laughed, in a sneering sort of manner and replied: 'I didn't ask um to go.' One of the Tommies who had been standing by shrugged his shoulders and observed: 'Swelp me, what can you do with a bloke like that?' So it was all the way. It was a bad day for recruiting.

The Parkham farmer's extraordinary response provoked an outcry and inspired a poem by Gerald M L Reade, of Alfington

Vicarage, Ottery St Mary. Published in *The Western Times*, it included the following verses:

> *Fair Devon's sons in days of old*
> *They sailed across the main,*
> *They feared no foe – they all were bold –*
> *They feared not death, nor pain.*
>
> *Fair Devon's sons in those great days*
> *Were bravest of the brave,*
> *To guard our shores in sailor's ways*
> *They braved a sailor's grave.*
>
> *Fair Devon's sons in days of plight*
> *Knew nought of fright or fear;*
> *They only knew that day or night*
> *The foemen might be near.*
>
> *But, now, alas! Another tale*
> *The rhymester has to tell.*
> *It makes true Britons' cheeks go pale,*
> *It does not sound so well!*
>
> *For now, the love of shop and farm*
> *Make some Devonians cold;*
> *And – much worse still! – the fear of harm*
> *Makes some no longer bold!*
>
> *You'll curse the day you did not go*
> *To fight for Britain's fame,*
> *To save old England from the foe,*
> *To save Fair Devon's name,*
> *And save your family from woe.*

A letter strongly defending Devon's farmers and their sons – written by my mother's grandfather, Daniel Arscott, who farmed over 100 acres at East Nutcott, Rackenford in North Devon – was published in *The Devon and Exeter Gazette* in December 1914. It said:

We have been hearing a lot lately about farmers' sons being shirkers as regards the war. It is not true of this part. Where would the small farmers be but for their sons working long days year in, year out, and most of Sunday as well, tending the cattle in all sorts of weather, and preparing for crops? The working man nowadays won't stay on the land to do it. He goes into the towns where he gets his half-day holidays. Where do the farmers and sons' half-day holidays come in?

The land was labour-starred (regarded as essential) before the war. Will those who want to take all the men off the land give us back our rent, rates and taxes, which are getting to such a pitch?

There's been talk about women doing the farm work; one can't get a servant in the house. No doubt lords and gentlemen can get them, and plenty of men, but not so the farmer. Devonshire is largely a farming county, but many men have left for foreign parts during the last three years. In fact, all the best young men go abroad.

Why did not the Government prepare, as the late Lord (Frederick Sleigh) Roberts (one of the most successful Army commanders of the 19th century) advised them, and keep up the Army? Why take all the men that are growing food for the people when there are so many thousands who are doing nothing?

A month earlier, at a meeting of the Tiverton Branch of the Devon Farmers' Union, Daniel Arscott asked how farmers could rise to the occasion and grow extra wheat for men on the front line without men and horses. His parish, with a population of 300, had supplied 20 men to the Army and all had come off the land.

Told that an Army officer blamed farmers for not allowing their sons to enlist, branch members hit back at claims of unpatriotic behaviour and passed the following resolution: 'We hereby affirm that in our opinion greater sacrifices in men and horses have been made by the farming industry than any other industry in England.'

The chairman of the Bideford branch of the Devon Farmers' Union said there had been 'unjust stigma' placed on farmers' sons. In an article published in the *Western Times* in January 1915, he said a good many farmers had made very great sacrifices and had scarcely men left on their farms to do the work that had

41

to be done, to say nothing of increasing the tillage as had been suggested.

But there was no let-up in the admonishments of farmers' sons. And a report in *The Western Times* in February 1915, recalling a 'bad recruiting day for the Devons' in the west of the county, included a warning that those who failed to fight in the war could miss out on the chance to have their own farm when the hostilities ended.

Despite all the eloquence of the speakers, the martial music and persuasion of the soldiers from the trenches, only two men were recruited. Even the heavens wept. Rain poured almost all day ... There was a big meeting at Holsworthy Drill Hall, and there was a good sprinkling of eligible young men. A Lieutenant Wreford did not mince matters. 'What', he said, 'do you think of yourselves – you men who will not come forward? You cheer, but what's the good of that. You read the newspapers and say: "we've done well today". You have done nothing. You are content for somebody else to stick in a rotten trench fighting for you while you stay comfortably at home.'

This outburst had some effect – six came forward from Holsworthy. Outside the town, a solitary magpie flew across the road. One of the superstitious Devons declared this to be an omen of ill luck. Perhaps he was right, for the rest of the day only produced two men. At Halwill Junction, one well-built young man was appealed to join, and replied: 'Not me – I've got nothing to lose.' But surely, said the recruiter, you recognise that you ought to help your country in her hour of need? 'No, I don't,' he replied. 'I don't care about my country.' And this dull-witted fellow laughed insolently, evidently imagining that he had said something really smart.

At St Giles-on-the-Heath, a steward of the Molesworth estate said the farmers did not send their sons because they claimed that they must have help to do their work. As a practical man, he knew that they must have labour on a farm, but those farmers who had sent their sons could get their work done. In future, if a man applied to him for a farm, he should ask what he did during the war. If the reply was that he stayed home with mother, and another said: 'I enlisted and did what I could', the man who joined the Army would be the one who would get the holding. He advised all landlords to do the same.

An article in *The Western Times* in September 1915 argued

that 'pushing the rake' was more important to a man at Combeinteignhead than 'pushing back the Germans'. A farmer's wife at Stokeinteignhead said that while two of her three sons had enlisted, other farmers had 4-5 sons who had not joined up. When it was suggested to her that the men may have been needed to work the land, she said: 'They are not on the land at all. They are out buying and speculating all day.'

More than one million British men joined the armed forces voluntarily by January 1915. But as thousands died in battles on the Western Front – and fewer volunteers came forward – conscription was introduced in 1916. The Military Service Act of January 1916 specified that single men aged between 19 and 41 were liable to be called up for military service unless they were married, widowed with children, serving in the Navy or Royal Marines, employed as clergymen or engaged in work of national interest. Conscription began on March 2 that year.

The act was extended to include married men on May 25, 1916. The age limit was eventually increased to 51. Thousands of men in Britain refused to fight. These conscientious objectors were mainly pacifists who believed it was wrong to kill another human being. Thousands of conscientious objectors agreed to carry out non-combat service, with many dying as stretcher bearers on the front line. Hundreds of men refused all service. Some received death sentences but were reprieved and given prison sentences instead.

Military service tribunals were set up across Britain – including rural, town and city areas in Devon – to adjudicate on claims for exemption from conscription into the British Army on grounds of performing civilian work of national importance, domestic hardship, health, and conscientious objection. About 750,000 men appealed against their conscription in the first six months of 1916. Most were granted exemption of some kind, even if it was only temporary. Only 2% of those who appealed were conscientious objectors.

Rural military service tribunals often came under fire for granting exemptions to men working on the land – frequently unfairly. In 1916, the South Molton Rural District Tribunal caused a national outcry when it granted exemptions to dozens of farmers. The exemptions provoked fury among soldiers on the front line and South Molton became known as 'the place to go to escape the Army'.

An article in *The Western Times* in March 1916, headlined 'The duty dodgers: what Devon lads in the trenches think of them', said 'London papers' had pointed 'accusing fingers' at the tribunal after it had allegedly granted 94 exemptions – 51 absolute, 26 conditional and 17 temporary – out of 111 cases it had recently considered.

But, said the newspaper, South Molton's 'unenviable reputation' had gone further than Fleet Street. Its decisions had been read with 'distressing feelings by Devon lads in the trenches'. And to prove the point, it published a scathing letter from three local soldiers who, *The Western Times* claimed, 'no doubt represented the opinions of scores of others'.

The letter stated:

On behalf of a few Devon lads in my company, I have been asked to write to you at our disgust at the shame that is cast upon our country by the large number of attested single men who appeal for exemptions and also of the tribunal that granted those wretched examples of men the chance of dodging their duty to the country and the wives and children of those men of Devon who have up to now given their lives.

If those men who are helping to make the war last longer by refusing to join up could hear the opinion of their fellow Devonshire men who are now enduring the hardship of winter warfare on the Western Front, they would not care to face them in a hurry. I wonder what they feel like when they read of our Devon battalions in the newspapers, or meet a wounded soldier? Do they faint? As a Beaford boy, I hope they will yet be compelled to earn the right to live near men who did not wait for … conscription before they did their duty. Pte G Smale, Pte F Collins, Pte A Mallett, all of 37th Division.

The outcry provoked a detailed and angry response from the tribunal clerk, Mr Fred B Wyatt. He said recent criticism had brought great discredit on the tribunal, whose members had attained an unenviable notoriety. A more 'abominable piece of injustice' he had not encountered. In certain newspapers, it was wrongly represented that (exemption) certificates were granted against the wishes of military authorities. He was sure military representatives would associate themselves with him in 'repelling the insulting suggestions which had been made'.

It was painful to think that London papers that circulated wherever the English language was spoken, should publish paragraphs stating that 'only three out of 111 men' were obtained for the Army. One of those papers came out with the heading: '105 exempt out of 111; where to go to escape having to be in the Army.'

He had written to the newspaper stating that the South Molton district was not the place for slackers; that there it would find an energetic recruiting sergeant and not a mild and soft tribunal. But so far as he knew, the letter was never published. He had read the criticism from three North Devon soldiers. 'I wish my voice could extend to the trenches,' said Mr Wyatt, 'and say that the whole thing is a travesty of the facts.'

He explained that, at the tribunal's March meeting, 'there were 31 cases of attested men in which certificates of absolute exemption were granted, and 12 cases of unattested men who received absolute certificates with the full approval and consent of the military authorities. Three temporary certificates were granted, to which the military authorities had consented, and 15 conditional certificates which the authorities were willing to be granted.'

Some 61 certificates were granted with the approval of the authorities and, 'if one took the trouble to investigate the matter, it was difficult to imagine that anything could have been done other than was done'. As for the 43 certificates granted to attested and unattested men, the acreage of the farms covered was 5,207. The tribunal had to consider that of the attested men to whom absolute certificates were granted, 23 were farmers in charge of 3,817 acres, or an average for each man of 166 acres.

Those certificates, therefore, were granted on the assumption that, each man could take charge of, cultivate and manage 166 acres. And the average age of those 23 farmers was 35. Only four of them were unmarried. Where there was any cause of complaint by any person whomsoever he failed to see. As for the 12 men not attested, the figures were still more striking. Of those men, eight were farmers in charge of 1,390 acres, giving an average of 174 acres per man. Only one of the eight was single.

Crediton's Rural Tribunal also found itself at the heart of controversy in early 1916 when it was accused of granting too many exemptions to farmers and agricultural workers. The accusation was made at a meeting of the nearby Tiverton District Tribunal. One of its representatives, a Mr New, asked what would 'become of agriculture if we lost the war, and weren't we likely to lose it if tribunals did like Crediton and let off 90% of the men'.

The outburst provoked a series of letters in local newspapers. One, by 'Fair Play', of Sandford, said: 'If the war is to be carried on, the question has to be settled: who are to go? Of course, the farmers say let somebody else go as we are short of labour. As I happen to know something of the labour required and employed during the past 20 years in the Crediton district, I feel sure the scarcity of labour is not anything like so much as represented. Among all the trades in the country districts, none is reaping so much a harvest through the war as the farming interest, and none sending so few of its sons ... While I have every respect for the farmers, there are many members of their families who could be spared.'

Tom Batting, chairman of the Crediton Tribunal, said Mr New's remarks demanded a reply as they seemed to 'cast a slur on Crediton Tribunal in unduly favouring agriculture at the expense of the country. I much deprecate the members of one tribunal criticising or, worse still, censuring the doings of another, as they cannot know the circumstances of individual cases.'

The tribunal had been asked to review a number of cases in the light of instructions that agricultural workers were 'entitled to be treated as starred (or exempted in the national interest) even though they may not be individually indispensable'. Mr Batting said because of this, 'one of the cases which had previously been dealt with, and refused, had to be acceded to, and the claim for exemption allowed, although the tribunal thought the man was not indispensable on the farm on which he was employed'.

He added: 'It is evident the government place much importance on the home-grown food supply, and recognise that this supply must suffer if the important men on the farms are taken. They are, therefore, making it very clear it is their wish that essential men on farms are to remain. Judging from the remarks of Mr New, he would denude the farms of labour and leave them crippled and maimed, buy – as long as there was any money to pay for it, and ship to take it – our food from abroad, and then, with a huge Army, find our money exhausted and our people starving. I am glad wiser counsels prevail, and that it is recognised that men, money, munitions, all combined, will win this war.'

The row over exemptions gathered pace in March 1916, when the fears of a member of the Crediton Tribunal, Canon Boles – a Church of England Canon – were reported in *The Western Times*. He spoke of his concerns that it was 'heading towards a position which, to his mind, was dangerous, if not entirely indefensible, and that was in entirely exempting a class of men and all their families from doing their duty to their country in naval and military service'.

As the war took its toll – with more and more men being conscripted into the Army – thousands of women were recruited to help keep Britain's farms operating and to grow sufficient food for soldiers fighting on the front line. Many farmers initially opposed the establishment of a Women's Land Army. But by the end of 1917, the WLA was pivotal in keeping farms and smallholdings in operation, with its members ploughing fields, growing crops, milking cows, bringing in hay and corn, and carrying out forestry work.

Part Two

THE GRANDSONS WHO DID NOT COME HOME

7

THE DAY DEATH VISITED JOHN AND HIS FAMILY

Rooks hovered noisily overhead in the strong winds sweeping across the open countryside. It was a cold October morning and heavy showers and a sharp chill in the air were a foretaste of the wet and wild winter to come.

John Roberts sat wearily on the gnarled old wooden bench outside his family farmhouse to eat his lunch, a large and stale chunk of home baked bread, Cheddar cheese and onions pickled by his daughter-in-law.

Wearing his favourite bowler hat, he brushed crumbs from his whiskers and tattered, weather-beaten overalls as he quietly looked out over the fields at Newland Farm, Witheridge, in the heart of rural Devon.

John was in his 87th year. He had worked as a farm labourer for more than seven decades and he was now spending his 'twilight years' with his youngest son Thomas and his family at a place he had grown to love.

But as he rose from the bench to take a short walk across the land, his thoughts were of different fields hundreds of miles away – in France, Belgium and other countries he had heard of but had never visited.

It was October 1915 and he had, at that stage, more than 20 of his grandsons involved in the Great War, many of them serving in the Devonshire Regiment, some who would be involved in some of the bloodiest battles in history.

Local newspapers had speculated that the number of John's grandsons fighting for 'King and country' could well be a record. John was justly proud of their bravery, but also feared for their lives and prayed for their safe return.

He had already been shaken to the core by the experience of losing one of his grandsons in May 1915. Jack Roberts, of nearby Cruwys Morchard, was just 20 when he died from injuries sustained on a French battlefield.

A widower for more than 15 years, John had had 15 children and had enjoyed watching his near 100 grandchildren grow up in the many small, rural communities in Mid and North Devon that he himself had lived and worked in all his life.

Although now retired, he still did a few 'odd jobs' at Newland, helping to harvest wheat and potato crops, and feed and look after the farm horses. He loved walking the land with the aid of a hand-carved walnut walking stick that belonged to his father.

John had often reflected on how he had reached such a great age when people he grew up and worked with had died in their 40s and 50s, some even younger, many worn out after working long hours as farm labourers.

Now, young men in their tens of thousands – brothers, cousins, friends looking for adventure and glory – were signing up to serve in a war that everyone had predicted would have been over by Christmas 1914.

Army recruitment campaigns were under way throughout Devon with senior officers and battle-hardened soldiers urging young farmers and workers in towns and cities to 'do their duty' and 'defend their country'.

John's grandsons – from Rackenford, Witheridge, Cruwys Morchard, Puddington, Washford Pyne, Sandford and Tiverton – were now serving in various battalions of the Devonshire Regiment, as well as the Royal 1st Devon Yeomanry, the Royal Engineers and Royal Field Artillery.

As he trudged slowly through the fields, with ever darkening clouds enveloping the skies above him, he wondered how many of his 'boys' would come home, when the fighting would be over and what toll the war would take on his family.

Riddled with arthritis and tired from his exertions, he decided to make his way back to the farmhouse as rain started to fall. Suddenly, a piercing scream shattered the silence that had accompanied him on his walk.

It came from the farmhouse and as John hurried back he heard cries of despair from his daughter-in-law Mary, who was standing outside the front door, shaking uncontrollably and holding a letter in her left hand.

John almost fell over as he approached her, dropping his walking stick, desperate to know what was upsetting her. His son, Thomas, raced across the farmyard to comfort his wife, fearing the worst as he looked into her crying eyes.

Mary couldn't speak. The letter she carried was crumpled and wet from her tears. Thomas removed it from her hand, read it slowly and dropped it to the ground. Barely able to talk, he told John that death had come to their door.

The letter stated: *'It is my painful duty to inform you that a report has this day been received from the War Office notifying the death of Private Albert Roberts (Thomas and Mary's son and John's grandson) of the 8th (Service) Battalion Devonshire Regiment ...'*

The chilling words were on an Army B104-82 Form, sent as standard by the British War Office to the next of kin to notify them of the death of a member of the Army – and ultimately distributed on an industrial scale as the war raged on for three more years.

The form, signed by the 'officer in charge of records', showed that Albert had died at a hospital near Boulogne and included the following words: *'I ... express to you the sympathy of the Army Council at your loss.*

'If any articles of private property left by the deceased are found, they will be forwarded to this office, but some time will probably elapse before their receipt, and when received they cannot be disposed of until authority is received from the War Office.

'Application regarding the disposal of any such personal effects, or of any amount that may eventually be found to be due to the late

soldier's estate, should be addressed to The Secretary, War Office, London, S.W., and marked outside "Effects".'

It was all so final. The wording seemed cold and inadequate to say the least. What a way to be told that a young man, a much-loved son, brother and grandson who had brought so much joy to his family, would not be coming home.

John had lost a second grandson and was inconsolable. He had watched Albert grow up as a toddler on Newland Farm and become a cattleman. He had been one of his favourite grandsons and he had now died from wounds in a French hospital aged just 19.

It was a sign of many tragedies to come for John and his family, his neighbours, friends, people across Devon and the rest of the United Kingdom. John would lose five more of his grandsons before the war would finally come to an end.

8

JACK — BAPTISM OF FIRE ON THE WESTERN FRONT ENDS IN TRAGEDY

A cool breeze caressed Jack's face as he looked up to a clear night sky filled with stars. Amid a brief but welcome silence, he closed his eyes and thought of the halcyon days of home. Of the green and golden fields of Devon, the wind rushing through the corn, and birds singing and flying so freely over the farm he had worked on.

He spent much of his life now in the barren trenches of northern France, caught up in a war where death and chaos were never far away. The deafening noise of artillery and machine gun fire and the carnage from desperate combat on the Western Front were the new and brutal reality for 20-year-old infantryman, Private John 'Jack' Roberts.

The horrors and mayhem of the Battle of Neuve Chapelle – the first major British offensive of the Great War – had provided a baptism of fire for one of the newest recruits to the 2nd Battalion of the Devonshire Regiment. He had been with the battalion for just a few weeks when he was thrust into the tumult and savagery of trench warfare in that three-day battle in March 1915 that claimed thousands of British lives.

Now, two months later, there was little time to reflect on the ferocity of that onslaught. For Jack was in the trenches again, not far from where he fought at Neuve Chapelle, ready for a major new attack on the Germans. It was just after dawn on May 9, 1915 and the sun had risen so brilliantly after a cold, dry night. Jack was among thousands of British troops poised to take part in what would become known as the Battle of Aubers Ridge.

In the lull before the assault, he had time to reflect on how in such a short space of time his life had changed so dramatically from being a farm worker in the heart of rural Devon to a volunteer in Lord Kitchener's British Expeditionary Force. A few short years ago he had been a cattle boy, herding cows with the aid of a large stick. Now he was armed with a Lee Enfield rifle, awaiting an order to advance on and kill enemy soldiers in a foreign country.

As he looked at his pocket watch, it was exactly 5am when the artillery opened fire on the enemy. The bombardment of the German front line and barbed wire entanglements bordering No Man's Land lasted 40 minutes. But the pounding proved far from devastating. For when the main assault started, infantrymen came under heavy machine gun fire and many soldiers were killed or wounded as soon as they went 'over the top' from front line trenches.

Hundreds of men were slaughtered by German marksmen as they ran into No Man's Land or became trapped on barbed wire that was still intact despite being hit by a wave of shrapnel bombs in the bombardment. When Jack and the 2nd Devons were ordered to advance, they came under unrelenting attack. Eight of their officers and more than 200 men of other ranks were killed or wounded while moving forward from assembly to first line trenches.

The huge number of British casualties, the lack of support for soldiers reaching the German front line and a paucity of fire power to counter the enemy artillery, led to the attack being stopped and ultimately abandoned within 24 hours. It took three days to remove the wounded from the battlefield to casualty clearing stations before many were then transferred to the large Army base hospital at Boulogne.

The Aubers attack was a 'bitter setback', C T Atkinson said in *The Devonshire Regiment 1914–1918*. 'Losses had been terrible.

The Devons, who had not got beyond the British front trenches ... had lost nearly as many as at Neuve Chapelle.' For these losses, there was nothing to show, no gains of ground, or the opportunity to repulse the enemy, Atkinson opined.

It is believed that Jack was among those seriously hurt on May 9 or the early hours of May 10. There are no records to show when he was injured or how. It is possible that he was wounded in the days after the Battle of Aubers Ridge. For his battalion suffered a number of casualties in the trenches from shell and gun fire on May 13, 14, 23 and 24.

What is known is that Jack lost his fight for life at Boulogne Hospital on May 30, 1915, two days before his 21st birthday. He had been in France for just 111 days, fought in two of the bloodiest battles of the war, witnessed great courage in the face of a formidable enemy and seen friends and fellow soldiers killed or badly wounded in wholesale front-line massacres.

The killing of two close friends from Devon in the final hours of the battle encapsulated the human tragedy at Aubers. Privates Frederick (Fred) Josiah Squire and Charles (Charlie) Walker – among four young men from Torbay who joined the 2nd Devons on the same day – died within seconds of each other, both shot in the head.

They were not the first of that group of four to die. Their pal Charles Henry (Harry) Hodson was killed in action at Neuve Chapelle. The sole survivor of those Torbay recruits, a Pte Richards, wrote to Fred's mother after his death to tell her what happened to him. His moving letter was published in *The Western Times* in May 1915, under the headline 'Chums to the end'.

He said he, Fred – who had been a conductor at Paignton on the local tramway before going to war – Charlie and Harry had 'always been together' since signing up, 'sharing each other's blankets and food and always marched in the same section'. Since Harry's death, 'Charlie, Fred and I have been chums'.

On May 9, 'we had orders to advance about 700 yards across open country, amid a perfect hail of bullets and machine gun fire. We all got over safely, and were together all the day. That night we had to line the parapet several times to repulse the

57

enemy. At 5.30 on the 10th we had orders to line the parapet again.

'Fred and Charlie stood side by side. Charlie was killed instantly, being shot through the head. He had hardly fallen when poor Fred fell across him, also shot through the head. Neither spoke, and death was instantaneous, so two chums died at the same moment. I took their personal papers, books and Fred's ring, and gave them to the officer. His belt, with about 1s 2d in French money and his cap badge I will bring home to you or, if possible, send by post.

'We tied them up in waterproof sheets and laid them side by side as two chums, and as two of the bravest of Englishmen. It will be a comfort to you to know that they were always brave and cheerful, and were very good men. They died good men. You can realise my own feelings when I say I have lost all here now. Please accept my deepest sympathy. I shall hope to see you when I return.'

The 2nd Devons had marched into assembly trenches just south east of Rue du Bois on the eve of the battle. At 6.15 the next morning, they moved forward to another block of trenches south of the Rue Petillon. 'Getting into these trenches was awkward as companies had to move … in file. It was here we suffered our first casualties, losing about 10 NCOs and men from shell fire,' their war diary recorded.

The battalion suffered their heaviest losses after 6.45am, as they were 'subjected to very heavy artillery fire and enfilade machine gun fire from a salient in enemy trenches on our right' in a 'difficult' advance. When Albert and his fellow soldiers reached the front line, they found the trenches 'full of men' of various battalions with scarcely an officer among them.

A further bombardment of enemy defences was ordered but was halted to prevent British troops 'in and in front of German trenches' being hit. After being 'heavily shelled all afternoon', the 2nd Devons were ordered to 'hold themselves in readiness to assault enemy trenches after dark', but this attack was cancelled.

Early the next day, the fighting came to an end as the battalion covered the Rifle Brigade's evacuation from the battlefield. It was a bitterly disappointing end to an assault that achieved high losses but no gains. The inadequate bombardment of enemy lines, hampered by a lack of field guns and shells, was blamed for the outcome – carnage on an industrial scale, with 11,000 British casualties in just 24 hours.

The attack on Aubers provoked an outcry over shortfalls in high explosives on the Western Front. *The Aberdeen Daily Journal* in May 1915 quoted a leading article in *The Times* which said:

'Men died in heaps upon the Aubers Ridge ... because the field guns were short, and gravely short of high explosive shells. Our sole purpose is to ensure that such a lamentable defect shall be made good as soon as possible. Manufacturer after manufacturer can relate how they offered to make shells, how their offers were coldly rejected and how after months had been lost they were implored to begin. The matter does not end there. Requests and warnings from the front about the need for high explosives have been grievously disregarded. The War Office thought it knew how to conduct the present forms of warfare better than the men on the spot.'

Jack was born in Witheridge, Devon on June 1, 1894. He was the second of three sons of Samuel Roberts, who was born in the village in 1864 and Maria Roberts (nee Morrish), who was born in Knowstone, Devon in 1871.

The year of his birth was noted for political upheaval, with the resignation of the great Liberal Prime Minister William Ewart Gladstone – and his replacement by Archibald Primrose, the 5th Earl of Rosebery.

One of Britain's best-known landmarks, Blackpool Tower, opened for the first time. The International Olympic Committee was founded in Paris by Baron Pierre de Coubertin, with the first modern Olympic Games being held two years later.

Jack was born in the same year as King Edward Vlll (who abdicated less than a year after taking the throne in 1936), Harold Macmillan, who became Prime Minister in 1957, and the American film director John Ford.

In 1901, when he was seven years old, Jack lived with his parents and two brothers – Sidney and Samuel Jnr – at Edbury

Farm, on the boundaries of Pennymoor and Poughill in Mid-Devon. His father worked at Edbury as a farm labourer.

Ten years later, Jack was working as a cattle boy at Lower Ford Farm, Cullompton. The farm was run by 32-year-old Harry Herbert Pearcey who had a wife, Amy, and a one-year-old daughter, Florence Emily.

Jack enlisted in the 2nd Battalion of the Devonshire Regiment in Tiverton, Devon and arrived in France on February 9, 1915. He was one of 35 recruits to officially join the battalion at transport lines seven days later. Based in billets at Rue du Bacquerot and near Merville during the month, he spent a number of days in the trenches, coming under enemy fire.

There was drama on February 26 when a wagon load of bombs blew up, fatally wounding two of his fellow soldiers who had been cycling close to the scene of the explosion. Nine men were killed in action or died of wounds in Jack's first 12 days on the Western Front – and another, Private James Curtis, of Appledore, was suffocated in his sleep by fumes from a coke fire.

In early March, the 2nd Devons – operating in France under the orders of the 23rd Brigade of the British Army's Eighth Division – marched to billets in Estaires in preparation for the Battle of Neuve Chapelle, a small village between Bethune and Lille. The battle marked the largest attack mounted by the British forces since the beginning of the war. The artillery bombardment of enemy lines was formidable, with more than 300 guns firing as many shells at German trenches in 35 minutes as were discharged in the whole of the Second Boer War fought in 1899–1902.

The 2nd Devons played a pivotal supporting role in the battle, between March 10 and 12, advancing on German lines, helping to bomb enemy soldiers out of trenches and to take prisoners. They also had to dodge shells coming from their own side as well as from the Germans, and suffered heavy losses from artillery and machine gun fire. In those two days, and in the following 48 hours, their casualties totalled 284. Five officers, including Captain Claude Alexander Lafone, and about 80 other ranks were killed. In all, almost 12,000 British officers and men were killed, wounded or reported missing in the battle.

A letter sent by Sergeant H Eames to his cousin in Barnstaple – and published in *The North Devon Journal* in April 1915 – told of the bravery of the 2nd Devons at Neuve Chapelle and how his fellow soldiers had endured terrible weather, punishing marches and fierce bombardments in the course of the battle.

He said the battalion marched 'practically all night' on March 7 and 8, a night 'a dog would not go out unless he was forced to do so, as it was raining torrents. But the boys were in the best of spirits, singing and whistling all along the road.' At midnight, on March 9, 'we moved up to take our positions', halting on the road to 'take some hot tea, which turned out to be the last hot stuff we had for four days'.

Sgt Eames told how the Germans 'rained shells into us ... using every big gun they owned' after he and his men were ordered to 'dig in' after attacking enemy defences. 'Really, I cannot explain the horrors of it,' he wrote. 'We remained in the firing line until the 15th when we were relieved, and went into billets for two days.'

Sergeant Robert Gilliland, of the 2nd Devons, who was wounded at Neuve Chapelle, described the fighting on March 12, 1915 in a letter to a friend in Exmouth which was published in *The Western Times* in April that year. 'From where I was I could see the whole front of our line,' wrote Sgt Gilliland. 'And as I saw the enemy again and again throw themselves against our front, I thought of the beach at Exmouth, where the waves roll in and back again.

'But their waves were very much diminished each time before the return journey. Their losses in killed alone must have been awful, and the prisoners we took were absolutely disheartened and scared out of their wits. The bullets fell all around us, over us, in front of us, behind us, and very often not more than half a yard away, but we stuck to the business, and I pride myself that (an) officer and I got our little crowd to (safety) without losing a single man.'

A military funeral was held for one victim – Private Arthur Turner – in Barnstaple at the end of March 1915. The former farm hand died at Shorncliffe Military Hospital in Kent from serious wounds in the aftermath of the battle. He had been transferred there after initially receiving treatment in Boulogne Hospital, and 'succumbed to his injuries' just two hours after being admitted.

The North Devon Journal reported that Pte Turner, who was 26 when he died on March 25, was the first Barnstaple soldier in the war to have his 'mortal remains … brought to his native place for interment'. His body was taken to the town's St Mary Magdalene Church where a short service was attended by members of his family before the 'fallen hero was honoured with a military funeral'.

There was a large congregation for a 'profoundly impressive' service conducted by the Vicar, the Rev R J E Boggis, and thousands of people lined the town streets leading to the cemetery where men of the Devonshire Regiment fired three volleys over his grave. The coffin was draped with the Union Jack on which rested Pte Turner's helmet, belt and bayonet. A bugler sounded the Last Post at his graveside.

Rev Boggis said: 'We sympathise with his kindred and his friends in their sorrow at losing a son, brother, a lover, a companion; and also, we share with them the pride in having given one to die for King and country. And we of Barnstaple assemble here to show honour, to manifest our admiration for bravery, to tell (of) our gratitude for one of those who have behaved themselves valiantly for their people.'

The cortege, on leaving the church, was headed by the firing party of the 3rd-6th Foreign Service Battalion 6th Devons. The coffin was carried in relays by members of the 6th Devons. Among the family mourners were Pte Turner's two brothers, Jack, serving with the 12th Welsh Regiment and Bertram, serving with the North Devon Hussars. Wounded soldiers being treated at the North Devon Infirmary and Red Cross Hospital also attended.

Another Barnstaple, or 'Barum' soldier killed at Neuve Chapelle was Private John William Turner, aged 21, of Pilton. He was shot in the head on March 11, just a few weeks after attending the funeral of his mother, Mary, in Devon.

The war diary for the 2nd Devons for the period of the Battle of Neuve Chapelle, shows that the 2nd Devons arrived at their assembly position, on the south side of Rue Tilleloy, in the early hours of March 10. 'Some difficulty was experienced in finding (our) way across country in spite of ground having been reconnoitred,' the diary recorded. A party of engineers 'crossing the line of march of the brigade' was given as the principal reason for this – with 'too narrow' bridges over ditches also being blamed.

The battalion learned that, in the attack, they would be in support of the 2nd Scottish Rifles and 2nd Middlesex Battalion. At 7.30am, wire breaking by the field artillery and bombardment of enemy positions began. At 8am, the 2nd Scottish Rifles launched their attack 'from our trenches, advancing in the most gallant manner in spite of heavy losses'. Half of the 2nd Devons' A and B Companies started their advance along Sign Post Lane (a communication trench) at 8.15am in support of the Scottish Rifles.

The remaining men of A and B Companies advanced along Rutland Row to occupy trenches vacated by the 2nd Middlesex. It soon became clear that the 2nd Middlesex were unable to advance, 'every man being shot down as he appeared over the parapet', the 2nd Devons' war diary recorded. 'B Company then made three attempts to cross to German trenches … all of which were frustrated, the men being all killed or wounded.

'Lieutenant (Reginald Plumtre) Bates led the first attempt and was killed, falling on German wire.' The officer in charge of machine guns was wounded and both of the 2nd Devons' machine guns were put out of action before they could be used. Men from A and B Companies followed the Scottish Rifles into the trenches and bombers were sent forward to try and clear the enemy out of their defensive positions.

At 9.30am, 2nd Lieutenant George Clinton Wright led a bombing party of five to clear enemy soldiers from a long stretch of trench to enable the advance to continue. He was shot in the back and killed by a wounded German officer in achieving his objective. 2nd Lieutenant Mark Gilham Windsor was wounded in the assault and subsequently killed by a shell when taken to a dressing station. Another officer, Lieutenant

Robert Owen Bristowe, was killed after A and B Companies captured a German trench.

Two more senior officers were wounded or injured before 2nd Lieutenant Cecil Jacob, the only officer left standing, took over command of B Company. In further advances, the 2nd Devons captured 'many prisoners' and a machine gun before beginning to 'consolidate' their position at 1.30pm. They came under heavy shell fire from British guns during the evening, preventing them from capturing more Germans 'on the run'. In the following two days, the battalion came under heavy artillery fire, suffering more casualties. Captain Lafone was killed by a shell splinter on March 12.

During the afternoon of that day, the battalion were ordered to help in an attack on enemy defences at Pietre-La Russee. An 'impenetrable fence' – a heavily wired thorn hedge – was discovered 100 yards from the German position and the attack was called off at the 11th hour. However, B Company, in an isolated position, and unaware of the halt to the assault, advanced close to the enemy line. They came under heavy fire and suffered 30 casualties before being led back to safety.

The fighting, hampered by poor communications between front line soldiers and the artillery, a lack of reinforcements and a lack of munitions, ended on March 13. On that day, the 2nd Devons, just south west of Pietre-La Russee, were in trenches with the 2nd West Yorkshire and 2nd Middlesex Regiments, where they were shelled at 'point blank range'. They remained in the trenches the following day before being relieved by the 1st Lincolns, marching to billets at Pont du Hem.

Neuve Chapelle provided a dreadful warning of things to come. Jack was just happy to have the chance to fight another day. But death and uncertainty were his constant companions. Two men from his battalion were killed on March 17. Three more were wounded ten days later when German soldiers hurled shells into trenches south of Bois Grenier – which the 2nd Devons had taken over just two days earlier. The trenches were shelled again the following day when an officer and one man were 'dangerously wounded'.

Relief from fighting on the front line came from stays in

billets – in Rue du Bacquerot, Estaires and at Bac St Maur. In early April, just before taking over trenches by Ancien Chartreux, the battalion were addressed by Field Marshall Sir John French, Commander-in-Chief of the British Expeditionary Force, who thanked the officers and men for their courage at Neuve Chapelle.

On April 18, the battalion moved into Brigade Reserve billets on the Rue du Quesney, near Fleurbaix before later marching into country billets near Doulieu. While there on May 1, Neuve Chapelle was rocked by a heavy German bombardment in the early hours. The following day, Jack and his battalion marched into more austere billets in a factory at Estaires, and on May 4 marched five miles in pouring rain to new trenches in the build up to the Battle of Aubers Ridge.

Jack's death was reported in *The Western Times* on Monday, June 14, 1915. The words *'died of wounds – Roberts, Pte J. 11889'* appeared under the heading 'latest list of casualties in county regiment'.

He died at No 13 General Hospital (Boulogne). Just over three months before his death, he completed a will in which he stated: 'In the event of my death, I give the whole of my effects or property to my father, S (Samuel) Roberts, 1 Higher Furse, Pennymoor, Cruwys Morchard, near Tiverton.' His father received a war gratuity.

Jack was buried at Boulogne Eastern Cemetery where the grave stones were laid flat on the ground because the sandy soil made it almost impossible for them to be erected upright. Jack's grave number is VIII.A.55. His headstone includes his service number and the date of his death.

Buried close to Jack is the Great War poet Julian Grenfell, a Royal Dragoons captain who died from wounds on May 26, 1915. Captain Grenfell composed one of the finest ever war poems, *Into Battle*, which was published in *The Times* newspaper on the day he died.

Jack is also remembered on Cruwys Morchard War Memorial, which honours eight men from the parish who died during the Great War. His name is etched in marble on a plaque within the parish's Church of the Holy Cross.

Jack's service number was 11889. His Great War medal card mistakenly states that he died of wounds on September 30, 1915. He was awarded three medals: The Victory and British War Medals and the 1915 Star.

9

ALBERT — CUT DOWN AT BATTLE OF LOOS

It was his 63rd day in France and a momentous one for 19-year-old Albert Roberts. He was about to take part in his first — and last – battle. The attack he was to be involved in would be heralded as one of the most remarkable of the Great War.

It was 6am, 30 minutes from 'Zero Hour' on September 25, 1915, and farmer's son Albert was standing in rain-soaked, muddy trenches at Vermelles in northern France, waiting for the signal to go 'over the top'.

Just a few days away from his 20th birthday, he couldn't imagine being in a bleaker, more inhospitable environment, starkly contrasting to the lush, green fields of Devon he had been working in just a few short years before.

Surrounded by the deafening roar of a huge bombardment of German defences by more than 500 field guns, he knew that his life would never be more under threat in the next few crucial hours, or perhaps, minutes.

Albert, who had arrived in France with the newly formed 8th (Service) Battalion of the Devonshire Regiment just two months earlier, was about to take part in the largest offensive yet of the war, the Battle of Loos.

It was not a day for faint hearts. The enemy trenches to be attacked were veritable fortresses. The dash across No Man's Land would be fraught with danger, with large sections of razor wire still in place and the German defences crammed with machine guns.

With the British forces using a chemical weapon for the first time at Loos – deadly chlorine gas – Albert and his men had to make that fateful infantry charge while wearing cumbersome, but potentially life-saving gas masks.

When this new weapon of mass destruction was discharged along the British front, fickle winds created a hazard for the 8th Devons, with the gas drifting back into their trenches and lingering over their attack zone.

Some men, finding the crude flannel masks – or 'P' Helmets as they were known – too hot to wear, and having difficulty in seeing through tiny eye pieces, were exposed to and overcome by powerful chlorine fumes.

As 'Zero Hour' arrived and the attack whistles blew, the 8th Devons suffered heavy losses within minutes when three of their companies, moving swiftly forward almost in one line, struggled to get through gaps in the razor wire in No Man's Land.

Officers and men were brutally cut down by artillery and machine gun fire. Undaunted, the battalion courageously continued to charge forward in a hail storm of bullets, helping to capture the trench from which they had come under murderous attack.

They reached it within a dozen minutes of starting their assault. In that short space of time, their numbers were decimated with most of their senior officers, including their commanding officer, Lieutenant-Colonel Alexander George William Grant, being killed.

The battalion captured four German field guns in their heroic assault. But now, with their casualties mounting and facing the real possibility of being completely wiped out on the battlefield, their fearless advance ground to a halt.

Albert and his men were not the only Devon boys at the heart of the battle. The 9th Devons, with whom the 8th would fight side by side for most of the war, were also in the thick of it. Both battalions suffered catastrophic losses.

A total of 19 officers and 620 NCOs and men of the 8th

Devons were killed, wounded or listed as missing at Loos – many of the casualties occurring in the first few hours of the battle. The 9th had 15 officers and 461 NCOs and men killed, wounded or 'missing in action'.

Albert was among those seriously wounded. He was taken by field ambulance to a casualty clearing station before being transferred to the Army base hospital at Wimereux, near Boulogne, where he died on October 3, 1915, three days before his birthday.

The nature of his wounds and exactly when and how he was fatally injured in action and taken to Wimereux are not known. He had been in France for just 71 days when his great adventure abroad ended in tragedy.

A picture of Albert was published in *The Western Times* on Friday, October 22 under the headline: 'Witheridge lad dies of wounds'. Two days earlier, in the same newspaper, his death was recorded in a roll of honour which also listed 28 others from his battalion as killed or wounded.

The immense courage of the 8th Devons in leading the attack on the German trenches – and in their daring capture of the enemy field guns in the assault – as they faced potential obliteration, cannot be over-stated.

The battle was their first major action since arriving on French soil. Their assault on the enemy was regarded as among the bravest and boldest of the whole war and would ensure that the part they played at Loos would never be forgotten.

At a lecture in Exeter in November 1920, reported in *The Western Times*, senior officer Lieutenant-Colonel Percy Reginald Worrall said the attack launched by the battalion was one of the 'finest incidents' of the war.

He believed it would be regarded as 'second only' to the heroic last stand by the 2nd Devons at Bois des Buttes in the Third Battle of the Aisne in May 1918 when more than 550 of their officers and men were killed or captured as they were surrounded by the enemy.

There was 'no finer page in history' than the gallant way the 8th Devons pressed forward at Loos when reduced to a fraction of their fighting strength, and captured the German field guns in an extraordinary bayonet charge, said Lt-Col Worrall.

When two of those guns were paraded through the streets of Exeter and presented to the county of Devon almost two months after the battle, thousands of people turned up to honour the 'local boys' who had fought with such honour.

Earl Fortescue, Devon's Lord Lieutenant, who received the weapons, said: 'Unless I am mistaken, it is almost without parallel in the history of our own or of any other army, that the remnants of a shattered battalion … should go on and capture a whole (artillery) battery.'

The Battle of Loos, which ultimately raged over 18 days, was the largest British offensive of 1915. Launched after a four-day artillery bombardment by hundreds of large guns in which a quarter of a million shells were fired to 'soften up the enemy', it resulted in more than 60,000 British casualties.

The following report on the 'memorable deeds' of the 8th Devons – nicknamed 'Buller's Own' after Crediton's Zulu War hero General Sir Redvers Henry Buller – published in *The Western Times* in April 1919, recalled the drama of the battle.

The 8th Battalion of the Devonshire Regiment have done many memorable things in the war, but nothing they did attracted more attention than their capture of four German guns at Loos … The attack was made by the famous 7th Division, and in the 20th Brigade, which was included in this Division, were not only the 8th Devons, but also the 9th Battalion. It was, however, the 8th who led the attack, and on them fell the brunt of the work, the 9th being in support and giving help at a time when it was desperately needed.

The final objective was Lens, that great coal centre from which the Germans were getting so much strength, and the loss of which was so keenly felt by the French. Between our lines and the final objective lay the village of Hulluch. The country around was most flat, but there was a slight depression leading to the village, and it was here that there was a battery of guns, the very guns which were finally captured. Although the final objective was Lens, the Devons were not expected to do as much as that. What they hoped to do was to push along the road, and, after capturing the village of Hulluch, they were to cross the canal and hold the opposite bank.

... The 8th Devons took up their position in the front line during Friday night, September 24. It was a miserable evening, rain fell incessantly – hardly conducive to the proper spirit for an attack. Yet these men were grim and determined, and thought nothing of the discomfort. All that night they were getting ready for the 'stunt', which was timed to commence at 6.30 next morning.

Orders were given out to the NCOs that the Devons were to keep to the left of the Hulluch road, while the 2nd Gordons (Highlanders), who were on the right, were to cross over to the other side of the road after the trenches had been passed. It was suggested to them that they were not likely to meet with any great opposition until they had passed the German third line trench, but it was pointed out that some way along the road there was a spot which might cause trouble. Observers ... had noted something, but they were unable to determine what it was. Subsequent events proved that their suspicions were well founded.

In the early hours of the morning – at 5.45 to be precise – our artillery put up what, in those days, was considered to be a very healthy bombardment, and this was directed with good effect on the German front line trench. Just before half past six, the gas cylinders in our own front line were opened. Our own men were already in their (gas) helmets, and very soon a greenish yellow cloud was drifting over so slowly towards the enemy. The weather was most unsuitable. Drizzling rain kept everybody thoroughly wet, breathing in those early-pattern gas helmets was difficult, and the wind was not strong enough to carry the gas towards the Germans sufficiently quickly ... Warning gongs were beating and (the Germans were) opening up a terrible machine gun barrage a quarter of an hour before the Devons clambered over the parapet.

... The attack with gas was not the success that had been anticipated. It lacked the element of surprise. A favourable wind was an important feature in the days when gas clouds were the vogue. In addition, it has to be remembered that this was the first time the battalion had attacked in helmets.

At 6.30 to the minute the boys in the front line climbed over the top and commenced to advance in waves. The first company to go over was C, and this was followed by the other companies in the order: A, D and B. As soon as they showed their heads above the parapet, the German artillery, which had already been lively, opened up in all *its fury. Undismayed, by short, sharp rushes the waves of Devons crept forward till they reached the dangerous point which had been indicated to them. On arrival, it proved to be a death trap.*

The artillery, which had otherwise done its work well, had failed lamentably at this spot, for it had left the wire uncut in many places. No blame attaches to the gunners, however, for it must be remembered that even in these days the supply of high explosive was limited and had to be used sparingly, and it was only high explosive which was of any use in clearing the way for an attack. All around this uncut barbed wire was a big nest of machine guns which swept the surrounding area. Men fell quickly and thickly, and the casualties were terrible. Among those killed within a few minutes of each other were the commanding officer, the second in command (Major Henry Charles Carden) ... and the Adjutant (Captain Arthur St John Mackintosh Kekewich).

After the barbed wire had been cut, the Devons rushed the front line, but with the exception of dead and dying it was found that the enemy had only left a few men here to keep up a fire while they were getting ready to make a show in the second line of trenches. Here, they had a number of machine guns and kept up a truly awful fusillade with them. As soon as this was discovered – for the men were falling fast now, and very few officers remained – the order was given for the Devons to lie down in the open and keep up as hot a fire as was possible on the German trench. The whole of the Scouts platoon, with the exception of Lieutenant (Douglas William) MacMichael and one man were killed. Then the diminishing numbers gathered themselves for a rush, and with it the Germans bolted back to their third line through their communication trenches, while the Devons followed them across the top.

Here was another grim struggle, and all the time the Germans were exacting a heavy toll ... for they had the advantage of cover in the trenches, while 'Buller's Own' had to go across the open, machine-gun swept ground on the top. Heartened by the progress they had made, and by the sight of the village of Hulluch in front of them, they soon gave the enemy the order to quit from his third line, and were quickly chasing them down the slope into the village itself. In this depression they found a battery of four guns, with the gunners still standing at their posts and serving them.

The capture of the guns was a thrilling incident. Although their presence had been keenly felt, no-one had seen them – no-one could see them – until they were quite close. The gas was moving so slowly that the attackers were still fighting in it, and on the brow of this depression, they suddenly came to the edge of this cloud. Weird, shadowy figures were working shoulder to shoulder, and when they came out into the clear daylight they lay flat on their stomachs for safety till enough of them could be collected to make another rush.

Almost as soon as they had got clear of the gas, they saw the guns. Sergeant (Reginald) Northam raised a shout of triumph which was muffled by his helmet, and roared 'come on boys'. The men, heedless of what they were facing, rallied to his call and dashed down on the guns. The gunners were, on the orders of (2nd) Lieutenant (F W) Trott – a gallant officer whose bandaged head and blood-stained face bore evidence of an early wound – taken prisoner and sent to the rear. Private Coombes, picking up a piece of chalk from the ground, wrote 8th Devons on each gun, and the remainder at full speed chased the Germans, who were scuttling into the village.

On the road, after sniping two Germans, Sgt Northam was himself shot through the head. He had behaved splendidly throughout, and was a source of strength and inspiration to all around him. Away on the left terrible havoc was being wrought by the concentrated fire from the Hohenzollern Redoubt.

The whole of Hulluch was reeking with gas, and from every corner window machine guns spurted death. The back of the town was packed with the enemy. They had expected the attack, and had made every preparation to resist it. So strong was their defence that within a very short time the Devons were only a handful of 50 men with Captain (Kingsmill Douglas Hoseason) Gwynn and 2nd Lt Trott, and at a quarter to nine the order was given to retire from the town and dig in just outside.

While they were falling back, more men fell. Captain Gwynn was wounded with a bomb, and 2nd Lt Trott took command. In order to be able to put up a better resistance, he withdrew again slightly, and the men who were left, firing from their knees, put up plucky resistance. Then 2nd Lt Trott was again wounded in the hand, and the charge fell on Company Sergeant Major (A) Bryant. By falling back, the Devons had lost the guns they had captured, and these were too good to lose,

73

so, reinforced by some of the 9th Battalion, who had come through and joined up with them, Sgt-Major Bryant led them with such effect that they took two lines of enemy trench, again securing the guns and holding on.

In the evening, the Germans had made a determined counter-attack, but still the Devons held on and drove the enemy back. In the night, the 9th Battalion took over the line, and many days later they were relieved by the Guards' Division, who despite repeated attempts, failed to take Hulluch. The Devons lost heavily when in the village in the morning from the shelling of our own artillery. Signals were sent back, but the barrage was not raised, and this was largely responsible for the Devons' retiring.

Reflecting on the 8th Devons' actions at Loos, C T Atkinson in *The Devonshire Regiment 1914–18*, said it 'spoke well for the battalion's training and for the spirit by which they were inspired, that, when nearly all of their officers had fallen with so many of the men, the survivors should have carried on the attack with such vigour and resolution.

'For the failure to exploit to the full the success of the first attack, the 8th and 9th (Devons) could not be held responsible. In capturing their objectives, and in retaining all but the most advanced positions reached, they had done all that could be asked of them.'

Atkinson said it was 'even more in the quality than in the quantity of their losses' that the 8th had suffered so much. 'To lose so many of their officers and NCOs who had borne the brunt of the work of raising and training the new battalion was a shattering blow.'

The war diary for the 8th Devons shows that they arrived in Vermelles, an old coal mining town about six miles from Bethune and 20 miles from Lille, on September 14, 1915. They found it in ruins, smashed by months of artillery fire.

The battalion moved into trenches there at 9.15pm on September 24 in readiness for an attack at dawn the next day. The trenches were waterlogged and mud-filled after repeated downpours and difficult to stand in or move around.

The diary recorded the following for the first day of the Battle of Loos:

As soon as our guns started the intensive bombardment, the German guns – scenting what was in the wind – replied with heavy and light artillery and caused some casualties, though not many. On the signal being given, C, A and D Companies seemed to go forward together in one line. This happened probably because A and D Companies started too soon. The result was great crowding towards the gaps in the wire and consequent increase in casualties – most of which occurred just outside or in the midst of the wire in front of the Breslau Trench.

During the advance from our own trenches to the Breslau Trench, every officer – save three – was either wounded or killed ... As soon as the attack reached the German trench the few Germans therein put their hands up and surrendered. The attackers then bore to the south east and crossed the Hulluch Road. No opposition was met with and Gun Trench was reached. The German gunners put their hands up and surrendered and so the battalion captured four field guns. These guns by their overheated state bore witness to the intensity of the German artillery fire. The charge towards the guns was led by Sgt Northam and A Company and 8th Devons was chalked upon them.

Then the advance proceeded to the crossroads west of Hulluch. The battalion here was about 100 strong ... All the machine guns were gone – two knocked out in the first advance and the other two seem to have been lost on the outskirts of Hulluch owing to a section getting too far forward and getting cut off. No advance was possible from these crossroads during the day for two reasons: 1, At first the artillery were still firing only just beyond the position and 2, no troops came up to reinforce. So the battalion dug themselves in just to west of road with their sight on the crossroads. The 2nd Gordons were on the right and no-one at all on the left.

At this place, Sgt Northam was killed by a sniper. At this time there seems to have been very few of the enemy in Hulluch or (nearby) Cite St Elie and lack of support alone kept the German line unbroken. All day this position was held ... At about 9.30pm the enemy coming from Cite St Elie got behind our position in estimated strength of a company and the first known of this was the interception of ration parties. A retirement was then made to Gun Trench in the course of which many losses were sustained owing partly to rifle fire and bombing by the enemy and partly from rifle and machine gun fire *from the Bedfords (Regiment) in Gun Trench who in the dark mistook friend for foe. The remnants of the battalion occupied Gun Trench and there dug themselves in, finding themselves with 2nd Borders on their left and the 6th Gordons on the right. Mixed up with the battalion were many of the 9th Devons and a few of other units. There was no more infantry action during the night.*

The diary recorded the following for the second day of the battle, September 26:

During the night Gun Trench was improved and by daybreak it afforded sufficient protection from rifle fire. The position was as follows … from Hulluch Road to 200 yards south were the 2nd Borders, about 250 strong. Then a mixture of 9th and 8th Devons, the latter about 50 strong with no officers and on the right, were the 6th Gordons. About 5.30am the reserve officers joined the battalion in the trench. The rest of the day was passed in this trench as orders were received from Brigade to hold on about 8am. There was no infantry action. The German guns were active but did not shell us at all. Very likely they didn't know we were there. There was a little sniping but most disconcerting was the fire and stray bullets coming from the direction of Fosse 8 (a slag heap), which was practically reverse fire. Owing to this one man was shot through the back of head and killed. Our guns were very busy shelling Cite St Elie and Puits … and it was a pleasant spectacle. We were relieved at 10pm.

Between September 27 and 29, the diary recorded that organisation had been restored as far as possible:

Battalion now 130 strong as many stragglers came in and about 50 men had spent yesterday in trench on north of road. Spent three very uncomfortable days: all ranks very tired and very dirty and weather was very bad. There was continuing fighting for Fosse 8 and also below the Loos ridge. The first of which could be plainly seen. German artillery were very active indeed and they had got up some of their bigger guns.

On September 30, the 8th Devons were in billets in Beuvry, a town near Bethune. The war diary recorded the following:

The men cleaned themselves up as well as possible. During the afternoon General (John Frederick) Trefusis (Commander of the 20th Brigade of the 7th Division) went round billets and congratulated them on their conduct in action.

The presentation of two of the captured field guns to the county of Devon in November 1915 was a spectacular and emotional ceremony. The *Devon and Exeter Gazette* reported that there was a 'huge gathering' at Northernhay, Exeter to witness the handing over of the weapons.

The ceremony took place in the roadway leading to the main entrance to the city's Queen Street Station. The guns were hauled through the streets by horses from the Royal Field Artillery at Topsham Barracks.

They were officially presented to Earl Fortescue by Colonel Walsh, commanding officer of the No 8 district (Devonshire Regiment). He said that 'great and valiant deeds' were done by the 8th and 9th Battalions and it was by those noble deeds that the Devonshire Regiment had again become famous in the British Army.

Many 'gallant and noble lives were lost', but it was hoped that the sorrows of the widows, children, mothers and fathers of those men who 'threw down their lives in such a cause' would be 'somewhat alleviated by the remembrance of their loved ones' magnificent deeds'. The guns would be a memento of those brave men, said Col Walsh.

Eight German guns in all were seized at Loos, four by the 8th Devons and four by the 2nd Gordon Highlanders. One was later presented to Queensland in Australia where it can be found today at the Queen's Park in Brisbane.

Presented by King George V, it was shipped to Australia by the steamer *Carpentaria* and unveiled by the Governor of Queensland, Sir Hamilton Goold on August 18, 1917. He said it would be forever kept as a memento of the war.

Albert was born in Rackenford, Devon on October 6, 1895 – when Victoria was Queen of England and Robert Cecil, the Marquess of Salisbury, was Prime Minister. It was a year that marked the founding of the National Trust and the publication of H G Well's masterpiece, *The Time Machine*. The first United States Open Golf Championship was staged at Newport, Rhode Island, and England's greatest cricketer W G Grace, scored his 100th century.

Albert was born in the same year as the legendary baseball

player Babe Ruth, the Italian actor Rudolph Valentino, the American heavyweight boxer Jack Dempsey, J Edgar Hoover, head of America's FBI, and King George VI.

Albert was the son of Thomas and Mary Ann (nee Morrish) Roberts, of Newland Farm, Witheridge. Just three years before the Great War, he worked alongside his father and brothers as a cattle man on the farm. Albert was from a large family. His parents had ten children in all, losing two in infancy.

Albert's oldest brother, Frank, a carter, would go on to serve in the Royal 1st Devon Yeomanry, one of Devon's oldest regiments of the British Army. Frank would survive the war – remarkably after suffering a gunshot wound to the head. Another of Albert's older brothers, Thomas, a farrier, served with the Army in Italy in the months after the war ended.

Immediately before the start of the war, Albert worked at two Devon rectories, in Meshaw and Thelbridge, for about three years. It is believed that he joined the 8th Devons shortly after their formation in Exeter in 1914 when the battalion were attached to the 14th (Light) Division. He sailed with the battalion from Southampton to Le Havre on July 25, 1915, arriving there the following day. Nine days later, the 8th Devons became attached to the 20th Brigade of the 7th Division of the British Army.

The war diary shows that the battalion travelled by train to Wizernes, a small village close to the Belgian border, on July 25, arriving the next morning. Officers and men went into billets and were inspected on July 30 when they were 'highly complimented'. They moved to billets in Carvin on August 4. Thirteen days later they travelled to Locon, five miles north of Bethune, where they suffered their first casualties two days later, with one man being killed.

On August 26, Albert and his fellow soldiers moved into the trenches for the first time, coming under attack from snipers and artillery fire in the following days. They were relieved on August 30, moving into billets before heading for Busnes, a small farming village eight miles from Bethune. Five days later they were in different trenches that were 'fearfully wet and muddy'.

One man was killed and one wounded before the battalion were relieved and moved into billets at Verquigneul, near the former coal mining town of Verquin on September 8. The 8th Devons moved 'unexpectedly' to Verquin five days later, before heading to the heavily bombed town of Vermelles in the run up to the Battle of Loos.

Albert made an informal will on May 18, 1915, just two months before arriving in France. In it, he stated that, 'in the event of my death, I give the whole of my property and effects to my mother – Mary Ann Roberts, Newland Farm, Witheridge, Morchard Bishop, Devon'. Mary received a war gratuity after his death.

Albert died at No 14 General Hospital (Wimereux) and was interred in the communal cemetery in the town, about five kilometres north of Boulogne. The cemetery contains 2,847 Commonwealth burials of the First World War, two of them unidentified. Buried among them is Lieutenant-Colonel John McCrae, author of the famous poem *In Flanders Fields*, who died in January 1918.

The poem read as follows:

> *In Flanders fields the poppies blow*
> *Between the crosses, row on row*
> *That mark our place; and in the sky*
> *The larks, still bravely singing, fly*
> *Scarce heard amid the guns below.*
>
> *We are the Dead. Short days ago*
> *We lived, felt dawn, saw sunset glow,*
> *Loved, and were loved, and now we lie*
> *In Flanders fields.*
>
> *Take up the quarrel with the foe:*
> *To you from failing hands we throw*
> *The torch; be yours to hold it high.*
> *If ye break faith with us who die*
> *We shall not sleep, though poppies grow*
> *In Flanders fields.*

Because of the sandy nature of the soil, the headstones lie flat upon the graves. Albert's (grave number five in plot 1, row K) includes the words 'Gone but not forgotten'. Albert is also remembered on the Witheridge War Memorial. His service number was 10851. He was awarded three medals: The Victory and British War Medals and the 1915 Star.

10

SAM — KILLED ON FIRST DAY OF BATTLE OF THE SOMME

He was known as lucky Sam – and for good reason. He was shot in the chest when attacking a German trench just days before Christmas in 1914. The bullet, fired from an enemy rifle, should have killed him. But he lived to fight another day because a tiny pocket book he kept in his shirt pocket took the full force of the blast.

Sam was critically injured, spending many weeks in intensive care in hospital. But, a year later, he fulfilled his promise to return to the front line, inspiring the many men around him. They were all keen to hear his remarkable story of survival – and they all hoped that some of his good fortune would rub off on them.

Particularly today.

It was the dawn of July 1, 1916, the first day of the Battle of the Somme. On what was a 'beautiful' and 'breathless blue morning', Corporal Samuel (Sam) Roberts stood shoulder to shoulder with his men of the 8th Devons in a 'reserve' trench near the village of Mametz, ready to join the largest offensive ever mounted on the Western Front.

On what would become the bloodiest and most disastrous day in British military history, his battalion, fighting side by side with officers and men of the 9th Devons, would play a pivotal role in the capture of the German-held village, about eight kilometres from the town of Albert in Picardy, northern France.

The young infantrymen from Devon would be among 100,000 British and French soldiers sent 'over the top' along a vast 23-mile front north and south of the Somme. In the days leading up the 'Great Advance', more than 1.5 million shells were fired to at best destroy and at worst seriously destabilise formidable German defences.

The bombardment was so enormous, its rumblings could be heard as far away as southern England. Confidence among senior British military chiefs that the barrage would 'crush' the enemy was so high, they told their soldiers that they would be able to walk across No Man's Land to occupy 'annihilated' German trenches.

But 21-year-old Sam knew from bitter experience there would be no room for complacency. That whatever toll the barrage may have exacted, the challenge in taking Mametz was likely to be formidable. He prayed that good luck would again smile on him and spoke encouraging words to anxious soldiers looking to him to lead them with bravery and determination.

In the lull before the assault, he looked across the vast panorama of the Somme, and thought of his older brother, John Francis (Frank), a lance-corporal. For he, too, would be fighting in the same battle that day, just a few miles away, with the 2nd Devons, who were to help lead an attack on the village of Pozieres, close to Albert.

In the countdown to the attack, and amid growing euphoria over the success of the bombardment on the enemy, Sam wondered if he and his men would be called into action. They would not be in the first waves of the advance. That 'honour' had been given to the 9th Devons, now minutes away from leaving their front-line trenches.

His heart was racing as a short but eerie silence was broken at 7.30am by piercing whistles, the signal for the assault to begin. There were loud cheers when word spread that the German artillery had been decimated. Hopes were raised as mines were blown under enemy positions at nearby Fricourt and smoke and gas were discharged to enable soldiers to venture into No Man's Land unseen.

Amid this early optimism, there was increasing concern among some senior officers that the 9th Devons would be walking into a death trap, that the barrage had failed to destroy a well defended enemy machine gun post at Mametz Cemetery, directly opposite the position from where the battalion would begin their advance.

In the days leading up to the attack, one of the 9th Devons' company commanders, 30-year-old Captain Duncan Lenox Martin, went to extraordinary lengths to demonstrate the potential threat posed by the gun post, believed to be hidden near a place called The Shrine – using his skills as an artist to make a detailed plasticine model of the area which he called the 'danger spot'.

When he showed it to superior officers, he was told that the bombardment would destroy all enemy positions. But the gun post survived the barrage. The 9th Devons were cut down as they headed into what became known as a 'valley of death' towards Mansel Copse, a plantation next to Mametz. And Captain Martin was among the first to fall, fatally wounded, at the 'danger spot'.

As the battalion's losses mounted, Sam knew it would only be a matter of time before he would be joining the fray. Later that morning, the 8th Devons were called into action. And disaster awaited them, many falling victim to the same murderous machine gun fire from The Shrine as they tried to cross about 100 yards of No Man's Land to enemy trenches.

The attack on Mametz – with the two Devonshire battalions, the 2nd Gordon Highlanders and the 2nd Borders operating under the orders of the 20th Brigade of the British Army's 7th Division – was one of great drama, huge tragedy and a missed opportunity, as the following extract from *The Long, Long Trail* reveals:

The 2nd Gordons moved off towards the enemy front line but their left company ran into uncut barbed wire, hidden in a dip. Surrounded by unexploded British shells, many men fell to German machine gun fire from 'The Shrine' … as the wire was negotiated.

Even so, the Gordons got as far as the second enemy position at Shrine Alley by 7.55am and maintained touch with the South Staffords (of 91st Brigade) further along in Cemetery Trench. They were unable to progress from there and spent much effort in clearing enemy dug outs.

Across the road, the 9th Devons advanced from a line some 250 yards behind their own front trench, so badly had this been damaged by shell fire. They were hit by heavy machine gun fire from Fricourt Wood, the German support trenches and from Mametz. At least half of their losses for the day were incurred before they had even reached Mansel Copse, just ahead of the front line. The survivors pressed on into the German front and support trenches, but by now all the battalion's officers had become casualties. As early as 7.40am the final company were ordered to advance but lost all their officers in crossing No Man's Land. The same thing happened to two companies of the 8th Devons when they were ordered to reinforce.

At 2.30pm, an attack was made by 21st Division on Fricourt. 7th Division organised a fresh attack to take advantage of it and assist the battalions now held up in Cemetery Trench, Shrine Alley and in the outskirts of Mametz. Two companies of 2nd Royal Warwicks and two of 8th Devons attacked at 3.30pm, after 30 minutes' artillery support. It was enough for the German garrison of Mametz: 200 of them emerged with hands up before the new attack had even reached the old German front line. By just after 4pm, the whole of Mametz had fallen and within another hour the situation was quiet. 7th Division reported that further advances towards Mametz Wood could be made if fresh troops could come up. But none did, and the moment – tragically – was lost.

Sam's luck ran out that day. He was killed in action in the advance on Mametz, just a few short yards from his own trench. He was one of more than 19,200 British soldiers to die on that most terrible of days. Another 40,000 British soldiers were wounded on the first day of the Battle of the Somme. Losses among the 7th Division alone totalled 3,380 officers and men, the vast majority cut down by machine gun fire.

Sam's body was retrieved and carried back to the front-line trench behind Mansel Copse where he had started his attack. He was among more than 160 officers and men of the 8th and 9th Devons to be buried there – a site which became The Devonshire Cemetery. The cemetery, where there is a headstone in Sam's memory, is one of the most famous on the Somme and is unique in being almost entirely devoted to a single regiment and its dead from one day of a battle that raged until November 18, 1916. The defiant and poignant ten-word message *'The Devonshires held this trench, the Devonshires hold it still'* – originally carved into a wooden cross – is inscribed on a permanent memorial at the cemetery, close to Mametz.

Between July 1 and 3, the 8th Devons suffered more than 200 casualties. Three officers were killed, including Captain Geoffrey Philip Tregelles, commander of the battalion's A Company, who was described as a man of 'remarkable quality and devotion to duty', and who had 'inspired' all those around him with his great spirit. More than 40 NCOs and men were killed and seven officers and 153 NCOs and men were wounded.

Among those who fought and died with Sam on July 1 were 2nd Lieutenant John Frederick George Rew, the grandson of a Newton St Cyres farmer; 17-year-old Private Robert Harenburg, of Honiton, one of the youngest to fall on the battlefield; 19-year-old Privates William Browning, of Dawlish and Reginald Victor Connett, of Plymouth; Private Mark Radford, 22, of Puddington, Private Sidney Boundy, 25, of Burrington, and Private Sidney George Morrish, 27, of Crediton.

The 9th Devons suffered a catastrophic 480 casualties, with eight officers and more than 150 other ranks killed. Nine officers and more than 260 NCOs and men were wounded and dozens more were 'missing in action'. Among the officers killed was Lieutenant William Noel Hodgson, who wrote one of the most moving poems of the Great War shortly before being killed on that fateful day. Lt Hodgson was killed by the machine gun at The Shrine while carrying grenades to men in captured trenches. The final verse of his 142-word poem, *Before Action*, read:

I, that on my familiar hill
Saw with uncomprehending eyes
A hundred of thy sunsets spill
Their fresh and sanguine sacrifice,
Ere the sun swings his noonday sword
Must say good-bye to all of this;
By all delights that I shall miss,
Help me to die, O Lord.

C T Atkinson, in *The Devonshire Regiment 1914–1918*, said the 7th Division had 'scored a big success' on the Somme, rendering Fricourt 'untenable', inflicting heavy losses on the Germans and forcing them to 'draw back hastily the bulk of their artillery'. In this success, the 8th and 9th Devons had 'played a prominent, if costly part'.

Sam's brother, Frank, survived the July 1 attack on nearby Pozieres in which the 2nd Devons had ten officers and 163 men killed in action, with another 20 dying from wounds. But two brothers from Bradninch, near Exeter, both died that day on the Somme. Private Thomas (Tom) Copp, aged 32, was fighting with the 9th Devons at Mametz when he fell. His 22-year-old brother, Sidney Archibald, was killed in action with the 2nd Devons near Ovillers.

It would be some time before their parents, William, an agricultural labourer and Polly, a charwoman, would know they had lost their sons. For the bodies of Tom and Sidney were never recovered. Although serving with different battalions, the brothers – today remembered on the Thiepval Memorial to the Missing – had remarkably similar regimental service numbers. Tom's was 20402 and Sidney's 20042, a coincidence that became a major talking point after their deaths.

Men of the 9th Devons to die on July 1 – and who would almost certainly have been known by Sam at home and at war – included Private John Henry Bradford, aged 20, of Shillingford, Private Albert Carpenter, 26, of Oakford, and Private Francis George Crook, of Witheridge. One of the oldest soldiers killed was 41-year-old Private Henry George Webber, of Chawleigh.

On July 28, 1916, *The Western Times* reported that many of

those killed – including Sam, Captains Tregelles and Martin and Lt Hodgson – were buried at the Devonshire Cemetery on the evening of July 4, in the presence of senior officers and many other soldiers who survived the carnage at Somme. Seven days later, *The Western Times* carried a report of Sam's memorial service at the parish church in Rackenford. The newspaper said 'there was a large congregation' at a service attended by Sam's parents and 'many other relatives'. Hymns played included *'Jesus, lover of my soul'*, *'Peace, perfect peace'* and *'They whose course on earth is o'er'*. The Rector, Rev H G Gifford, played Chopin's *'Marche Funebre'* (Funeral March) as an introductory voluntary and Handel's *'Dead March from Saul'*, with the congregation standing throughout the two pieces.

The war diary for the 8th Devons gives a valuable and insightful, though in many ways very understated, account of the part they played in the Battle of the Somme on July 1 and in the run-up to the attack. The night before the battle, the battalion paraded at 11pm and marched into their positions in the trenches at 3.45am the following morning. A and C Companies were in the 'Lucknow Redoubt', B Company in 'Peronne Avenue' and D Company in 'Ludgate Circus'.

At 7.30am, Zero Hour, B and D Companies moved to reserve and support trenches and A and C Companies were in 'Lucknow Lane', according to a report produced by Lieutenant-Colonel Boucher Charlewood James, commanding officer of the 8th Devons. Three hours later, B Company were 'sent forward' to support men of the 9th Devons and Gordon Highlanders marching on Mametz, moving via Mansel Copse into a dangerous hollow on the Bray-Fricourt Road.

'This company did not move again as a whole until 4pm when all their officers had been wounded and CSM (Company Sergeant Major Walter) Holwill assumed command,' reported Lt-Col James. C Company took up the reserve trench position vacated by B Company. D Company were made available to support the Gordon Highlanders 'if required' and at 10.45am, two of their platoons were 'sent forward'.

Twenty-five minutes earlier, Lieutenant-Colonel Henry Limes Storey, commanding officer of the 9th Devons, 'ordered the advance of the 8th Devons' A Company (from a reserve trench) to support the right of the 9th Devons'. Lt-Col James wrote: 'No information of this move was given to battalion HQ. They moved in the direction of the Halte (the old railway halt at Mametz). The four officers of this company were either killed or wounded and I got no information as to the whereabouts of this company until late in the evening when 2nd Lieutenant (Samuel Hugh) Duff reported to me he had picked this company up.'

At 3.30pm, C Company, the last of the 8th Devons in the reserve trench were 'given orders to proceed to Hidden Wood via Mansel Copse. The company sent two platoons over the top of reserve trench but Lieutenant Saville, seeing numerous casualties, took the remainder of the company (via an alternative route) and proceeded to his objective with practically no casualties at all,' wrote Lt-Col James.

At 4pm, he sent 2nd Lt Duff to 'collect B Company and push on in support of C Company to Hidden Wood'. Twenty minutes later, 2nd Lt Duff reported that he had 'found remnants of B Company in Mametz Trench'. They were working through the trench with the Gordon Highlanders in the direction of Dantzig Support and Hidden Wood.

At 5.10pm, 2nd Lt Duff joined up with 2nd Lieutenant Horace Joseph of C Company and men from the 9th Devons. Lt-Col James wrote: 'We have worked under the bank to Halte and beyond, and are now working round to Hidden Wood (between Fricourt and Mametz). I have taken and sent back many prisoners from under the bank, including four (German) officers.

'The nature of the engagement was affected by mopping up parties not clearing the trenches, leaving machine guns and snipers. The bank by the Halte was entirely disregarded and all dug-outs in Dantzig Trench were found occupied; the enemy using the bank above could concentrate an enfilade fire (shooting straight down the trench) on troops advancing to Hidden Wood or Mametz.

'Also, the traverses (a projection of sandbags built into a trench to make them less vulnerable) being fire-stepped (a step on the forward face of a trench from which men stood to fire), they could shoot down the valley to our lines. A machine gun was found at the Halte which had fired a great quantity of rounds. The enemy had taken advantage of this high bank to make it an impregnable position.'

War correspondent Sir Herbert Russell recalled the 'cataclysmic' first day of the Battle of the Somme in an article marking the 10th anniversary of the start of the offensive – published in *The Western Morning News and Mercury* in 1926. 'I shall never forget the perfect peace of that July dawn, save for the rumbling mutter of the artillery,' he wrote. 'Larks rose out of the dew-sodden grass about me and soared, trilling. It was a breathless, blue morning – a shocking contrast of the peace of God and the brooding fury of Hell.

'An old peasant woman trudged past me – why she had not been evacuated miles back goodness alone knows – and with an air of supine unconcern murmured "*Un bean temps, m'sieur*" (a beautiful time), looked across the silvery vista and shuddered. The cataclysm broke loose in a sudden great belching of woolly smoke. The roar of the intense bombardment was strangely subdued (from my viewpoint) on the Albert Ridge. Yet the earth was violently trembling under my feet. Archies (artillery fire) were bursting like scattering snowballs over my head, and more than once falling fragments screeched uncomfortably near.

'Then came a sudden, dreadful silence … a staccato voice called out "Now they're going over!" … a faint whirr, like the racing of a clock which has suddenly lost its pendulum, was borne on the soft song of the summer wind. The machine guns … Back at advanced GHQ, they told us the day had gone well. The stark, terrible truth had not yet been collected.'

Sir Herbert said that when he retired to his room on the eve of the battle, he lay down but could not close his eyes. 'One takes curious notice of infinite trifles under tense conditions, and I found myself measuring the hum of a very persistent bluebottle against the muffled rataplan of the guns. But like a terrible oppression upon my soul lay the thought that within a few hours 20,000 splendid men, now in the full tide of young life, would be lying stark corpses, with God alone knew how many more strewn maimed and mangled upon the smoking earth,' he opined.

On the 20th anniversary of the battle, a Letter from London, published in *The Devon and Exeter Gazette* in July 1936, said the offensive may have been magnificent, 'but it was more assassination than war. It achieved nothing to compensate for the gallant fighting personnel thrown away or the brave high spirits it well-nigh quenched.'

A remarkable chance meeting of a soldier from Sam's battalion and a German PoW who helped him on the first day of the Battle of Somme was reported in *The Western Morning News and Mercury* in October 1927. Thomas Knight, a tailor, living in Newton Abbot, was recognised in the town by a captured German soldier who, with three others, had helped to save his life by carrying him to safety on a stretcher when he was seriously wounded at Mametz. 'Mr Knight … was leaving work when he was excitedly held up by a man speaking in broken English,' said the report. 'He asked me if I remembered him,' said Mr Knight, the German reminding him how he had helped him that day.

Sam, born in the hamlet of Cove near Tiverton on March 6, 1895, was one of seven children of John and Elizabeth (nee Morrish) Roberts. The family lived for many years at Blindwell Cottage, Rackenford. Sam was one of three brothers to fight in the Great War. Frank survived the early days on the Somme but was killed by a shell just over two months after Sam's death. The third brother, William Ben Roberts, a lance-corporal in the Royal Engineers, survived the war.

Sam had another brother, Charles and three sisters – Alice Maud Mary, Elizabeth Kate and Amy Daisy. Sam worked with his father as a labourer at Sydenham Farm – then run by the Beedell family – in 1911, when he was 16. He enlisted in the Army at Blackawton in about 1913, initially joining the 2nd Battalion of the Devonshire Regiment. He served in Cairo, helping to protect the Suez Canal, before heading for France with his brother, Frank.

Sam sailed from Cairo to Southampton on the troop carrier *SS Osmanieh* on September 13, 1914, arriving at the British port on October 1. He went to Romsey and later Hursley Park, near Winchester before marching to Southampton 'in torrents of rain and through a sea of mud' in the early hours of November 5 to Southampton.

The war diary for the 2nd Battalion – under the orders of the 23rd Brigade in the 8th Division of the British Army – show that Sam and Frank sailed to Le Havre on the Blue Funnel Line's merchant ship, *SS Bellerophon*. On November 7, the battalion were transported by train to billets in Neuf-Berquin in northern France before marching 11 miles four days later to Neuve Eglise, the men staying in farm buildings there.

They went into the trenches for the first time on November 12 and experienced 'heavy shelling on both sides' the following day. There was two inches of snow on the ground on November 19 when the battalion lost their first soldier. Over the next ten days, in freezing conditions, seven men were killed and 11 wounded. More than 50 men were treated in hospital on November 30 for frost-bitten feet caused by standing in ice-covered trenches.

The 2nd Devons faced more heavy shelling on December 1 and five men were wounded by snipers on the following two days. Sam and his battalion moved into billets at Pont Rirchon on December 9 before returning to 'very wet' trenches three days later. Relieved on December 14, they went to the Brigade Reserve on La Bassee Road in northern France before returning to the trenches three days later.

Sam miraculously escaped certain death on December 18, 1914 when the 2nd Devons attacked German defences at a farm complex known as the Moated Grange, situated between Neuve Chapelle and Armentieres. Shot in the chest, he was one of more than 120 casualties in the advance. A bullet – believed to be from a sniper – first struck a military hand-book kept in Sam's breast pocket, saving his life.

In an assault in which a German trench was captured, three officers and more than 50 NCOs and men were killed. Many more were wounded by rifle and machine gun fire as they became caught up in wire in No Man's Land. Sam, removed from the battlefield seriously injured, was later transported back to England for medical care, becoming a patient at St Mark's Hospital in London for several weeks.

The war diary for the 2nd Devons reveals that their advance began at 4.30pm on December 18, 15 minutes after a 'heavy bombardment' of enemy lines. The following extract highlights the drama and tragedy of that day.

D Company, under Captain (Claude Alexander) Lafone, took German trench. C Company, under Major Goodwyn, started but owing to latter being wounded at once and not having had time to explain scheme to his officers sufficiently (company commanders attending a 'conference' about the attack 'only got back to their companies about 10 or 11 minutes before operations were to commence'), the company lost direction, got too much to the left and were caught up in barbed wire, losing heavily. Captain (Charles James) Spencer and Captain (Reginald Benjamin) Featherstone were killed. Captain (Ronald George) Legge missing, believed killed. Major (J F) Radcliffe DSO, Major Goodwyn, Lieutenants Park, Andrews and Case wounded, and 121 NCOs and men killed, wounded and missing. We took 27 prisoners in the trench and many Germans were killed and wounded.

Captain Featherstone, of Westward Ho! was 30. He and Captain Spencer were veterans of the Second Boer War. Captain Legge was killed in action. He was 36 and had married Phyllis Ford, the daughter of the Rev Mortimer Ford, of Yarcombe, Devon, four years earlier. Among the NCOs and men who were killed was Lance-Corporal Ralph Hewitt, of Exmouth, one of three brothers who lost their lives in the war – one of whom, Leslie, died on the same day two years later.

The fallen also included 42-year-old Private William Frederick Horsam, of Teignmouth, who left a widow and seven children; Private William Braund, of Bow, near Crediton; Private Alfred Chudley, aged 33, of Morchard Bishop; Private George Frederick Knapman, a 32-year-old former postman from Ashburton; Private Percy Thomas Lang, 22, of Braunton; Private Thomas Arthur Luxton, 22, of Bideford; and Private Daniel Passmore, 21, of Crediton.

The wounded were removed from the field of battle in the early hours of the following day. The 2nd Devons, in the captured German trench, were later relieved by the 2nd West Yorkshires and returned to their own trenches before going into billets at Pont Rirchon. Just hours later, men of the 2nd West

Yorkshires suffered heavy casualties when they were bombed out of the trench taken by the 2nd Devons and returned to their original lines.

C T Atkinson, in *The Devonshire Regiment 1914-18*, said that, in an effort to maintain 'complete secrecy', company commanders of the 2nd Devons were not issued orders for the attack on Moated Grange until about two hours before it was to take place. 'As they had then to regain the front line over a sea of mud and along water-logged communication trenches', it was not 'wonderful that there was all too brief a time to issue orders to the assaulting companies, C and D, and to explain to platoon and section commanders what exactly they had to do. There was not enough time even to cut our own wire properly.

'Looking back at the attack now it is extraordinary to contrast the scanty preparations possible for an operation in which a whole battalion were engaged with the elaborate training and systematic working out of tasks and plans which a much smaller operation would have involved two winters later,' commented Atkinson.

'But the Devons were ready, and after 15 minutes' accurate and vigorous bombardment, C and D went over the top. C, led by Major Goodwyn, on the left of the Moated Grange, came almost at once under heavily enfilade fire from their left, while their progress was hampered by fences, which ran diagonally across their line of advance. Almost inevitably the company swerved to their left towards the fire and ran into barbed wire in front of the main German trench. A burning rick, ignited by the Germans had lit up the ground to be traversed and in consequence the company suffered very heavily.

'... D, on the right, under Captain Lafone, were more fortunate. The configuration of the ground covered them from the enfilade fire which had mowed C Company down, while a couple of reconnaissances made by 2nd Lieutenant Cox before the attack, had located some wire, which was successfully avoided. A small trench just south of the Moated Grange was rushed and the German line east of the farm was reached. A sharp tussle followed in which D inflicted many casualties and captured nearly 30 prisoners,' wrote Atkinson.

'B Company now followed across and all ranks promptly set to work to consolidate their gains, as owing to C's losses it was clearly impracticable to push on against the next line. The trench taken was about 150 yards long, and its condition showed how effective our bombardment had been, as it was full of killed and wounded ... Every effort was made by B and D, now joined by the survivors of C under Lieutenant Joy, to render the position defensible. They were under considerable shell fire and sniping and several more casualties occurred.'

The *Western Times* in January 1915 reported Sam's admission to St Mark's Hospital and added: 'Had it not been for a book which he carried in the breast pocket, and through which a clean hole was made by the bullet, the shot would probably have proved fatal.'

St Mark's – based at the college of that name in Chelsea – first took men from the Western Front in September 1914. Many of them arrived in a 'terrible condition, their clothes stiff with mud and blood from wounds which were often septic'. Most of the men were treated for upper body shrapnel wounds. But by January 1915, when Sam was a patient there, 22 soldiers blinded on the front line had also been admitted to St Mark's.

Sam was invalided out of the Army for almost a year before joining the 8th Devons towards the end of 1915. He was promoted to lance-corporal and within weeks became a corporal, a promotion reported in *The Western Times* in January 1916.

He spent Christmas of 1915 at Ailly-sur-Somme in northern France – he and his fellow soldiers enjoying a 'plentiful supply of turkey and plum puddings.' It was a stark contrast to the previous year when he had been fighting for his life. Sam was in Fourdrinoy on the Somme on New Year's Day 1916. Three days later, his battalion marched 15 miles to Pont-Remy on the northern bank of the Somme and were based there for 24 days for training before marching the 17 miles to Ailly-sur-Somme.

In February 1916, the 8th Devons marched to Cardonette. They were in billets at La Houssoye before marching to Meaulte, a village just south of Albert. They were in the trenches for eight days before heading to billets at Ville-sur-

Ancre. On February 20, Sam and his men marched to Becordel, a village close to Albert, and moved into trenches two days later. One man was killed and six wounded when they came under artillery and heavy machine gun fire.

In March 1916, the battalion were based in Meaulte and Becordel, spending a number of days in the trenches. The following month they moved to Vaux-sur-Somme for front line training, with the four companies later being based at the nearby Grove Town and Bois de Tailles Camps. They spent much of May and June in camps and trenches in the Somme area before finally moving into assembly trenches near Mametz late on June 30 in readiness for the start of the Battle of the Somme.

Sam's medal card shows his service number (9306), that he was awarded the Victory and British War Medals and the 1914 Star, and was 'killed in action'. He is buried in plot A, row 2 of the Devonshire Cemetery. He is remembered on two war memorials in Rackenford, on a granite monument on the outskirts of the village and on a brass plaque in All Saints Parish Church.

Notes

- *SS Osmanieh* was sunk off Alexandria on New Year's Eve 1917, with the loss of almost 200 lives after striking a mine laid by a German U-boat.

- Two altar fronts commemorating Captain Tregelles, of the 9th Devons, were dedicated at his local church, in Newport, Barnstaple in January 1917. The Vicar, the Rev W Richards, said Captain Tregelles was a devout and sincere churchman. He was preparing to become a priest in the church when the war broke out and he volunteered for service. His chief concern was to do his duty well even at the supreme cost of self-sacrifice. Before leaving the last time for the front, Captain Tregelles had knelt before the church altar to receive Holy Communion, according to a report in *The North Devon Journal* in January 1917.

11

JOHN FRANCIS 'FRANK' — SHELLED WHILE ENJOYING A CUP OF TEA

After a brutal two years on the front line in France, Lance-Corporal John Francis 'Frank' Roberts had every reason to believe that he would survive the Great War – and return home to Devon to perhaps get married and have children.

Against all the odds, he had remained uninjured in four of the bloodiest battles on the Western Front between 1914 and 1916 which claimed the lives of hundreds of officers and men serving with him in the 2nd Devons.

He fought side by side with his brother, Sam, at the Moated Grange, between Neuve Chapelle, in December 1914 – seeing him shot in the chest and miraculously being saved by a pocket book which had taken the full force of the bullet.

Frank took part in one of the most extraordinary events of the war, the 'Christmas Truce' of 1914 when British and German troops stepped out of their trenches, shook hands, exchanged cigarettes and gifts, and buried their dead.

He narrowly avoided injury or death when shrapnel grazed his shoulder as he charged enemy lines at the Battle of Neuve Chapelle in March 1915. He had another narrow escape the following year when he was side by side with his school friend, Private Archie Snell, when he was hit by shrapnel.

Frank was involved in the attack on Aubers Ridge in May 1915. He survived the massacre of the 2nd Devons in Mash Valley on the Somme on July 1, 1916 – the day on which his brother was killed in an attack on nearby Mametz.

Seventy days later, on September 9, 1916, Frank was taking a well-earned break with his men in a trench in northern France – enjoying one of the few luxuries available to him and his men, a mug of hot tea.

Without warning, a shell burst over the trench, firing its lethal load into him. Frank, described by his commanding officer as 'one of the very best, and a soldier through and through', was killed instantly. He was 25.

It is almost impossible to imagine the extent of his experiences in France – from savagery and devastation, to colossal courage and deep personal loss – in what must have felt like a lifetime of horror on the front line.

The events of July 1, 1916, when the 2nd Devons suffered catastrophic losses in an attack on formidable German defences between Ovillers and La Boiselle, perhaps offer the most graphic example of what he endured.

The 2nd Devons and officers and men of the 2nd Battalion of the Middlesex Regiment – both an integral part of the 23rd Brigade of the 8th Division of the British Army – led the assault with astonishing bravery that day.

They were given the incredibly difficult task of crossing more than 800 yards of No Man's Land in Mash Valley to capture enemy front lines near Ovillers and to then advance across open country to the south of Pozieres.

More than 1,000 officers and men from both battalions were slaughtered or wounded in No Man's Land in the face of unrelenting machine gun fire. The few who managed to reach enemy trenches were killed.

The dramatic story of the 2nd Devons' involvement in the advance is told in a special operations report contained in the battalion's war diary and written by their commanding officer, Lieutenant-Colonel A J Sutherland.

The British artillery started a bombardment at 6.30am which lasted for an hour. In the final moments of the barrage, the battalion's A and B Companies moved closer to the enemy trenches, closely followed by C and D Companies.

The advance was carried out in 'four consecutive waves, in the most perfect order', wrote Lt-Col Sutherland. However, Temporary Captain E G Roberts, commander of A Company was badly wounded by shell fire while leaving the front line and 2nd Lieutenant Arthur Carey was killed.

A mist drifted over No Man's land just before the attack, making observation 'very difficult'. At 7.30am, as the barrage ended Captain James Allfrey Andrews, in charge of the front line, was shot in the head and killed as he gave the order to advance.

As the 2nd Devons dashed to the German trenches, 'the enemy opened a terrific machine gun fire from the front and from both flanks, which mowed down our troops', reported Lt-Col Sutherland. Only a few reached the German lines alive. They 'put up a determined fight against enormous odds' but were killed in their endeavours.

Hundreds were lying dead or wounded in Mash Valley, opposite the enemy defences. The 2nd Devons were not the only ones 'cut to pieces'. The 2nd Battalion of the Middlesex Regiment and 2nd Battalion of the West Yorkshire Regiment were also decimated by machine gun and shell fire.

Runners sent out to find out what had happened were killed or wounded, but the grim reality of the carnage in Mash Valley gradually emerged as wounded men began to crawl back to their trenches in small numbers.

'No accurate information could be ascertained as to the exact number of casualties the (2nd Devons) had suffered, although it was clear that there were very few left that had not been hit,' wrote Lt-Col Sutherland. The wounded, stranded in No Man's Land, came under fire from snipers.

'When it was quite clear that we were not holding the front line, the barrage was brought back on the German front line trenches, and the 2nd Scottish Rifles were moved forward ... and were told to hold themselves in readiness to advance.

'During this time, the hostile shelling had increased and the front line systems of trenches were very badly knocked about.

The enemy used a very high proportion of lachrymatory (tear gas) shells which caused a great deal of inconvenience to anyone not wearing gas goggles.

'The enemy continued to confine his shelling practically entirely to our front line, support and communication trenches. About mid-day orders were issued ... that no further advance would take place till further orders,' reported Lt-Col Sutherland.

As the wounded continued to crawl back to their lines, there were difficulties in evacuating them to the Regimental Aid Post because the badly damaged trenches were too narrow to get a stretcher through – and stretcher bearers had to run the gauntlet of machine gun and shell fire.

Amid the chaos, the wounded, many bandaged by the medical officer, were eventually carried to the aid post on the backs of stretcher bearers and regimental pioneers from the 2nd Devons' headquarters and in waterproof sheets.

By late afternoon, those still standing in the 2nd Devons were told that they would be relieved that night. They were moved into dug-outs by 10pm and were later transferred to bivouacs at nearby Millencourt.

The battalion had ten officers and 163 NCOs and men 'killed in action' that day. Another 20 died from wounds during the following two weeks. Another 200 or more were wounded. The 2nd Middlesex suffered more than 650 casualties.

Two of the 2nd Devons' Lewis guns were 'lost'. The remaining six were recovered in daylight under heavy fire. Two were brought in by privates who were 'the only men left of their teams', wrote Lt-Col Sutherland.

The body of one soldier of the 2nd Devons who was reported missing on July 1, 1916 was found 12 years later. *The Western Morning News and Mercury* in March 1928 reported how a couple in Brixham were notified by the War Graves Commission that they had discovered the body of their son, Private Ernest George Vass, 'in scattered graves at La Boiselle'.

His remains were exhumed and 'reburied reverently' at Serre Road Cemetery, Beaumont Hamel. Pte Vass's identity was established through a disc and wrist watch he was wearing, both of which had been forwarded to his parents, Arthur James and

Maria Vass. Pte Vass, who was a painter and decorator by trade, was 23 when he was killed.

Among the fallen of July 1 were 2nd Lieutenant Eric Melville Gould, a member of an old and respected Barnstaple family, who volunteered for service after moving to Canada. A relative of the world famous political cartoonist and caricaturist Sir Francis Carruthers Gould, whose work was published in the *Pall Mall Gazette* and *Westminster Gazette*, 2nd Lt Gould had been in France for just two months when he was killed in action.

Other officers killed that day included 19-year-old 2nd Lieutenant Cecil Victor Beddow, the second son of Dr Josiah and Grace Mary Beddow, of Pynes House, Thorverton, who had been in France for just six weeks; Plymouth-born 2nd Lieutenant Edward Arthur Jago, who was 20; Captain Alban Preedy, 23, the son of the Rev Canon Arthur Preedy, Vicar of Saltash; and 2nd Lieutenant George Sholto Douglas Carver, the son of William and Beatrice Carver of South Stroke, Exmouth, who was 29.

Lance-Corporal William Cann, aged 30, of Thorverton, reported as missing in August 1916 in *The Western Times*, but whose death on July 1 was later confirmed, had been wounded in action twice before. 'He has had thrilling escapes', said the newspaper. 'On one occasion, a bullet passed through his shoulder and missed a vital part only by an ace.' At least five men from Crediton lost their lives that day – Privates Fred Cann, aged 23, Frederick Drew, 28, John Elston, 41, who had a wife, Lavinia, John Evans, 25 and Lewis Albert Keen, 24. One of the youngest to fall was 17-year-old William John Pugsley, of Lapford.

CT Atkinson, in *The Devonshire Regiment 1914–1918*, said more formidable defences had seldom been assaulted than the German lines against which the British 'hurled themselves' on July 1. The German fortifications had been strengthened by 'unremitting labour, by lavish expenditure of materials, by skilful turning to account of every natural feature, by the employment of every device known to the field engineer'.

That any defences could have existed under the 'hammering to which the British bombardment had subjected them was almost incomprehensible; that any defenders would survive to offer any opposition let alone a vigorous and effective resistance, seemed hardly possible'. Yet, survive they did, the enemy reducing the 2ⁿᵈ Devons to a 'mere wreck' and shattering the infantry of the 8ᵗʰ Division, said Atkinson.

On July 2, 1916, the 2ⁿᵈ Devons received orders to move to the coal mining town of Mericourt and over the next few days travelled to Ailly, Soues, Longeau and Dieval before arriving in billets in Barlin, in northern France, on the 7ᵗʰ. Three days later, the battalion were inspected at Barlin by senior commanders of the 8ᵗʰ Division who congratulated officers and men on the 'splendid work' they had done and the 'wonderful bravery shown by all ranks on July 1'.

Frank and his men were back in the trenches close to Cuinchy, near Givenchy, on July 14. The following day, their trenches were attacked by enemy bombers and came under fire from aerial darts, rifle grenades, shells and trench mortars.

Two men were killed and five wounded on July 16 when the battalion were shelled and attacked with rifle grenades which caused 'considerable damage' to their front, support and communication trenches and to dug-outs.

Further German attacks were repelled but trench mortars and aerial torpedoes fired by the enemy on the night of July 17 caused further serious damage to trenches and killed two more men and wounded five others.

An enemy mine was exploded opposite A Company the following day. It appeared to 'burst backwards' burying several German soldiers, as well as 'entombing' four of a garrison of men from the 2ⁿᵈ Devons.

A platoon led by 2ⁿᵈ Lieutenant R J Andrews occupied part of a crater created by the explosion and inflicted heavy losses on the enemy, wrote Lt-Col Sutherland. The battalion lost one officer and five men in and after the explosion and 15 were wounded.

2ⁿᵈ Lt Andrews was later awarded the Military Cross for 'conspicuous gallantry' at Cuinchy. Six other soldiers from the battalion were also honoured for showing 'great courage and coolness' in helping the officer confront the enemy.

Another man was killed and 13 were wounded on July 19 as the 2nd Devons endured another barrage from shells, aerial torpedoes, trench mortars and rifle grenades. A 12-man enemy patrol were 'caught' by bombers and 'driven back to their own lines'.

The battalion successfully exploded a mine opposite A Company lines on July 21. Nine men were wounded after the enemy 'opened heavy fire' on battalion positions with minenwerfer mortars, rifle grenades and machine guns.

A party of 10-15 Germans – who 'with the exception of one man, believed to be an officer, were in short sleeves and wore no boots and were armed with revolvers, clubs and bombs' – raided one of the 2nd Devons' trenches on July 29. 'This party was immediately attacked and driven out, but managed to drag away one of our sentries who was cut off and ... clubbed,' wrote Lt-Col Sutherland.

Sixty-pounder trench mortars were fired at enemy lines in an unsuccessful attempt to cut wire entanglements. The battalion came under heavy fire from 'shells of all calibre' during the day and faced more hostile bombardments the following morning. One man was killed, 13 wounded and one man was taken prisoner on July 29 and 30.

Frank and his men moved into billets in Annequin and Fouquieres in early August 1916. One man was killed when they went back into the trenches on August 11. The battalion captured four members of a German raiding party the following day.

Heavy artillery, trench mortar and rifle fire resulted in more casualties on August 13 and 14. Two were killed, including 2nd Lieutenant William Herbert Lesley Vesey-Fitzgerald, and 11 others were wounded. Another man was killed in attacks on August 20.

The following day, several men were buried, but escaped alive, when a German mine was exploded in front of trenches defended by the 2nd Devons. One officer and nine NCOs and men were killed and 20 were wounded in enemy bombardments on August 21 and 22.

The battalion moved into billets in Sailly-Labourse on

August 23 and over the next two days took part in the Divisional Horse Show – winning first prizes in light, heavy draught and charger competitions.

On September 1, 1916, Frank and his men moved into reserve trenches. Four days later, they relieved the 2nd Scottish Rifles in trenches in the Hulluch Alley area. Two patrols were sent out during the night in an attempt to capture a prisoner, but without success.

'Several bodies were found out in No Man's Land, having been there for some months,' wrote Lt-Col Sutherland in the war diary. Pocket books and shoulder straps brought in identified them as Royal Scots.

Enemy artillery fire and minenwerfer mortars caused a 'considerable amount of damage' to trenches guarded by the battalion on September 8. 'Our Lewis guns dispersed several hostile working parties during the night,' recorded Lt-Col Sutherland.

On September 9, the 'enemy was fairly active with his minenwerfer, doing considerable damage again … in his attempt to find our trench mortar positions. Our Stokes (mortars) were very active and caused a great amount of damage to enemy trenches. This he attempted several times during the night to repair, but was prevented from doing so by our Lewis guns.'

The war diary recorded three casualties for that day – one man being killed and two wounded. The man who died was Frank. His full name was John Francis Roberts, but everyone knew him as Frank.

The *Western Times* in October 1916, reported that he was 'instantly killed, together with his officer, when having tea in the trenches, by the bursting of a shrapnel shell'. The 2nd Devons' war diary does not record the death of an officer that day. It does report the killing of 2nd Lt Gilbert Hosegood on September 10 – from machine gun fire while leading a night patrol.

Frank's death was first reported in *The Western Times* in September 1916. 'The sad intelligence came to Rackenford last week that Lance-Cpl John Francis Roberts, better known as Frank, of the Devons, met his death in action in France,' said the newspaper

'According to a letter received by his parents from the officer commanding the company, "Frank suffered no pain, being instantly killed by a shell. He was one of the very best, and a soldier through and through". With this high opinion, all who knew the brave fellow will agree.

'Only as recently as July 1, his younger brother, Corporal Sam Roberts gave his life for his country, a memorial service being held about six weeks ago. It is exceedingly deplorable to have to mourn the loss of two sons in so short a time, and the family have the fullest sympathy of the parish, and of all their friends.'

Frank's memorial service echoed that of his brother. 'At the commencement of the service, the Rector, Rev H G Gifford, rendered Chopin's most affecting *Marche Funebre* and at the close the *Dead March from Saul*, the large congregation remaining standing as a mark of respect to the memory of the gallant fallen soldier,' reported *The Western Times* on October 6.

He is one of 2,134 soldiers commemorated at Vermelles British Cemetery, near Lens. The town was at the centre of some of the fiercest fighting in 1914 when it was in German hands for three months before being recaptured by the French.

The cemetery was started in August 1915 and was known as the Gloucester Graveyard after being laid out and fenced by the Pioneers of the 1st Gloucesters. At that time, there was not a single property in Vermelles which had been left undamaged.

He and his brother are also commemorated on the granite Rackenford War Memorial at Rackenford Cross – and on a brass memorial plaque in the local parish church naming eight men from the village who died in the Great War.

Frank was born at East Mogworthy, Rackenford on April 24, 1891, just a month after the Great Blizzard brought the South West of England to a halt. Much of Devon was covered in snow up to four feet deep. Drifts more than 20 feet high were recorded across the county and snow up to 300 feet deep was said to have built up in a deep ravine on Dartmoor in fierce gales.

Many rural communities were cut off in the Great Blizzard which claimed the lives of more than 200 people and thousands of horses, cattle and sheep. Storms off the south coast led to the loss of several ships. Twenty-three people died when the *Bay of Panama*, a merchant vessel, was driven on to rocks off Nare Point, Cornwall.

A train plunged into drifting snow near Meldon Junction, Okehampton, trapping passengers, who had no food and water for 16 hours. Six men and women, again without food or drink, were trapped in a blizzard-hit train near Princetown for 36 hours before they were found and saved by a local farmer who had been rescuing sheep.

Weddings, christenings, funerals and many other family events had to be postponed. The *Totnes Weekly Times* reported on a bridegroom in North Devon who 'in spite of almost Herculean exertions', had been unable for three days to get within three miles of the village where he was due to get married.

Frank was born in the same year as actor Ronald Colman, star of numerous classic films, including *The Prisoner of Zenda* and *Random Harvest*, and Henry Tandey, of Leamington, Warwickshire, one of the most decorated British soldiers of the Great War, who received the Victoria Cross, the Distinguished Conduct Medal and Military Medal.

The eldest son of John and Elizabeth (nee Morrish) Roberts, who lived at Blindwell Cottage, Rackenford for many years, little is known about Frank's early days. At the time of the Census in 1901, when he was aged nine, he was described as a visitor at Little Rackenford, next door to Windsor Cottage where his parents and family were then living.

In 1911, he was a private with the 2nd Devons in Malta. They were based there between 1910 and 1912 before moving to Egypt. The *Devon and Exeter Gazette*, in January 1912, reported the departure of the battalion from Malta after a farewell inspection by the Governor of the island, General Sir Henry Macleod Leslie Rundle.

The inspection, in the square of the magnificent Grand Master's Palace in Valetta, attracted 'great interest' from a huge crowd who had gathered to say goodbye to the 2nd Devons. The balconies of the palace, home to the Governor, 'were thronged with the wives and families of the officers', reported the newspaper.

The Governor, who was born in Newton Abbot, Devon, and fought in the Zulu War in 1879, the First Boer War in 1881 and the Anglo-Egyptian War in 1882, said: 'I feel I am voicing the sentiments of the whole island when I say how much we regret losing you from this command. My regret at losing you is tempered by the knowledge that you leave this command in a high state of efficiency – fit to go anywhere and do anything your King and country may ask of you. As a Devonshire man, I wish you goodbye and Godspeed.'

He paid tribute to the battalion's commanding officer, Lieutenant-Colonel W T Bartlett, who was unable to lead his men at the inspection after being injured by the fall of a temporary bridge. The 22 officers and 738 men of the battalion paraded 'in summer-like weather' under the command of Major J F Radcliffe.

A Devonshire Regiment band 'played several airs – a different one for each company' – as the inspection took place. The 'talented musicians' of the band, said the newspaper, had 'often delighted Malta audiences'. The Governor was given a traditional 'three cheers' by the 2nd Devons before they returned to their St Andrew's Barracks via Strada Reale, Porta Reale and the small town of Pieta.

Frank's medal card confirms that he went to France with his battalion – and with his brother – on November 6, 1914. Just weeks later, Frank took part in the 'Christmas Truce' of 1914.

The war diary for the 2nd Devons for December 25 that year records an 'informal armistice during daylight'. It adds: 'Germans got out of their trenches and came towards our line. Our men met them – in No Man's Land – and wished each other a merry Christmas, shook hands, exchanged smokes etc.'

But the truce – which caused consternation among many senior officers and government officials – was short lived. The war diary for the 2nd Devons records that at about 7.30pm on Christmas Day, with a hard frost setting in, sniping began again. One man – Devonport-based Private Richard Gregory – was killed and another wounded.

Frank's close shave at Neuve Chapelle was recorded in *The Western Times* on November 19, 1915. Reporting his first visit home from the trenches in France for 12 months, the newspaper said: 'He had a narrow escape when charging at the Battle of Neuve Chapelle, when a piece of shrapnel grazed his shoulder.'

On the same day it reported the death of his brother, Sam, in July 1916, *The Western Times* told how Frank had been next to his school friend, Private Archie Snell, when he was wounded in the left arm by shrapnel. 'Comrades at school, they were again comrades in the field of battle,' said the newspaper.

It is likely that Archie was wounded in the attack on the Somme on July 1 that year. On May 27, 1918, he was involved in the greatest of all last stands made by the Devonshire Regiment in the Great War – at Bois de Buttes – when the 2nd Devons came close to annihilation.

More than 550 of their officers and men were killed or captured in brutal combat with the Germans. The battalion's gallantry in the face of overwhelming odds led to them being awarded the French military decoration, The Croix de Guerre, for heroism.

Archie was one of the survivors, and was taken prisoner. *The Western Times* in December 1918 reported that he had been held by the Germans at Lorraine where he lived on a menu of 'horse flesh, spinach soup and black bread'. When freed, he walked to the French lines and arrived at his parents' home in Devon on December 4 that year.

Frank's medal card reveals his service number (8885), that he was 'killed in action' and received the Victory and British War Medals and 1914 Star. His father, John, 'the sole legatee', received a war gratuity. Frank's headstone at the Vermelles British Cemetery is the 16th in Plot 5, row B.

Notes

- A memorial to Captain James Allfrey Andrews, of the 2nd Devons, who was 26 when he died on July 1, 1916 was erected within the St Mary the Virgin Church, Salehurst, East Sussex. He was the son of Lieutenant-Colonel James Andrews and Mrs Emily Andrews.

- A chapel in memory of 2nd Lt Edward Arthur Jago, of the 2nd Devons killed on July 1, 1916, and his brother, Captain Henry Harris Jago, also of the 2nd Devons, who was killed in action on April 28, 1918, was dedicated at Emmanuel Church, Plymouth on December 21, 1919. The chapel, in the north transept, was dedicated by the Archdeacon of Plymouth, the Venerable Arthur Perowne. The ceremony was reported by *The Western Morning News* the following day. It said the chapel was separated from the north transept aisle by a 'beautiful screen of carved oak'. Shields bore the initials of the two brothers and regimental badges and the places they fell were also commemorated. Edward and Henry were the sons of Mr and Mrs W Henry Jago, of Mannamead, Devon. The chapel, with an altar, reredos and prayer desk, included the following wording: 'Lovely and pleasant were they in their lives, and in their death, they were not divided.'

12

WILLIAM — STRUCK DOWN BY HEART DISEASE IN MESOPOTAMIAN DESERT

He was stepping into new territory – a desert country where the Turks, Arabs and sickness were the enemy. It had taken more than a month to reach this, his final destination, a remote and bleak camp on the banks of the River Tigris.

Corporal William Henry Kingdom arrived in a storm-lashed Sheikh Sa'ad in Mesopotamia on the last day of March in 1916 after spending more than a year in India with the 1/4th Battalion of the Devonshire Regiment as they prepared for war.

William had entered what is now Iraq amid one of the darkest eras for the British Army in the Great War. They were struggling against a battle-hardened Turkish army in the harsh climate and unforgiving terrain.

A hundred miles south of Baghdad, in the British-Indian Garrison at Kut, thousands of soldiers and civilians were starving, dying from wounds and disease and coming under constant attack as they were besieged by the enemy.

The siege ended disastrously on April 29, 1916 with the garrison surrendering to the Turks and survivors, many suffering from dysentery, scurvy and malaria, being marched to imprisonment – many not surviving the journey after being tortured and humiliated.

William, a Tiverton-born gardener, had joined the 1/4th Devons in December 1914. The battalion, a territorial force, at that stage were based in Ferozepur, India, coming under the orders of the 3rd (Lahore) Infantry Division.

When he and the 1/4th Devons were 'mobilised' in February 1916 – travelling by train to the Pakistan city of Karachi and then sailing to the Mesopotamia 'theatre of war' – they were attached to the 41st Indian Infantry Brigade.

They arrived at the Magil Camp, near Basra on March 2 that year and then journeyed up the 1,150-mile-long Tigris River to Sheikh Sa'ad, where, just over two months earlier, British and Indian forces had been involved in a three-day battle against the Turks, suffering more than 4,000 casualties.

At Sheikh Sa'ad, William and his men helped to defend desert out-posts and redoubts on the outskirts of the Army camp at which they were based, and worked on improving trenches, perimeter defences, roads and 'bunds', or embankments.

They frequently toiled in blistering temperatures and many fell victim to dysentery, cholera and heat-stroke. Hundreds fell sick, with increasingly large numbers admitted to hospital in the late spring and summer months.

In early May 1916 – and weeks after being joined by almost 200 officers, NCOs and men of the 2/4th and 3/4th Devons – the 1/4th Devons were transferred to the 37th Indian Infantry Brigade of the 14th Indian Division in Mesopotamia.

William fell seriously ill that month and lost his fight for life on May 27, 1916, aged 26. His death, from heart disease, at the 'regimental detention tent' at Sheikh Sa'ad, was recorded in the 1/4th Devons' war diary by the battalion's Adjutant, Major John Morth Woollcombe.

William's death certificate showed that he suffered from heart failure as he 'died of disease' that day. He completed an 'informal will' on April 10, 1916, just 47 days before his death, leaving his worldly possessions to his wife, Louise.

Sheikh Sa'ad was the principal front line Royal Flying Corps (RFC) base on the River Tigris. Author Paul Knight, in his book, *The British Army in Mesopotamia in 1914–1918*, said 'it was not a salubrious location'.

He wrote: 'The camp (there) was situated between two hospitals. The one located downstream was the cholera hospital, and there was a daily procession of funerals, which did little to lift spirits. There was no fresh food. They were all on half rations. Corned beef was liquid and could be poured out of the tin.

'The only cool water from a porous earthenware "charri" hung from the tent overnight where evaporation provided cool water, but only if drunk before the sun rose. Tinned fruit was issued in an attempt to prevent scurvy, but without success, and both scurvy and jaundice were common.'

Lieutenant-General Sir Percy Lake, commander of the Mesopotamian Force, said in a despatch published in *The London Gazette*, that there was an outbreak of cholera in Mesopotamia at the end of April 1916. The intensely hot weather the following month 'rapidly increased' the number of those falling sick and the heat was 'aggravated at the front by the total absence of shade'.

A report in the *Western Daily Press* in July 1916, written by Edmund Candler, a representative of the British Press with the Expeditionary Force in Mesopotamia, provided a graphic account of the kind of challenges faced by the 1/4th Devons. He wrote:

There is no respite or truce in the plagues of Mesopotamia, and the only normal thing in the country on which one can count is that the plague cycle is unbroken and continuous, that the plagues overlap.

The plagues of May are dust, heat and flies; and the greatest of these is flies. The flies in the tents, dug-outs and trenches, unless seen, are unbelievable. To describe them is to hazard one's reputation for truth.

You cannot eat without swallowing flies. You wave your spoon of porridge in the air to shake them off; you put your biscuit and your bully-beef in your pocket, and surreptitiously convey them in closed fist to your mouth – but you swallow flies all the same.

They settle in clouds on everything. As I write I cannot see the end of my pen. I overtook a squadron of cavalry the other day, and in that state of semi-coma, in which the heat wraps one, I thought that they were wearing chain armour. I had walked my horse beside them some minutes before I discovered that what looked like mail, was the steely blue metallic of flies.

The Mesopotamia variety is indistinguishable from the English house-fly, except that many of them, one in 20 perhaps, can bite or sting. Those apparently are not a different species – only more impregnated with vice.

At night the flies disappear, and the mosquitoes and sand flies relieve them, completing the vicious circle ... In one camp, I struck a species (of mosquito) which could bite through cord riding breeches. Sand-flies are another and more insidious plague. A net with a mesh fine enough to exclude them is suffocating, and they keep one awake at night with a hose of thin acid, playing on one's face.

Candler described Mesopotamia as a 'country of excess' where 'nothing is ever moderate'. He wrote:

There is something almost biblical in the way the gods of this ancient land have conspired to punish us. There is malice in the sky and soil. Malice of heat and drought; hunger and thirst; and flies; damp and cold, and mire; flood, hurricane and rain; fever and ague.

You eat sand, breathe sand, lie in sand, have sand in your ears, eyes and clothes. Sand-flies by night, flies by day, until they shrivel up; sand and suffocation by day and night.

There are different kinds of discomfort, different kinds of heat, the moist and tropical heat of the swamps of the Euphrates and the Shatt-al-Arab, the parched and desert heat of the Tigris and the Karun. Each variety has its attendant insects and peculiar ailments, which often take the form of boils and eruptions.

The *North Devon Journal* in July 1916 reported how Barnstaple soldier Private Thomas Green, recuperating at home from wounds he had received in action, had endured 'on many occasions' temperatures of 148 degrees in the shade in Mesopotamia.

British and Indian troops served in Mesopotamia between 1914 and 1921. Initially sent there to secure oil supplies from neighbouring Iran (then known as Persia), they fought a determined and well trained Turkish army supported by Arab troops.

William was one of more than 12,000 soldiers who died from sickness in Mesopotamia in the Great War. His death was reported in *The Western Times* on June 30, 1916 in just 31 words: 'News has been received from the War Office that Cpl W Kingdom of the Devons, a native of Tiverton, has died on service. He leaves a widow and two young children.'

He is remembered on the Basra Memorial in Iraq which honours more than 40,000 members of the Commonwealth forces who died in the war in Mesopotamia. Originally situated on the main quay of the naval dockyard at Magil, a few miles north of Basra, it was designed by Edward P Warren and unveiled in 1929 by Brigadier-General Sir Gilbert Clayton, the British High Commissioner for Iraq.

Almost 70 years later, in 1997, the memorial was re-erected near Nasiriyah, on the banks of the Euphrates River, where, in the Gulf War in 2003, a battle was fought between Iraqi and invading US forces. Sadly, the memorial is deteriorating, with the names of many of the fallen now illegible, and the Commonwealth War Graves Commission is unable to maintain or restore it while political instability and conflict persists in Iraq.

Including a 252ft long courtyard, the memorial is surrounded on three sides by a colonnade and is enclosed on its front by an iron fence and gateway. The colonnade, made from stone quarried in India, is a semi-octagonal arched recess in the centre of which stands a 55ft high obelisk – a 'Cleopatra's Needle' – which 'stands out boldly in the skyline'. The names of those commemorated, including more than 150 officers and men of the Devonshire Regiment, are inscribed on panels of English slate mounted on the walls of the colonnade.

William was born in Hensleigh Cottage, Tiverton on May 6, 1890 – a year in which the Forth Bridge, spanning the Firth of Forth in Scotland, was first opened and 176 men and boys were killed in an underground explosion at the Llanerch Colliery in Abersychan, Monmouthshire.

Also born in 1890 were crime writer Agatha Christie, actor and comedian Stan Laurel, the American comedian, Groucho Marx and Dwight Eisenhower, who, in 1953, became the 34th President of the United States.

William was the son of George and Lucy Kingdom (the daughter of John Roberts), and was one of 11 children. His brother, Walter, was killed in action in the aftermath of the Battle of Epehy in September 1918.

William and his father worked as domestic gardeners in the run-up to the war. The family lived at Howden Cottage in Tiverton in 1911. In 1901, when William was 11, he lived with his family at Bushment Cottage, Tiverton. At that stage, his father was a general labourer. Ten years earlier, the Kingdoms lived at Ditchets Cottage in Tiverton.

William married Louise Clarke at St Paul's Parish Church in Tiverton on January 1, 1912. He was 23 at the time and Louise was 30. They lived in the town, at 15, Sharlands Square. They had a son, William Albert H Kingdom, who was born on April 30, 1912 and a daughter, Doris Ada, who was born on August 2, 1916.

William volunteered to join the 1/4th Devons who in August 1914 were based in Exeter as part of the Devon and Cornwall Brigade of the Wessex Division. The battalion moved to Plymouth and then Salisbury Plain before sailing for India in November 1914.

In India – where, according to a report in *The Western Times* in December 1915, the battalion were a 'trifle scattered' – William and his men were 'trained in all the arts of warfare' and in constructing trenches.

In that year, the 1/4th Devons were at Amritsar, near Lahore, a city famous for its golden temple and a 'hot-bed of disaffection', on garrison duty at the frontier station in Peshawar, at Ferozepur Fort and Arsenal, and at the Gough Barracks, on the outskirts of Ferozepur.

In the latter part of 1915, the battalion were busy building deep trenches in India. However, officers returning from duty in France 'told them they would not be able to anything like it' on the Western Front, because they would not have the time to do so and 'if they went down so deep they would be striking water levels and get flooded out'. In January 1916, the battalion, while in Ferozepur, were put through the 'Kitchener Test' – a three-day war simulation trial involving long marches, shooting practice, tent pitching and 'attacks' on native regiments.

The 1/4th Devons' departure from India to Mesopotamia was reported in the *Devon and Exeter Gazette* in March 1916. It was, said the newspaper, 'an occasion of many expressions of regret and congratulation, both official and private, the battalion having smartly carried out their duties while in the "Land of Regrets," and, at the same time, played a prominent part in the social life of those among whom their lot has been cast since their arrival at Ferozepur'.

On the eve of their departure, Brigadier-General William Cross Barratt, who commanded the Lahore divisional area, wrote to the 1/4th Devons' commanding officer, Lieutenant-Colonel Hugh Leonard Acland Troyte: 'As the 1/4th are about to leave India on field service in a few days, I am writing to ask you to convey to all ranks of your battalion my sincere thanks for their services while they have been stationed in this divisional area. At the outbreak of war, your battalion were not only one of the very first territorial units to be ready for service, but you were also able to supply drafts to bring other units up to strength. Please accept my congratulations on the state of efficiency you have maintained in the battalion during their service in this country.'

Brigadier-General A H Eustace, a former commander of the Ferozepur Brigade, also wrote to Lt-Col Troyte, to congratulate him and his battalion on being selected for active service. He had 'very pleasant memories of his associations with the 1/4th while they had been in India, having performed splendid work for the Empire'. He had always been struck by the bearing and behaviour of the men, and was sure they would add to the magnificent achievements of their county. The Devons had made numerous friends in India, and their doings on active service would be watched with special interest, not only by their friends at home, but also by those to whom they were now bidding goodbye.

The Rev E F Muspratt, Chaplain, paid a 'glowing tribute' to the support given by the Devons to church work in Ferozepur. They had ... rallied around him splendidly and their behaviour had had a marked influence upon the people of the district. There was great regret at the Devons' departure. Ferozepur, he said, would 'never forget them, and in the campaign in which they were to participate the prayers and thoughts of those they were leaving would always be with them'.

Brigadier-General Robert Mitchell Betham, Commander of the Ferozepur Brigade, said how proud he had been to have the battalion under his charge. They had done 'exceedingly well' in their military work and had been honoured during their stay in India by being called upon to garrison one of the most important centres. The 1/4th's efficiency had been marked in everything they had been put to do, and now the greatest honour had 'fallen to their lot' – they had been selected for active service, and if they did as well in the firing line as they had in their work in Ferozepur the Devons would play an important part in achieving ultimate victory. He could not speak too highly of the behaviour of the Devons – no commander could wish for a better set of men.

The Kitchener Test was designed to prepare the 1/4th Devons for their transfer to Mesopotamia. The battalion received an order to 'mobilise' on February 4, 1916 and 17 days later William and his fellow soldiers left by troop train for the city of Karachi.

The war diary shows that the battalion comprised 27 British officers, 593 British NCOs and men, one Indian officer, and 24 Indian 'followers', or non-combatants. They took with them 14 riding horses, or cavalry chargers, 12 mules and two machine guns.

The train journey was in itself a challenge. 'Latrine accommodation on the train was entirely inadequate for the number of men, some of the carriages having no latrines whatever,' wrote Major John Woollcombe.

The battalion arrived in Karachi on February 23 and embarked on *HT Vita*, a British Steam Navigation Company troop ship, to sail to Mesopotamia. The 390ft long vessel, built in 1914, could carry more than 3,000 soldiers.

Also on board the *Vita* – which was converted to a hospital ship later in 1916 – were a half battalion of the 2/4th Ghurkha Rifles, detachments of the 16th and 19th Mules Corps and the 37th Infantry Brigade's Signal Section. The passengers included

Brigadier-General A Cadell, commander of the 41st Indian Brigade, an infantry brigade of the British Indian Army, and Lt-Col Acland Troyte.

The *Vita* arrived at No 3 Wharf at Magil, near Basra, on February 28. After the horses and mules were unloaded, the soldiers were forced back on board by heavy rain. 'That night, owing to a bad storm and the ship only being moored forward to the stump of a palm tree, she broke the moorings and drifted down stream,' wrote Major Woollcombe, in the 1/4th Devons' war diary.

The vessel had to be anchored 'mid-stream' and much of the following day, March 1, was spent 'disentangling the ship's chain which had fouled another'. The ship was unloaded by midnight and Major Woollcombe praised the 'great assistance and kindness shown to all ranks by the master and ship's officers during the time we were on *HT Vita*'.

One of the battalion's cavalry horses died from 'accidental strangulation' on the night of March 1-2. After finally leaving the ship on the morning of March 2, the battalion marched to No 3 Camp Magil where they remained for the next 22 days. During this period, they were engaged in field work, marches and drill and in building 'bunds' (embankments or walls, probably to surround fuel tanks).

On March 23, William and his men were on the move again. They embarked on a river steamer – *HT P23* and two barges – at Magil's No 3 Wharf for a week-long journey up the River Tigris to Sheikh Sa'ad. Before the journey, all the 1/4th Devons' rifles were exchanged at the Ordnance Depot in Ashar for weapons capable of firing .303 Mark VI and Mark VII ammunition. And all the remaining 13 cavalry horses were handed in to the Remount Depot at Makina Masus, near Basra, 'according to instructions received'.

The loading of baggage and rations and embarkation of troops on the ship was not completed until the early hours of March 24 – and proved a dangerous experience. Major Woollcombe noted in the war diary: 'The whole of the stores of men (on upper and lower decks) had to pass across one narrow plank, and be

117

lifted over some iron railings on the ship. This was a matter of considerable danger in the dark and one man fell into the river and was nearly drowned.

'The hold was very cramped and great difficulty was experienced in stacking things in it, added to which the electric light on the ship was out of order and could not be used. The lack of assistance on the part of the officers of the ship was very noticeable. The labour of embarking was greatly increased owing to orders given by the embarkation staff to stack the baggage and rations opposite the wrong jetty.'

An early warning of the sickness perils to come came just before the ship sailed when one of the battalion's officers, Lieutenant – later to become Captain – F A Thoday was admitted to hospital suffering from dysentery.

The vessel left Magil at 6am on March 24. Two days later, she ran aground. All troops had to disembark the *HT P23* and one of the river barges to enable her to be refloated, a task that took three hours to complete. William and the 1/4th Devons reached the city of Amarah on March 27, where one man was admitted to hospital suffering from diphtheria.

They reached Ali Gharbi on March 30 and arrived at Sheikh Sa'ad the following day, at about 6.45pm, when a 'bad storm' prevented them from disembarking until the morning of April 1. The battalion marched to Sheikh Sa'ad Standing Camp. With them there were the 6th Cavalry Brigade, the 39th Infantry Brigade, the Cavalry Field Ambulance, the 64th Pioneers (an infantry regiment of the British Indian Army) and a battery of the RFA.

April proved a gruelling 30 days for William and his men. Primarily engaged in improving trenches and the camp perimeter, they also helped in the construction of a new redoubt on the outskirts of the camp, replacing a damaged 'bund' at nearby Gomorrah and improving a road between the camp and Gomorrah.

Armed with rifles and machine guns, they defended outposts, redoubts, Picquets (early warning of attack lines) and blockhouses (reinforced observation points) throughout the month. They also became an integral part of a 'moveable column', established in the 'event of a move from camp being necessitated'.

Their camp and out-posts frequently came under fire from Arab snipers and on April 3 shots were fired at an enemy aeroplane, believed to be German, passing over Sheikh Sa'ad. The 1/4th Devons were 'stood to arms' at 4am on April 7, minutes before shrapnel shells were seen 'bursting' close to an out-post manned by their soldiers.

The officer in charge of B Company, in command of 'No 2 Post', on the fringes of Sheikh Sa'ad, said a 'Turkish gun opened fire' on them in a brief attack on the afternoon of April 7 at a range of about 5,000 yards. A Turkish patrol 'sniped' men while they washed and fired at a ration party as it approached the post. On April 9, a party of Arabs 'approached the post but galloped off on being fired at', leaving a sword behind.

A Turkish deserter, a junior cavalry officer, was brought in by the battalion's cavalry patrol on April 11. He had with him a horse, saddle, sword and a day's rations with rum. He was 'put under escort' and his horse was retained by Lt-Col Acland Troyte 'for his use', by permission of the general officer commanding lines of communication and defences.

Two days later, 400 enemy horsemen were seen moving south of a post manned by the 1/4th Devons, about three miles west of Sheikh Sa'ad camp. On April 20, the battalion were ordered to provide 200 men to observe enemy infantry moving close to a redoubt manned by the 1/4th Devons, but there was no confrontation.

The arrival at Sheikh Sa'ad on April 15 and 16 of almost 200 soldiers from two Devonshire territorial battalions – 100 NCOs and men of the 2/4th, from Wellington, Madras and two officers and 95 NCOs and men from the 3/4th Devons – caused controversy from the time they reached the area to reinforce the 1/4th Devons.

Major Woollcombe said in the war diary that 'no official intimation was received with regards to these drafts until after they had landed at Sheikh Sa'ad. It would have been a matter of some convenience had it been known that we might expect reinforcements.'

Concerns over the physical fitness and abilities of the 3/4th Devons came to a head on April 23. On that day, the NCOs and men from the battalion were 'struck off all duties' to undergo a course of physical training, musketry, drill and instruction in fieldwork. On April 24, Major Woollcombe voiced his disquiet in a confidential letter to the general officer commanding lines of communication and defences at Sheikh Sa'ad.

He said he considered the 'draft sent to me from the 3/4th Devons (117 strong when leaving England and quickly hit by sickness) is very unsatisfactory'. Many of them were 'mere lads and I am certain are physically incapable of standing the life here. It seems to me unfair both to the individual man and to the battalion that such men should be sent out from England. My medical officer quite agrees with me in these remarks and I feel it my duty to report the matter.'

Major Woollcombe said the 'draft from 2/4th Devons were of a very different quality and appear to me to be excellent in every respect. I am certain it would have been very much in the interest of the service if my strength had been made up entirely from the 2/4th Devons and the men sent from the 3/4th Devons had gone to the 2/4th Devons until they had been trained and acclimatised and had time to develop.'

Amid the heat and plague of flies and other insects, sickness increasingly took its toll. Ten of the 1/4th Devons were admitted to hospital in April. Four officers and 46 other ranks were admitted in May. In the four months after William's death, more than 460 officers and men, including Lt-Col Acland Troyte, were admitted to hospital.

In May, up to an eighth of the 1/4th Devons were on sick parade – during which they reported to their medical officer as unwell. Their reinforcements, particularly men from the 3/4th Devons, were harder hit, with up to a third of their number on sick parade. The 2/4th Devons fared better, but had up to 17% of their men registered as sick.

Two soldiers 'accidentally drowned' while bathing in the Tigris in May – Exeter-born Private Harold Gregory, of the 2/4th Devons, who died on May 1 and whose body was not recovered, and Wigan-born Private William Smallshaw, of the 1/4th Devons'

GRANDAD'S SHARE

Mr. John Roberts, of Witheridge, has thirty grandsons on active service.

Above left: The picture of John Roberts as it appears on Witheridge Historical Archive – and the remarkable caption. **Above right:** My parents, Sydney and Sarah Helena (Nellie) Roberts. My father was John's great-grandson. Note the family resemblance. **Below:** My parents on their wedding day in 1939. With them on the left are my father's brother, Dick, and his sister, Vera. On the right are my mother's brother and sister, Jack and Elsie.

Above: Boulogne Eastern Cemetery in France where Private John 'Jack' Roberts is buried. Picture supplied by The War Graves Photographic Project.
Below left: Jack's grave at Boulogne Eastern Cemetery where the headstones are laid flat because of the sandy soil. Picture supplied by The War Graves Photographic Project. **Below right:** The memorial to the eight men from Cruwys Morchard who died in the war, at the village's Church of the Holy Cross. Jack's name appears as John on the memorial.

Pte. Albert Roberts, 8th Devons, son of Mr. and Mrs. Thomas Roberts, of Newlands, Witheridge, who died of wounds on October 3rd. He was within three days of his 20th birthday when he died. A brother is serving with the 1st Devon Yeomanry. For three years he was employed at the Rectories at Meshaw and Thelbridge.

10851 PRIVATE
ALBERT ROBERTS
DEVONSHIRE REGIMENT
3RD OCTOBER 1915 AGE 19

GONE BUT NOT FORGOTTEN

S/3402 PRIVATE
G. GRANTHAM

Above left: How Private Albert Roberts' death was announced in *The Western Times* on October 22, 1915. Image © Trinity Mirror. Reproduced with permission of the British Newspaper Archive. **Above right:** Albert's grave in Wimereux Communal Cemetery, France. Picture supplied by The War Graves Photographic Project. **Below:** Wimereux Communal Cemetery where, again, the headstones lie flat upon the graves because of the sandy soil. Picture supplied by The War Graves Photographic Project.

Above: St John the Baptist Church, Witheridge, showing the war memorial.
Above right: The names of men from the parish who died in the Great War, including Private Albert Roberts, 19.
Right: The granite cross above the names of Witheridge's fallen.

Above: Samuel 'Sam' Roberts (middle row, second left), among children with a perfect attendance record at Rackenford School. The picture was taken in about 1906 when he was 10 or 11 years old. Ten years later, he was killed on the first day of the Battle of the Somme. Picture from *Rackenford – a Short History*, by Sarah Child. **Below left:** Sam's grave at the Devonshire Cemetery, Mametz. Picture supplied by The War Graves Photographic Project. **Below right:** Named on Rackenford War Memorial – Sam and his brother, John Francis 'Frank' Roberts.

Above: The Devonshire Cemetery, Mametz. Picture supplied by The War Graves Photographic Project.
Left: Rackenford Parish Church where (*below*) is another memorial to Sam and John Francis 'Frank' Roberts and six other men from the parish.

To the Glory of God

AND IN HONOURED MEMORY OF THE FOLLOWING MEN OF THIS PARISH WHO GAVE THEIR LIVES FOR KING AND COUNTRY DURING THE GREAT WAR OF 1914-1919

CAPT THE REV GERALD J. LESTER RECTOR & CHAPLAIN 4TH HORSE.
PTE HARRY BOUNDY DUKE OF CORNWALLS L.I.
PTE DAVID FOOK 2/4 OX & BUCKS. L.I.
CORPL FRED GREENSLADE MILITARY MOUNTED POLICE
PTE CHARLES NOTT 1ST ROYAL DEVON YEOMANRY.
PTE FREDERICK GILBERT PINCOMBE 7TH WORCESTERSHIRE REGIMENT
L. CORPL JOHN FRANCIS ROBERTS 2ND DEVON REGIMENT
CORPL SAMUEL ROBERTS 8TH DEVON REGT

THEIR NAME LIVETH FOR EVERMORE.

Left: Vermelles British Cemetery in France where Lance-Corporal John Francis 'Frank' Roberts is buried. Picture supplied by The War Graves Photographic Project.

Right: Rackenford War Memorial, on the outskirts of the village. **Below:** John Francis 'Frank' Roberts' grave at Vermelles British Cemetery. Picture supplied by The War Graves Photographic Project.

Above: The Basra Memorial where Corporal William Henry Kingdom is remembered. **Below:** William's name among the dozens of Devonshire Regiment soldiers commemorated on the memorial, in Iraq.
Pictures supplied by The War Graves Photographic Project.

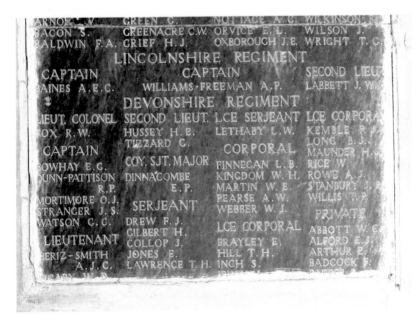

Above: Vis-en-Artois Memorial, where Private Walter Kingdom is remembered.
Below: How his name appears on the memorial. Pictures supplied by The War
Graves Photographic Project.

Above: Brandhoek New Military Cemetery No 3, in Belgium, where Rifleman Sidney Roberts is buried. **Left:** Sidney's grave. Pictures supplied by The War Graves Photographic Project.

Above: The Memorial chapel at All Saints Parish Church, Dulverton, where Rifleman Sidney Roberts is commemorated. **Right:** The chapel's memorial plaque, which includes Sidney's name.

1914 - 1918

FREDERICK PARKHOUSE
SIDNEY ROBERTS
HERBERT H. RUDD
JOHN SANGER
H. ST BARBE SYDENHAM
ISAAC SAUNDERS
JOHN TARR
CECIL TEE
EDWARD W. WHITE
FRANCIS J. WILLIAMS

Above left: All Saints Parish Church, Dulverton, where Rifleman Sidney Roberts is remembered in the memorial chapel.
Above: Dulverton War Memorial where (*left*) Sidney's name is listed among the fallen of the Great War.

Left: The war memorial in Oakford, which also commemorates Rifleman Sidney Roberts, of the Queen's Westminster Rifles.

Right: The plaque on Oakford War Memorial bearing Sidney's name.

IN SORROW, IN GRATITUDE, IN HOPE.

1914 - 1918	
W.BROOKS	F.E.BULLER
A.CARPENTER	J.HEYWOOD
J.MIDDLETON	F.REED
W.REED	S.ROBERTS

1939 - 1945	
W.H.COLLINS	C.J.CURTIS
J.C.MIDDLEDITCH	S.D.C.SMITH

TO THE GLORY OF GOD
AND IN MEMORY OF THOSE FROM
THIS PARISH WHO GAVE THEIR LIVES
FOR THEIR COUNTRY 1914-1919

W.Brooks   J.Middleton
F.E.Buller   F.Reed
A.Carpenter   W.Reed
J.Heywood   S.Roberts

Left: A plaque in St Peter's Parish Church, Oakford, remembering eight men from the parish who lost their lives in the war, including Sidney.

Above: Archibald 'Archie' Roberts, of the 13th Hussars, survivor of two of the greatest cavalry charges during the war. Picture kindly supplied by Lynne Roberts, Archie's grand-daughter.

Above: The certificate awarded to Private Archie Roberts, of Thorverton, on being honourably discharged from the 13th Hussars in 1918. He also received a Silver Badge for 'serving with honour' and becoming disabled while serving with the regiment in Mesopotamia. Picture kindly supplied by Lynne Roberts, Archie's grand-daughter.

Left: John Francis Bryant Roberts and family, pictured outside Woodbine Cottage, Sparkford in about 1927. John was a private in the 9th Devons during the war. He is pictured with his wife, Edith Mabel and their children, William, Ellen, Bert, Arthur, Alf and Elsie. They had two other sons, Charles and Sydney. Photo kindly supplied by Nicole Vallins.
Below: St Mary Magdalene Parish Church, Sparkford. John is buried in the churchyard there.

Above: Private George Burnett Roberts, my grandfather, who served in the Army Service Corps, joining at the age of 17 in 1915.

Left: George Burnett Roberts, at Newton St Cyres.
Below: George at work on Home Farm, Newton St Cyres, where he was employed as head cowman and farm bailiff.

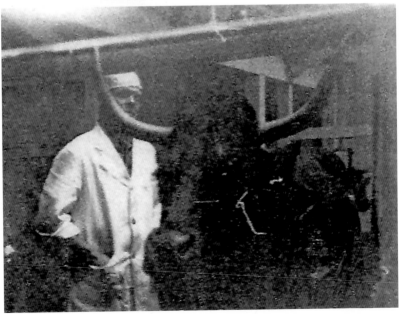

Above: Lilian Ellen (nee Arscott), wife of George Burnett Roberts.

Above: George Burnett Roberts with his four children on a day out on the beach – Dick, Margaret, Vera and my father, Sydney. **Left:** George and Lilian Ellen's grave at Newton St Cyres Churchyard.

Above: My father, Sydney George Roberts who handed down to me the tunic buttons from his father's WW1 uniform.

Above: Benjamin James Roberts, son of John Roberts who had 30 grandsons in the Great War, and father of George Burnett Roberts, who served in the Army Service Corps between 1915 and 1918. Benjamin, who farmed at Mariansleigh for many years, died in 1947.

Above: Elizabeth (nee Burnett) Roberts, wife of Benjamin, and mother of George Burnett Roberts. Elizabeth died in 1930.

SERVED

PTE. R. MANLEY.	R. F. A.
PTE. E. C. MORRISH.	COLDSTREAM GUARDS.
PTE. P. NOTT. M.M.	IRISH GUARDS.
ST⁰. F. V. NOTT.	R. N.
LCPL. A. NOTT.	1ˢᵀ R. DEVON Y⁰.
PTE. W. NOTT.	1ˢᵀ SOMERSET Y⁰.
SERGᵀ A. J. NICHOLS.	M.M. 16ᵀᴴ DEVONS.
GN⁰ E. NICHOLS.	R. M. A.
PTE. F. NICHOLS.	14ᵀᴴ M. G. C.
LCPL. E. OSMOND.	R. E.
LCPL. B. ROBERTS.	R. E.
PTE. J. SLADER.	8ᵀᴴ DEVONS.
CPL. G. SNELL.	13ᵀᴴ HUSSARS.
PTE. A. SNELL.	2ᴺᴰ DEVONS.
PTE. C. SINGERTON.	Nᴼ DEVON YEO.
LCPL. C. SANDERS.	R. E.
PTE. L. SNOW.	8. DEVONS.
2ᴺᴰ LIEUT R. TURNER.	9ᵀᴴ DEVONS.
PTE. I. TURNER.	1ˢᵀ R. DEVON YEO.
PTE. A. TURNER.	MIDDLESEX REGᵗ.

Above: The 20 men from Rackenford who served in the Great War – and survived. Remembered on the war memorial on the outskirts of the village, they include Lance-Corporal Ben Roberts – brother of Sam and John Francis 'Frank', who were both killed in 1916 – and Private John Slader, an uncle of my mother's, who served in the 8th Devons, and survived the war.

Left: The plaque at St Swithun's Church, Sandford, listing the names of dozens of local men who fought and, in some cases, died on the Western Front and in many other theatres of war. **Below:** How Henry 'Harry' Roberts' name appears on the plaque.

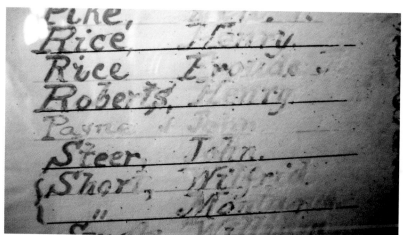

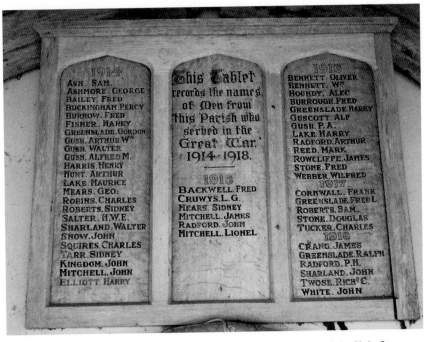

1914

ASH. SAM.
ASHMORE. GEORGE
BAILEY. FRED
BUCKINGHAM. PERCY
BURROW. FRED
FISHER. HARRY
GREENSLADE. GORDON
GUSH. ARTHUR Wᵐ
GUSH. WALTER
GUSH. ALFRED M.
HARRIS. HENRY
HUNT. ARTHUR
LAKE. MAURICE
MEARS. GEO.
ROBINS. CHARLES
ROBERTS. SIDNEY
SALTER. H.W.E.
SHARLAND. WALTER
SNOW. JOHN
SQUIRES. CHARLES
TARR. SIDNEY
KINGDOM. JOHN
MITCHELL. JOHN
ELLIOTT. HARRY

This Tablet records the names of Men from This Parish who served in the Great War. 1914-1918.

1915

BACKWELL. FRED
CRUWYS. L.G.
MEARS. SIDNEY
MITCHELL. JAMES
RADFORD. JOHN
MITCHELL. LIONEL

1916

BENNETT. OLIVER
BENNETT. Wᵐ
BOUNDY. ALEC
BURROUGH. FRED
GREENSLADE. HARRY
GUSCOTT. ALF
GUSH. P. A.
LAKE. HARRY
RADFORD. ARTHUR
REED. MARK
ROWCLIFFE. JAMES
STONE. FRED
WEBBER. WILFRED

1917

CORNWALL. FRANK
GREENSLADE. FRED L.
ROBERTS. SAM.
STONE. DOUGLAS
TUCKER. CHARLES

1918

CHANG. JAMES
GREENSLADE. RALPH
RADFORD. P.H.
SHARLAND. JOHN
TWOSE. RICHᵈ C.
WHITE. JOHN

Above: The magnificent tablet erected in the porch of the Church of the Holy Cross in Cruwys Morchard in honour of 54 men from the parish who served in the war – and survived. They include Sidney and Sam Roberts – sons of Samuel and Maria Roberts – who went to war in 1914 and 1917 respectively. Inside the church is a plaque honouring the eight local men who died in the war, including Sidney and Sam's brother, Jack.

HORWILL WILLIAM HENRY
LEACH FRANK
ROBERTS WILLIAM
SMITH THOMAS
SMITH REGINALD
SOUTHCOTT WILLIAM HAROLD
SOWDEN THOMAS
STENTIFORD FRANK
TUCKER HERBERT FRANCIS
VODDEN HENRY
WEBBER FREDERICK
WILCOX ALFRED

Above: Morchard Bishop War Memorial on which (*left*) Sergeant William James Roberts, of the 1st Battalion Coldstream Guards, is remembered.

Above: The county memorial to Devon's fallen heroes, close to Exeter Cathedral. It honours 11,601 servicemen and women who died in the Great War.

Above: The magnificent war memorial in Exeter's Northernhay Gardens. It is crowned by a spectacular bronze 'Victory' figure and features four seated statues representing the sailor, soldier, nurse and prisoner of war.

Above: The soldier on Exeter War Memorial in the city's Northernhay Gardens, commemorating almost 1,000 men from the city who lost their lives between 1914 and 1918.

Above: The grave of Henry and Mary Roberts – parents of Archie, Harry and Walter Roberts, who all survived the war – at St Swithun's Churchyard, Sandford.

Above: The house at Farthing Park Farm, Morchard Bishop, where I was born and grew up. My father, Sydney Roberts and four of his six children (including myself) are pictured, along with master thatcher Dick Frost. Farthing Park was the home of Sgt William James Roberts, of the 1st Battalion Coldstream Guards, who was killed in action in France in 1914.

A Company, who had a home in Lyme Regis, who died on May 12.

NCOs and men of the battalion worked up to ten hours a day during the month on constructing front line trenches. Because of the amount of digging required, and with sickness levels increasing, it 'became necessary' on May 5 to restore to service the men of the 3/4th Devons who had not been involved in any duties for 12 days.

The 1/4th Devons moved camp at Sheikh Sa'ad to the brigade reserve area west of Shahaniyah Canal on May 4, one of three local relocations in 18 days. Between May 15 and 20, 150 of their men were involved in working on a new Ordnance stores at the junction of the Tigris and the Shahaniyah Canal.

A Turkish deserter, a cavalry sergeant, 'gave himself up' to the officer in charge of A redoubt – one of two defended by the battalion – on May 7. He had with him a German Mauser rifle, a horse and 'some papers'. He was 'detained in battalion guard tent' and handed over to the officer in charge of the 1/2nd Ghurkhas on the morning of May 8.

On the day of William's death, the war diary recorded that the 1/4th Devons' A Company relieved D Company in the two redoubts defended by the battalion. Five men were admitted to hospital and more than 40 were on sick parade.

The battalion moved away from Sheikh Sa'ad on June 13 to Twin Canals. Two days later, a small convoy – sent out to recover stores left at Sheikh Sa'ad – was attacked by a party of about 25 Arabs. One soldier and one orderly were killed in the assault, two more were wounded, and one orderly was reported as 'missing'.

The 1/4th Devons moved to the Sinn area later in June. One of their men was severely wounded while on Brigade Guard on September 6. Another was killed by a sniper on October 8. The battalion moved into front line trenches in January 1917. One man was killed and an officer and 14 were wounded in an attack on January 29, and five men were wounded on the last two days of the month.

On February 3, 1917, the 1/4th Devons (and the 1/2nd Ghurkhas) led a daring and successful attack on the Turkish defences at Hai Salient, near Kut. Four officers – including Major Woollcombe, who had been promoted to second in command of the battalion in July 1916 – and 63 men were killed. Six officers and 149 men were wounded.

William was one of many young men from the Westcountry to die from heart disease while on duty. In December 1916, *The Western Times* reported that Private Leonard F A Baker, of Pilton, near Barnstaple, had died at Alexandria in Egypt from 'heart disease and dropsy', aged 34.

Private Samuel Sanders, aged 35, of Barnstaple, died in 1918 at a casualty clearing station in France from heart valve disease. 2nd Lieutenant Ricardio Sidney Rowse, of the 5th Duke of Cornwall's Light Infantry, died suddenly from heart disease at a Royal Army Medical Corps Camp in Tavistock in 1915.

Sergeant George Kerswell, of Braunton, was admitted to a field hospital in Mesopotamia in 1916 suffering from heart valve disease. He survived to return home for sick leave after being transferred to hospitals in Cairo and Alexandria, Egypt and then journeying to England as a patient on a hospital ship.

In making his will, William wrote: 'In the event of my death … I leave all my property to my wife, Louise Kingdom.'

His medal card confirms his service number (3598) and that he was posthumously awarded two medals: The Victory and British War Medals. The card does not mention his death or when he joined a 'theatre of war'.

William's name appears on the 11th panel (on the left-hand side) of the re-sited Basra Memorial.

Notes

- Major Woollcombe was from Ashbury, near Hatherleigh in Devon. In 1921, a bronze memorial tablet in his honour was erected in the Church of St Mary the Virgin, Ashbury by officers, NCOs and men of the 1/4th Devons. The following year a service was held at the church for the dedication of a new window in the north sanctuary of the church in memory of Major Woollcombe.

- In 1924, a tablet in memory of Lt-Col Acland Troyte, of Huntsham, Devon – who was killed by a shell at St Venant, France in April 1918 – was erected at St Michael and All Angels Church, Bampton, near Tiverton, by officers, NCOs and men of the 1/4th Devons. A sermon was delivered at the unveiling of the tablet by the Rev Arthur Charles Vodden, of Cullompton. It was a poignant moment for him for he had served under Lt-Col Acland Troyte with the 1/4th Devons in Mesopotamia. As a lieutenant, he was among the officers seriously wounded at Hai Salient on February 3, 1917. Later promoted to captain, he was at college preparing for ordination at the outbreak of the war in 1914. Ordained deacon in 1918 and priest in 1919, he became curate of St Andrew's, Plymouth, spent three years in Nairobi and was a vicar of a number of parishes, including Newport, Barnstaple and St Luke's, Mamingham, Bradford. He was a chaplain to the forces. In his later years, he lived in Paignton in Devon and died there in 1970, aged 79.

13

WALTER — KILLED JUST 52 DAYS BEFORE THE WAR ENDS

He was close to the German army's last great stronghold on the Western Front – the formidable 90-mile long Hindenburg Line. Believed by many to be 'virtually impregnable', Private Walter Kingdom knew it would have to be broken to bring the war to an end.

Walter, serving with the 1st Battalion of the Loyal North Lancashire Regiment, was about to take part in the Battle of Epehy, a key offensive in the campaign in the final months of the Great War to break the vast defences of the Hindenburg Line.

Built in just five months during 1916 and early 1917, with the help of tens of thousands of prisoners of war, the German fortress – also known as the Siegfried Line – stretched from Arras to beyond St Quentin on the French-Belgian border.

It included a huge network of heavily protected machine gun and artillery fire posts, enormous belts of impenetrable barbed wire entanglements, deep trenches and bomb-proof dug-outs and tunnels, and anti-tank ditches.

Tiverton-born Walter had been at war in France for about 18 months, initially serving with the 8th (Service) Battalion of the Carlisle-based Border Regiment before joining the 1st Loyal North in February 1918.

Walter's battalion took part in an attack on German outposts in front of the Hindenburg Line when the Battle of Epehy – led by the British Fourth Army, under the command of General Henry Rawlinson – was launched on September 18, 1918.

The assault began amid heavy downpours and fog-like conditions, with an artillery and machine gun barrage. British soldiers advancing on the flanks, including the 1st Loyal North, had limited success as they came under heavy fire.

But two Australian divisions at the centre of the advance forced their way some three miles into enemy territory, capturing thousands of German troops – an attack that would prove crucial in planning a breakthrough assault on the Hindenburg defences.

The 1st Loyal North suffered heavy casualties as they led the attack on the German outposts, advancing at 5.30am in 'thick mist and rain', when 'no land marks were visible', commanding officer Lieutenant-Colonel Thomas R Forsyth-Forrest recorded in the war diary.

The battalion's first objective was to capture the German-held Villemay trench, near Holnon village. Within an hour, one of their leading companies (D) reported this had been achieved, but officers and men of the advancing C Company were held up by 'very heavy machine gun fire'.

At 8am, B Company were ordered to join the assault on Villemay trench to go to the aid of fellow soldiers under un-relenting attack – and to try and establish contact with D Company in continuing the advance.

But on securing the battalion's position in the trench, officers and men of B Company came under heavy machine gun fire as German soldiers launched a counter-attack, emerging in large numbers from the nearby Arbousiers Wood.

Despite putting up strong resistance – during which Captain Russell Medley Leake was killed – they were 'forced to give ground'. Amid the fierce fighting, D, C and A Companies were withdrawn from dangerous positions.

Further attempts by officers and men of A Company to enter the trench were thwarted by continued machine gun fire. As darkness fell, C Company fought their way into the trench but found it 'impossible' to hold their position and had to withdraw.

During the night of September 18-19, the battalion 'took up a position to form a defensive flank in the high ground'. But officers and men 'lost their directions' in the face of severe enemy fire and poor visibility.

Lt-Col Forsyth-Forrest's operations report said the 'wide frontage' of the advance on September 18 had 'made it extremely difficult under the most trying of circumstances to keep touch and direction', although 'every effort was made to do so, by means of compass patrols and scouts'.

He said any advance beyond Villemay trench would have been 'impossible' because the Germans had not been forced out of key defensive positions at Arbousiers Wood and at the nearby Fresnoy-le-Petit redoubt.

In the period September 17-24, the build up to the Battle of Epehy, the battle itself and the aftermath, the 1st Loyal North had two officers and 48 NCOs and men killed in action. Seven officers and 180 other ranks were wounded, one officer and nine others were reported missing, and 21 were believed to have been gassed.

Walter survived the Battle of Epehy but was killed in action in the aftermath, on September 20, 1918 – just 52 days before the Great War ended on November 11. He was just 20 years old. His death came more than two years after his brother, Corporal William Henry Kingdom, died – from heart disease – while serving with the 1/4th Devons in Mesopotamia.

Just a few weeks before engaging the enemy at Epehy, Walter had fought at the Battle of Drocourt-Queant, the most northerly section of the Hindenburg Line, between the French towns of Drocourt and Queant. The 1st Loyal North were among armoured and infantry units advancing behind an artillery barrage, with tanks destroying enemy posts along the way. The offensive, led by the British Army's 1st and 4th Divisions and the 4th Canadian Division, led to the capture of more than 6,000 German soldiers.

On the night of August 31-September 1, the battalion marched to assembly positions south east of Gwemappe, a village about eight miles from Arras. 'At 5am the barrage opened and at 10.45am the battalion moved forward in artillery formation to consolidate their first objective (a ridge near the village of Dury) which the Canadians were reported to have taken', Captain Douglas Stephenson wrote in the 1st Loyal North's war diary.

With A and B Companies in the front line, and C and D in support and reserve, 'the objective was reached about 1pm when it was found that the fight was still in progress. The battalion accordingly withdrew about 200 metres and laid down in artillery formation under cover of the ridge,' recorded Captain Stephenson. 'At about 4pm, orders were received to withdraw a further 1500 metres. This was done and the battalion remained in the positions throughout the night. The casualties sustained were very light, a number being caused by bombs and machine gun bullets from low flying aeroplanes.'

The following day, September 2, the 1st Loyal North went 'into reserve' in the Drocourt-Queant line. A bomb was dropped on D Company's ration party the following night, wounding 14 soldiers. A company quartermaster sergeant and another sergeant later died of their wounds. Between September 1 and 8, 12 NCOs and men of the battalion were killed, and one officer and 47 other ranks were wounded. Nine men were gassed and one was listed as missing.

Born on March 27, 1898 in Ashley, Tiverton, Walter was one of 11 children of George and Lucy Kingdom (the daughter of John Roberts), of Howden Cottage, Tiverton. In 1911, his father and elder brother – William Henry – were gardeners. Walter was 13 at the time and a schoolboy. He lived with his family at Bushment Cottage, Tiverton at the time of the 1901 Census. He was just 19 years old when he went to war, in France, in April 1917.

Walter enlisted in the Army in Tiverton and ended up in the ranks of the Carlisle-based 8th Borders after their numbers were decimated in a series of brutal battles in France. In 1917, he fought with the battalion in the spectacular attack on the Messines Ridge, a German stronghold south-east of Ypres, and in the gruelling Third Battle of Ypres, which lasted for more than three months. Battlefields were turned into a quagmire in unrelenting rain in this major offensive and heavy artillery fire wreaked havoc on British and German forces, killing or injuring hundreds of thousands of men.

Walter joined the 7th Loyal North in early 1918. He was among hundreds of men posted to the regiment's 1st Battalion in February that year when the 7th were disbanded. It was month of change not just for Walter but for his new battalion – for they were transferred to the 1st Infantry Brigade of the British Army's 1st Division after a 'record' four years' continuous service with the division's 2nd Brigade.

He fought at Givenchy in April 1918, in the Battle of Bethune, when the 1st Loyal North suffered heavy casualties in an enemy attack. His battalion took part in two daring night-time raids on German machine gun posts in a remote area of Belgium, regularly came under artillery and machine gun fire on the front line on the French-Belgian border – and even came under attack in their own billets in Noeux les Mines, a town close to Bethune.

When he joined the 8th Borders, the battalion, frequently facing driving winds, blizzards, heavy snow and sleet, moved between different areas on the French-Belgium border, including Ebblinghem, Nortbecourt, Acquin, Borre, Outtersteene, Neuve Eglise, Wulverghem, Steenje and Erquingheim. There were practice attacks, bombing competitions, firing and bayonet exercises – and continuous work in trenches in preparation for one of the most explosive attacks of the war.

Four men from the battalion's C Company were killed and six wounded when a shell burst over them as they marched from Ravelsburg to Neuve Eglise on May 30, 1917. Six days later, just after midnight, Walter and his battalion were in an assembly trench at Messines Ridge, waiting for the start of an offensive designed to destroy key German defences that had been a major thorn in British and French operations since the 1914–18 War began.

At 3.10am on June 7, 1917 there was an almighty roar as a series of mines were simultaneously exploded in tunnels under enemy positions, killing thousands of Germans. The blast, which created a series of huge craters, was so loud it was heard hundreds of miles away. The 8th Borders were involved in the following attack which led to the capture of the Wytschaete-Messines ridge south of Ypres and of 7,000 enemy troops.

The 8th Borders left their assembly trench at 7am to take part in the assault. C and D Companies led their lines, with A and B Companies in support. Their task was to consolidate a line just east of the Messines-Wytschaete road but the battalion's war diary said they 'had to help clear several pockets of enemy left by advanced troops'. They reached the line at about 8.30am and 'began consolidation'. The 'enemy shelled very heavily at intervals all the day and night'. Four platoons were 'sent forward' in support of the 11th Battalion of the Cheshire Regiment. By the end of the following day, the 8th Borders had suffered heavy casualties. One officer and 13 NCOs and men were killed, and two officers and 65 other ranks were wounded.

The enormity of the attack at Messines was described in *The Western Times*, in June 1917, in a report by a special correspondent. 'At the pre-arranged moment, the biggest thing ever attempted in mining operations rent the sky with a terrible glare and an ear-splitting crash as a long series of mines, some of which were dug over a year ago, were blown along the enemy positions.

'For the past seven days, a preliminary bombardment of appalling intensity has been in progress. The villages of Messines and Wytschaete have totally vanished. From the north of Hill 60 to the south of Ploegsteert, the enemy's terrain looks like the face of the long valley at Aldershot after an August field day. People who saw Vimy Ridge after the Canadians had taken it said that the worst of the Somme battlefields could not compare with the much-pocked surface of that famous hump. Those who see the Messines Ridge will draw a similar comparison between it and Vimy. The spectacle this morning (June 7) is incredible. The whole geography of the district has been churned and blown and furrowed out of recognition,' the newspaper reported.

On June 9-11, the 8th Borders were 'resting' in the brigade camp in Neuve Eglise before moving back to the Messines trenches on the 12th. An officer was killed on patrol the following day and another was killed and three others wounded in action on the 14th. Later, in June, the battalion moved to Sec Bois, Merville, St Hilaire and latterly Erny St Julien where, the war dairy recorded, an 'attempt was made to clean filthy billets'.

In July 1917, the 8th Borders moved to Ypres in the run up to a battle that would begin on the 31st of that month and end in November 1917. The third major offensive in Ypres since 1914, it was conducted in appalling conditions, with attacks constantly delayed on battlefields reduced to mud baths.

Walter and his men had a mainly supporting role in the offensive. On July 31, they were in the Belgian Chateau area, near the front line, 'moving from the assembly area at 7.40am to a position of readiness,' the war diary recorded. 'During the night, we took over the line gained by the 2nd West Yorks Regiment, the 8th Division (of the British Army) having attacked during the morning.' The battalion suffered nine casualties.

It poured with rain when the 8th Borders were ordered to support the 23rd Brigade of the British Army in holding Bellewaarde Ridge, close to the Ypres-Roulers Railway, in the early hours of August 1, 1917. Men were suffering from exposure and extreme cold while the enemy continuously shelled their position. Two parties totalling about 100 men were 'sent forward at night' to help dig support trenches on the west slope of Westhoek Ridge.

Attacks were frequently postponed because of deteriorating weather. Enemy artillery fire continued to take its toll. A battalion officer was killed on August 3 and another died of wounds on the 9th when the 8th Borders were relieved by the 3rd Worcesters and being transported to the nearby Winnipeg Camp via the Menin Gate at Ypres and Belgian Battery Corner. They were back in the trenches three days later, on the eastern slope of Westhoek Ridge where rain continued to fall heavily.

The battalion moved to the Steenvoorde area on August 20. The following day Field Marshall Douglas Haig, Commander in Chief of the British Army in France and Flanders, carried out the annual inspection at which the 8th Borders were 'complimented' on doing a good job. There was welcome respite from bombardment and the mud-filled trenches in the next few days as Walter and his fellow soldiers took part in specialist and 'recreational training', with the battalion scoring the highest points in athletic races and finishing equal first in transport events.

The battalion were moved to another camp – Dominion – on September 1, 1917 and marched to Chateau Segard in the Dickebusche area where men went into bivouacs. An enemy plane heavily bombed the surrounding area during the night of September 2, but there were no casualties. The 8th Borders came under heavy bombardment when they moved into front line trenches in the Glencorse Wood area the following day – and also when they returned to the Winnipeg Camp.

They were bussed to Pradelles on September 12 and then marched to Steenbecque and Marles-les-Mines. Here, they had another chance to recover from the stresses of the preceding days, with shooting, tug-of-war, wrestling and football competitions organised. They marched to Noeux les Mines on September 27 and were in Le Preol on October 5. Later that month, they were in trenches in the La Bassee Canal area.

The battalion came under gas attack on November 6, with a 'large number of gas shells fired' into support lines between 2am and 3am. On the night of November 10 and 11, the 8th Borders launched a raid on enemy trenches. Gas projectors and mortars were fired at 2.20am as two fighting patrols 'went over under cover of smoke', the war diary recorded. There was 'practically no retaliation' and no machine gun fire and no enemy was found in the front line. The raid occurred as the Third Battle of Ypres (or Passchendaele) ground to a halt.

Any relief from the terrible conditions suffered by the soldiers was brief as rain gave way to snow and freezing conditions in December as the 8th Borders moved to Erny St Julien, Goniecourt, Beugnatre and Lagnicourt. They spent December 22, 1917 improving and deepening trenches and were heavily shelled by the enemy the following day. They moved to Vaulx-Vraucourt on the 27th and were there at the dawn of 1918.

After his brief transfer to the 7th Battalion of the Loyal North Regiment, Walter was among a detachment of 200 soldiers who joined the Regiment's 1st Battalion, at Wieltze near Ypres, in early February 1918. The day before his arrival, the 1st Loyal North suffered 13 casualties when they were shelled in dug-outs near the village. Three men were killed in or died after the attacks and ten were wounded.

Three men were killed and eight wounded when their positions were shelled later in the month. The battalion moved into a siege camp just south of the Belgian village of Elverdinghe on March 4 and five days later marched to the front at Langemarck, relieving the 12th Highland Light Infantry. 'The relief was completed without any special incident although the (Germans) appeared to be engaged on an area shoot, possibly owing to the amount of talking about the relief over the telephone which went on between the battalion and their brigade,' Lieutenant-Colonel Noel Clive Phillips (commanding officer of the 1st Loyal North before being succeeded by Lt-Col Forsyth-Forrest) recorded in the war diary.

The battalion then came under the orders of the British Army's 3rd Brigade who were in charge of the whole divisional sector. 'Generally, the method of holding the line as taken over was found to be very badly organised,' wrote Lt-Col Phillips. 'Enemy machine guns were found to be very active with direct fire onto the front posts of the left company and indirect fire upon our back areas, which caused us several casualties.' Two men died and 15 were wounded by the time the 1st Loyal North moved away from the front line.

The battalion's B Company, with artillery support, launched a raid on an enemy post at nearby Gravel Farm on the night of March 24-25. Three German soldiers were killed, one was captured and four others fled when the raiding party, which suffered two minor casualties, crossed a stream under cover of darkness and rushed the enemy's defensive position.

On the night of April 6-7 – three days before the start of Battles of the Lys, in which the Germans launched offensives to capture important railway and supply routes and cut off the British Army at Ypres – the 1st Loyal North led a second raid on Gravel Farm. One of two fighting patrols from A and D Companies, supported by artillery fire, came under attack from bombs and machine gun and rifle fire when they tried to breach wire defences, but had to withdraw when they could find no way through. An officer and five men were wounded.

Walter and his fellow soldiers moved to Houchin, near Bethune, by bus on April 11 and marched to Beuvry the following day. They were confined to billets, taking shelter in cellars, as they came under heavy shell fire over the next three days. Ten men were wounded in the bombardment. On April 16, the battalion were in the front line in the La Bassee Canal sector, near Givenchy where less than 48 hours later they would be fighting for their lives – and highly praised for their courage.

After enduring a heavy bombardment in the early hours of April 18, Walter and his men then had to fight off waves of German soldiers racing across uneven ground and pouring into their trenches in a series of sustained attacks. 'The enemy attacked from the north, filtering into our trenches under cover of the high ground at Givenchy,' Major G A Battcock recorded in the battalion's war diary. 'He (the enemy) succeeded in reaching and occupying the main line of resistance before counter measures could be taken. Vigorous counter attacks by C and D Companies eventually succeeded in ejecting the enemy from our main line. By 11am, he was only holding a few isolated points in our outpost line.'

Casualties were strikingly high in the fierce fighting in the trenches. By the time the battalion were relieved and moved back to Houchin and then billets in Noeux les Mines, two officers and 46 NCOs and men had been killed, five officers and 105 NCOs and men had been wounded and five officers and 189 NCOs and men were listed as missing. Twenty-eight honours were awarded to officers and men for their bravery at Givenchy, with four receiving the Military Cross and two the Distinguished Service Order.

In May 1918, the battalion fired almost 600 gas projectors into enemy rear positions at Auchy les Mines. In June, a reconnoitring patrol of two officers and three men ran into and were bombed by an enemy post in the Hohenzollern sector. 'Two men were wounded and one missing. Every effort was made to recover the latter without success,' the war diary recorded. Another two men were killed and one wounded when the battalion came under shell fire in Cambrin, a village near Bethune, in July.

There was a welcome break from hostilities at the end of July when the 1st Loyal North played the 6th Lincolns and 1st Camerons at football, winning both matches 3-1. They won cross country and quarter mile races and finished second in a tug-of-war contest at a divisional show held near the old coal mining town of Bruay in early August 1918.

Their billets at Noeux les Mines came under heavy attack on August 11, forcing them to move into open country west of the town. Just over an hour after the shelling stopped and the battalion moved back into the billets, a new attack began just as rations and dinners were being served, killing five men and wounding 22 others. Walter and his fellow soldiers moved to billets in Predefin on the 19th before taking the train to Arras on the last day of the month.

Walter is remembered on the Vis-en-Artois Memorial, near Arras, in France. It bears the names of more than 9,000 soldiers who fell between August 8, 1918 and the last day of the war, November 11, 1918, and have no known grave. His name is on the seventh panel of an impressive memorial wall that stands up to 26ft high. At its centre is a stone of remembrance representing St George and the Dragon.

A war gratuity was paid after Walter's death to his father, George. Walter's medal card lists his regimental numbers for the 1st and 7th Loyal North (28711) and the 8th Borders (34535). Commonwealth War Graves Commission records also show he had earlier served with the Hussars (with the regimental number 35283), with whom he probably completed his initial training. He was awarded the Victory and British War Medals.

14

SIDNEY — FATALLY WOUNDED IN BATTLE OF LANGEMARCK

He was close to a place likened to 'hell on earth'. The landscape, a grey, battle-scarred wilderness, could not have been more desolate. A once green and lush environment had been reduced to an apocalyptic scene dominated by shell craters, muddy ground and vast, foul-smelling muddy pools.

There was hardly a blade of grass growing anywhere. Artillery barrages had turned thousands of trees in woodlands into blackened, lifeless splintered trunks and stumps. There was a terrible stench that never seemed to go away – the pervasive smell of death and the whiff of high explosives, gas and stagnant water.

Rifleman Sidney Roberts had fought in the toughest of terrains, on the Somme and on the Arras front line. He had seen towns, villages and countryside destroyed and disfigured in 'scorched earth' campaigns. But he was shocked by the devastation and bleakness of his latest destination, the outskirts of the Belgian town of Ypres.

Serving with the Queen's Westminster Rifles, he had arrived here in August 1917 after a number of weeks away from the front line. For a brief while he had been able to escape the horrors of the trenches to focus on rifle, musketry, bayonet and bomb throwing training – and on watching and taking part in football matches, swimming competitions and his brigade horse show.

Now, he was back to the grim reality of attritional war, preparing to take part in the Third Battle of Ypres. His battalion had travelled by train from Abeele Station on the French-Belgian border to Ouderdom, and had then marched to the ruins of Chateau Segard near Voormezeele, camping there on the night of August 11.

The following day Sidney marched via cross-country tracks to the British-held Yeomanry Post, about 1,000 yards north east of Zillebeke Lake, a barren and dismal area frequently shelled by the German artillery and surrounded by dug-outs. One of his officers and four of his fellow soldiers were wounded as guides led his battalion to Glencorse Wood in the evening to take over front-line trenches.

Glencorse was hardly recognisable as a wood. It had been obliterated in a series of bombardments and attacks in two brutal years of combat. Torrential downpours of rain in late spring and the summer months had left the ground wet and boggy, with huge and putrid pools of water scattering the landscape on every side of the shattered woodland.

On the night of August 13, the Queen's Westminster Rifles were ordered to establish defensive posts in the wood, 100 yards from their front-line trenches. Heavy enemy artillery fire delayed attempts by the battalion's A Company in achieving this objective. But officers and men of B Company succeeded in creating a forward post in the face of fierce shelling.

Seven men were killed and two wounded in the advance. As shelling continued unabated through the night, 'through it all men hung on to their lonely shell holes with heroic endeavour', wrote Major J Q Henriques in his acclaimed book, *The War History of the 1st Battalion Queen's Westminster Rifles, 1914–18.*

He told of a corporal and seven men of the Queen's Westminster Rifles who were holding a small post in front of the line 'and, cut off from all communication with their company, without rations and exposed to the full fury of the enemy's artillery and machine gun fire, their position seemed hopeless. Their orders were to hold the post, and for over 30 hours, they clung on expecting to be overwhelmed at any moment.

'When the peril the men were in became clear, Sergeant (Edward) Yarnold volunteered to make an attempt to get a message to the men to withdraw. With conspicuous courage, he made his way across the open, exposed to machine gun fire, and succeeded in reaching the post in safety. The men then withdrew and on their way back to the front line five men out of the eight were hit and lay helpless where they fell. Sgt Yarnold got back unwounded, though his clothing was pierced by bullets. Calling for volunteers, as soon as he had regained the line, he went out again with a few brave men and brought in the wounded.'

The barrage took its toll with casualties rising dramatically during the night of August 13 and the following day. Twenty-four men were killed and 51 wounded before the Queen's Westminster Rifles were relieved by the 2nd Londons on the night of August 14 and moved into trenches at Half Way House, a vast underground shelter containing bunks for hundreds of soldiers.

Three more men were killed and 12 wounded amid heavy enemy fire on August 15. The following day, Sidney and his battalion took part in the Battle of Langemarck – part of the Third Ypres offensive. D Company, commanded by Captain E Brimelow, were ordered to act as 'moppers-up' in an attack led by the 2nd Londons, Queen Victoria's Rifles and the London Brigade.

Major Henriques recalled how the Queen's Westminster Rifles 'took part in a combined attack, delivered by the British and French armies on a wide front east and north of Ypres. British soldiers were given the task of capturing Glencorse Wood, advancing to the edge of (the adjoining) Polygon Wood and establishing a line inside the wood itself.'

Reliving the drama of the day, he wrote:

By 2am on August 16, troops were in position for the attack. But the Queen's Westminsters suffered heavy casualties from shell fire during the hours previous to the attack. Later that morning the 2nd Londons had taken Glencorse Wood and were pushing towards Polygon, with the Queen's Westminsters following closely behind. German resistance increased and the Queen's Westminsters were sent forward to assist the leading waves. Very severe and confused fighting took place and the advance was finally held up in Polygon Wood.

By 7.10am, the assaulting troops, who were under machine gun fire not only from their front, but from the rear on both flanks, were suffering very heavy losses. The troops, fighting stubbornly all the way, were gradually forced back into Glencorse Wood where the remnants of the 2nd Londons, Queen's Westminsters and other units were rallied on rising ground. Here, they succeeded in establishing a line of posts. The enemy were kept at bay until 4pm when they were driven back to the trench where they had assembled in the morning.

Although three companies of the Queen's Westminsters were not called upon to take any active part in the day's fighting, they all suffered severe casualties. One company were employed under very heavy fire in carrying up small arms ammunition during the attack, and the other two had taken shelter from the terrific storm of shells which fell all day in a portion of the tunnel under the Menin Road where their HQ was located.

The roof of the tunnel was quite thin and afforded no protection from a direct hit, even from small calibre high explosive shells. Every shell that burst in the neighbourhood caused the tunnel to reverberate with the sound and the beams and supports to groan and crack, while the roof threatened to fall in at any moment. To add to this nightmare experience, the floor was covered with several inches of water and the whole place was in complete darkness, save for a few guttering candles which flickered and threw strange shadows on the walls.

During the day, the enemy secured a direct hit on one of the entrances … but very fortunately only one casualty resulted from it. One shell broke through the roof above the Queen's Westminsters and a good many men were wounded or hurt.

The Queen's Westminsters suffered 160 casualties on August 16. One officer and 28 NCOs and men were killed and another officer died of wounds. Four officers and 109 NCOs and men were wounded and many others were reported as missing.

Rifleman Raymond Norrington was among those killed in the tunnel dug-out. He was just 20. An article in *The Suttonian*, a magazine published by Sutton Grammar School, of which he was a pupil, recorded how a heavy calibre shell landed on top of the shelter, 'smashing the place in completely. Most of the bodies were got out, but not all, owing to the situation of the place, and the fact that the other companies of the battalion had to move forward in support of the attack.'

The Battle of Langemarck – and the 'struggle about Glencorse Wood' – was 'one of the most heroic as well as one of the bloodiest days of fighting in all this war,' wrote Philip Gibbs in the book *From Bapaume to Passchendaele*. 'The ground was hideous, worse than in the winter on the Somme ... The courage of men who attacked over such (boggy) ground was great courage. The grim, stubborn way in which our soldiers made their way through these bogs and would not be beaten, though they slipped and fell and stuck deep while the enemy played machine-gun bullets on to their lines and flung high explosives over the whole stretch of bog-land through which they had to pass, is one of the splendid and tragic things in our poor human story.'

The men of the London regiments – 'the Queen's Westminsters and the old 'Vics' and the Rangers and the Kensingtons – fought forward with a wonderful spirit which is a white shining light in all this darkness, through Glencorse Wood and round to the north of Nuns' Wood, avoiding the most deeply flooded ground here, where there was one big boggy lake.'

They faced formidable German counter-attacks. 'The Londoners were exhausted after their dreadful night and all this fighting over foul ground; they were in exposed positions, and they were shut in by the most terrible gun-fire ... Our airmen, flying low, saw small isolated groups of London boys fighting separate battles against great odds. The enemy was encircling them, and they were trying to hold rear-guard positions, so that their comrades could withdraw in good order,' wrote Philip Gibbs, one of five official British reporters during the Great War.

Two more men of the Queen's Westminster Rifles were killed on August 17, 1917, before they left the trenches and moved back to Chateau Segard. Sidney died of wounds that day – ones he had sustained in action in the Battle of Langemarck.

It is not known whether he was wounded on the battlefield or in the tunnel under the Menin Road. He was 28.

Sidney was buried at Brandhoek New Military Cemetery (No 3), four miles from Ypres (now known by the Flemish name of Ieper). He is one of 975 soldiers interred there, 852 of them British. He is remembered on two war memorials – at the village of Oakford in Devon and at nearby Dulverton in Somerset.

He was born at Down Cottage in Cruwys Morchard, in Mid-Devon, on February 24, 1889 – when Victoria was Queen and Robert Cecil, Marquess of Salisbury, was Prime Minister. The Eiffel Tower in Paris opened that year. Preston North End became the first winners of the Football League in England and Birmingham was granted city status. He was born in the same year as Charlie Chaplin, one of the great comic actors of the silent film era, and the Second World War Nazi Germany leader Adolf Hitler.

Sidney was one of eight children of Charles and Eliza (nee Bryant) Roberts, who both died before the war broke out in 1914. At least two of his brothers also fought in the Great War and survived – his eldest brother, John Francis Bryant, who was in the 9th Devons, and his younger brother Archibald, who served with the 13th Hussars.

In 1891, aged two, Sidney was living with his family at Down Cottage, Cruwys Morchard, where his father worked as an agricultural labourer. Sidney attended Cruwys Morchard School and in 1901, he was living with his family at Slade Farm in Washfield, Devon, where his father was now employed as a dairyman. In 1911, aged 21 and single, he was working as a groom at the George Hotel in Broad Street, South Molton, which was owned by Somerset-born Hamlet Beater Rather.

Sidney enlisted in the Army in Tiverton, initially serving with the 2/5th (Territorial) Battalion of the Royal West Kent Regiment. The battalion were formed at Bromley in September 1914 and were transferred to Ascot in November that year, becoming part of the 2nd Kent Brigade of the 67th or 2nd Home Counties Division. The battalion were based in Tonbridge, Ashford and Canterbury in Kent in 1915 and 1916 and were disbanded in November 1917.

He joined the 1/16th County of London Battalion (the Queen's Westminster Rifles) in 1916, when he was 27 – arriving at their camp one mile east of Bapaume, a farming and industrial town in northern France, on September 1. The battalion were part of the 169th Infantry Brigade of the 56th (London) Division of the British Army.

Just a few days later, he was involved in the Battle of the Somme – in brutal trench warfare at Leuze Wood, near Ginchy.

He moved with the battalion from the village of Domvast to the Somme town of Corbie on September 2 and marched to Happy Valley near Longueval two days later. It was wet and cold when he arrived in the valley – which was captured from the Germans a number of weeks earlier – and many men had to bivouac in the open because of a shortage of tents.

Sidney moved to trenches near Maricourt on September 6. It was a 'very cold night and nobody got much sleep', the battalion's war diary recorded. 'The guide could not find the trenches and … the battalion did not settle down till about 4am.' Ten men were killed in the trenches in the following two days and one officer and 17 other ranks were wounded.

On September 9, two battalions of the 169th Brigade – the Queen Victoria's Rifles and London Rifle Brigade – led an attack on Leuze Wood. At 7.30pm that day, the Queen's Westminster Rifles, in the Malz Horn trenches at nearby Trones Wood, were ordered to advance to Leuze Wood to 'drive out' any enemy forces and capture a trench on the east side of Leuze.

'We had a severe barrage to get through in passing over the Falfremont Farm line but escaped with few losses and got into the wood at just before 11pm and found the Victoria's in it but in want of help,' Lieutenant-Colonel Rupert Shoolbred, commanding officer of the Queen's Westminster Rifles recorded in the war diary.

D Company lined the eastern edge of Leuze as A Company supported the Queen Victoria's Rifles in their advance. C and B Companies were kept in reserve. At about 1am on September 10, orders were received from the 169th Brigade 'that the enemy trench on the south-eastern side of the wood (Loop trench) must be taken before dawn'.

With two officers and 40 men killed or wounded in pitch-black conditions, Lt-Col Shoolbred wrote: 'The night was very dark and the enemy were pouring heavy shells into the wood without cessation and the position from which to attack ... as well as the exact bearing of the trench and its distance from the wood were unknown.'

Maps at his disposal were known to be inaccurate – and a runner provided the only communication between the battalion and the brigade, a journey which was taking more than an hour each way to complete. 'It was impossible to arrange an earlier hour than 7am for the attack,' Lt-Col Shoolbred recorded in the war diary.

Ten minutes before the attack, he received a message that an artillery barrage would be arranged to help the advance. A thick mist now covering the area had reduced visibility to 40-50 yards. The advance on German lines – led by C and D Companies in 'waves of platoons' – was hampered by a less than adequate bombardment of the enemy.

The two companies almost reached their objective when they were 'held up' by rifle and machine gun fire. The German trench was strongly defended and officers 'were obliged to withdraw the remnants of their companies' – the strength of each had been reduced to about 25 men – towards their initial assembly position.

After B Company were pushed forward to guard against a German counter-attack, a bombing attack was launched by the Queen's Westminster Rifles and the 2nd Londons in a last-ditch attempt to take the German trench. An artillery barrage 'working up and along the trench' was not successful in 'keeping the enemy's rifle fire down'.

The 2nd Londons 'pretty well made their objective' but they retreated when their captain was killed, bringing the Queen's Westminster Rifles back with them. They suffered heavy losses in the attack and 'retirement'. Four officers and 116 NCOs and men were killed during the day and the previous night. Five officers and 166 NCOs and men were wounded.

'From start to finish, we had, as it turned out, no chance,' recorded Lt-Col Shoolbred. The battalion had been 'ordered to attack from a wood we had never been in before on a black, dark night and on to a position we were unable to properly locate and then, owing to the breakdown of communication, launched in the morning to the attack without the artillery barrage'.

After 14 hours of 'exceedingly heavy shelling', the battalion were 'sent to it again to bomb up a trench, which as a trench, hardly existed, with hardly any trained bombers to lead the attack'. Lt-Col Shoolbred, who lived in Devon and who was renowned for being forthright, commented: 'It is no wonder that both the attacks failed.'

He paid tribute to the 'extreme gallantry and devotion' of Captain Albert Ramsbottom of the Royal Army Medical Corps, Sergeant G C Cordery and all stretcher bearers who, without exception, 'attended to the wounded under such shell fire as we have never experienced before for the whole 20 hours we were in the wood, and practically all the time in the open'.

The survivors of B, C and D Companies were re-organised to line the eastern edge of the wood until they were relieved in the evening and moved to the nearby Citadel camp. They remained there until September 13 when they moved into trenches outside Hardecourt before going back to trenches near Faviere Wood the following day.

On September 15, 1916 – the start of the Battle of Flers-Courcelette on the Somme, in which tanks, or Armoured Caterpillar Motor Cars as they were known then, were used in the war for the first time – the battalion moved into trenches in Angle Wood Valley, near Leuze Wood, ready to play their part in this latest offensive.

On the evening of September 17, the battalion received orders to attack a German trench along a sunken road from Bouleaux Wood – adjoining Leuze Wood – to the village of Combles. Two of their companies went 'over the top' at 5.50am the next morning and almost reached the German front line when they came under heavy machine gun fire.

Unable to get into the enemy trench, the survivors of the two companies – three officers and 90 men – withdrew to the assembly trench. 2nd Lieutenant Eric Jones was killed 'practically in the German trench. He was probably the only

143

man who reached it and was turning round to encourage his men on when he was killed,' wrote Lt-Col Shoolbred. Three officers and 34 NCOs and men were killed in the attack, 48 were wounded and 14 were reported as missing.

The battalion withdrew to Angle Wood Valley on the night of the 18th. Over the next eight days, three of their men were killed and 16 wounded before they marched to the village of Meaulte, near Albert on September 27. Three days later, the Queen's Westminster Rifles were back in front line trenches, east of the small village of Morval on the Somme.

Thirteen of their men were killed, 41 were wounded and eight were reported as missing as they were heavily shelled in the trenches on the opening three days of October 1916. One man was killed when they moved to trenches east of the village of Lesboeufs on October 8 and three men were killed and 40 wounded in heavy artillery attacks the following day – their penultimate day on the Somme.

On October 11, the battalion travelled by bus to La Chausee-sur-Somme. They later marched 21 miles to the village of Huppy and travelled by train to Berguette on October 23. Officers and men were billeted in factories and barns in the farming village of Calonne-sur-Lys, near Bethune, the following day before moving to the town of Lestrem and then to billets in Bout Deville.

They were in trenches in front of Neuve Chapelle on November 3. A wiring party was attacked on November 7 by a 'strong enemy patrol' and a sergeant was taken prisoner. Sidney and his battalion moved into support billets at Croix Barbee two days later, returning to the trenches on November 16 in 'cold and frosty weather'.

The Queen's Westminster Rifles returned to Bout Deville on November 21, marching to Robermetz just outside Merville on the 27th. They moved to reserve billets in Pont du Hem, a hamlet on the main road from La Bassee to Estaires on December 9. Back in the trenches on December 15, three of their men were killed on December 16 and 17. They spent Christmas at Pont du Hem.

On January 12, 1917 – the day after the battalion held a

boxing tournament at Bout Deville – a billet occupied by a platoon of B company was destroyed in a fire that raged for five hours. No-one was injured in the blaze. The Lewis guns were saved from the wreckage but the majority of soldiers' kit and possessions were lost.

The following day, an officer and 23 men, including Lewis gun teams from B, C and D Companies, were due to take over three posts in an abandoned German front line trench. But one of the posts was 'rushed' by the enemy shortly before the Queen's Westminster Rifles moved into position and was left in German possession.

Heavy snow and freezing conditions offered new challenges in the days ahead as the battalion carried out wiring and other work. It was so cold towards the end of January that men brought blankets to the trenches to help keep the frost at bay. Amid hostile shelling and defensive tasks, the men had the opportunity to take advantage of an 'excellent slide' made along a flooded ditch near battalion HQ.

Sidney and his fellow soldiers moved to billets in the farming town of Laventie on February 1, 1917. One man was killed when the Germans 'heavily strafed' the front line later that day. Trenches the battalion moved into on February 20 were 'beginning to show signs of wholesale collapse as a result of thaw and rain', the war diary recorded.

The first eight days of March proved immensely testing and exhausting for the Queen's Westminster Rifles when they marched almost 100 miles on leaving Laventie. They 'trekked' to Bout Deville, St Floris, near Bethune, Pernes, Willeman, Bonnieres, Sus St Leger and, finally, Gouy-en-Artois, a village about 15 kilometres south west of Arras.

Lt-Col Shoolbred said the 98-mile march – which had left the battalion just 21 miles from their starting point – had put a 'very big strain on men who had been in trenches continuously since November 29 and who had no marching at all since that date'. About 40 men had dropped out of the journey through exhaustion.

Officers and men arrived in 'uncomfortable' and 'cold' billets in the village of Simencourt on March 8 and moved to Achicourt, near Arras, six days later. They were back in front line trenches on March 18. The following day, an officer reconnoitring a position for the battalion HQ, found an 'excellent German dug-out' ideal for use as a base.

The dug-out contained an officers' mess room 15ft below ground with sleeping quarters further down comprising four rooms, each of which was equipped with a stove. However, while telephone wires were examined, a fuse was found at the opening to the dug-out leading to a mine. More mines were found at two other entrances.

It appeared that a German officer had been captured in Beaurains, a village on the outskirts of Arras, just before he had blown up the dug-out. It had been used 'up to the last minute as bread, butter, salt and pepper' were found on a table within it, wrote Lt-Col Shoolbred, who added: 'All other dug outs in the village seem to be very thoroughly blown up.'

Three men were killed and two wounded during hostile artillery fire on March 22. An officer was killed by a shell the following day and three men were wounded. The battalion moved into billets in Achicourt on March 24 and worked on digging and wiring new communication trenches in the following seven days.

On April 1, 1917, the Queen's Westminster Rifles marched 10 miles to the hamlet of Monchiet for battle training before returning to Achicourt six days later. Enemy shell fire wreaked havoc on April 8, causing devastating blazes which killed and wounded many men, destroyed billets and a convoy of lorries carrying ammunition.

A barn adjoining A Company's billets caught fire at 1am in a shell attack on Achicourt. Soldiers prevented the fire from spreading. But at noon, a shell exploded on B Company's HQ, 'causing part of the building to collapse' and 'inflicting many casualties on a platoon of men of this company who were taking shelter in the building', Lt-Col Shoolbred recorded.

Two hours later, a lorry loaded with British artillery ammunition was hit by shell fire and 'immediately burst into flames'. The blaze quickly spread to 20 other lorries. The ammunition began to explode and fire spread to and destroyed houses in Achicourt Square and a large quantity of stores and equipment were buried beneath the ruins. One officer and 16 men were killed and 31 NCOs and men wounded.

The battalion later moved to a 'reserve area' west of the town of Beaurains. On April 11, Sidney and his fellow soldiers moved to trenches near Neuville Vitasse, a village five miles from Arras, to take part in the First Battle of the Scarpe – part of the two-month long Arras offensive in which there were almost 160,000 British casualties.

The Queen's Westminster Rifles were to support an attack led by the 169th Brigade on the village of Cherisy and a wood just north of the community of Fontaine les Croisilles. They moved to the assembly area near Wancourt at 9am on April 13. When the attack was delayed, they relieved the London Rifle Brigade at Wancourt Tower Ridge.

At 10pm, the battalion received orders that, with the Queen Victoria's Rifles, they would lead an 'independent and apparently isolated attack' the following morning. Lt-Col Shoolbred observed in the war diary: 'The men were ... entirely whacked (having had about one hour's sleep out of 24 during the past three days) and there was no time or possibility of any proper explanation to them of their objectives – or of more than the mere organisation of the advance to the attack and the objective, which no-one had ever seen.

'These objectives were firstly the establishing of a position along the ridge some 500 yards west of Cherisy – a ridge running north east and south west and parallel to and 1,000 yards from the Tower Ridge on which we were established. And, secondly, the capture and consolidation of the village of Cherisy itself and the establishment of strong points on the northern flank of our attack and of outposts along the line of the Sensee River to the east of the village.'

Lt-Col Shoolbred wrote that 'the enemy was known to be digging in on the ridge west of Cherisy, some 1,000 yards in front of the Wancourt Tower Ridge and parallel to it, but the strength of his artillery or of his dispositions for defence were entirely unknown, though during the last few days he had been showing a much stronger resistance than at any period

147

since the beginning of his withdrawal from the … front.'

The attack began at 5.30am on April 14, with A and B Companies of the Queen's Westminster Rifles forming the first wave of the advance and C and D Companies leading the second wave. 'It was a beautiful morning and quite light with the remains of the moon to help the dawning day,' Lt-Col Shoolbred recorded.

The enemy launched an attack against Wancourt Tower at the same time as the battalion made their advance. A German artillery barrage began minutes before a British bombardment of enemy lines – which was described as 'negligible' by officers leading the Queen's Westminster Rifles' assault – got under way.

'It certainly did not keep the machine gunners' heads down or stop their fire,' reported Lt-Col Shoolbred. The battalion, with 497 officers and men in action, suffered catastrophic casualties as they came under heavy and unrelenting machine gun fire from their rear and from both flanks.

Despite the losses, the men of A and B Companies reached, and took cover in, an enemy practice trench, but were 'no longer in sufficient strength to press the attack any further'. C and D Companies were digging-in close by. Lieutenant W G Orr, in command of C Company, sent a messenger to report his position but he was killed before he reached battalion HQ.

Lt Orr and his men were attacked at about 11am but drove off the enemy with Lewis gun and rifle fire. His company were almost wiped out during the day. At dusk, he was one of only 27 still standing. The number included three officers from the Durham Regiment and a few survivors from the Queen Victoria's Rifles.

Lt-Col Shoolbred reported that the Queen's Westminsters had been hampered by the 'immense difficulties of the hurried issue of orders (for the attack) and of the absolute impossibility of any sort of reconnaissance of the ground (on which they had been operating)'. There was also a lack of communication from the front.

When an officer – 2nd Lieutenant A M Mackle – went out in the early afternoon to bring back survivors from the front, only

65 men of the Queen's Westminster Rifles returned. 'At this time, we had no knowledge of the men of C Company ... who were maintaining themselves in the German practice trench,' wrote Lt-Col Shoolbred.

Lt Orr, praised for behaving with the 'greatest gallantry', withdrew his men from a perilous position at dawn as they were 'practically surrounded by the enemy'. Three officers and 92 NCOs and men of the Queen's Westminster Rifles were killed in action on April 14, or later died of wounds. A further seven officers and 164 other ranks were wounded or reported as missing.

The following day, Sidney and his depleted battalion marched back to trenches in the old German front line, 500 yards south of Beaurains. On April 20, the remaining officers and men were transported to the town of St Amand. They marched 12 miles to the village of Wanquetin, about 12 miles from Arras, four days later and moved to Bernaville on April 26.

Two days later, they marched to the Harp, a formidable old German trench system near Tilloy before moving to the nearby Brigade HQ on April 29. Three men were killed and five wounded on May 1, 1917 as the battalion carried out the grim task of collecting the dead while facing severe shelling of their trenches.

Thirteen more men were killed and two officers and 39 others wounded in the following ten days. On May 19, the battalion marched to Arras and then to billets in the village of Duisans. After a series of training and rest days, they returned to the Harp trench system on June 8, 1917. In the run-up to August, they moved to Achicourt, Gouy-en-Artois, Sus-St-Leger and Wizernes.

Almost a year before losing his life in France, Sidney had told his older brother Bertie, who lived at Exworthy Cottage, Oakford, Devon that, in the event of his death, he would leave everything he had to him. Statements – from Bertie and Sidney's friend, James Bowen, of Bampton – confirming this were forwarded to the War Office in 1918.

The statements were supplied because a will made by Sidney while in active service was missing at the time of his death. Bertie said that he and Sidney had had a 'conversation the last night he was home on leave, in September 1916'. Sidney had told him he had made a will stating that if he never came home 'all I have belongs to you'. The evidence was accepted and Bertie received Sidney's war gratuity and personal effects.

Sidney's medal card shows that he was awarded the British War and Victory Medals. It includes his service numbers (7122 and 553492) for the Queen's Westminster Rifles. Commonwealth War Graves Commission records include his service number (4127) for the 2/5th Battalion of the Royal West Kent Regiment. He is buried in Plot 2, Row F, Grave 15 at Brandhoek New Military Cemetery (No 3).

Note

- Lt-Col Shoolbred lived at Rose Ash Barton, near Witheridge, and also had a home in London. He was the owner of James Shoolbred and Co Ltd, a furniture manufacturer and repository based in Tottenham Court Road, London. The son of Dr John and Mrs Jane Wilkin, he died in 1946.

Part Three

THE GRANDSONS
WHO SURVIVED

15

ARCHIE — SURVIVOR OF TWO OF THE GREATEST EVER CAVALRY CHARGES

There can be few more magnificent – and terrifying – sights than a cavalry charge. Proud, swashbuckling soldiers with swords in hand galloping majestically across open ground towards their enemy.

The towering courage of mounted officers and men as they stormed forward amid a formidable barrage of rifle, machine and field gun fire from heavily guarded trenches and barricades, almost defies belief.

The Charge of the Light Brigade at Balaclava during the Crimean War is remembered as one of the most heroic, daring – and deadly – in the history of military conflict. It is immortalised in paintings, poetry and books.

It is hard to imagine that in the highly mechanised Great War of 1914–1918, with heavy artillery used to such devastating effect on the Western Front in France and on battlefields in the Balkans and Mesopotamia, the cavalry still had an important role to play.

But they did, particularly in the deserts of Mesopotamia, the country we know today as Iraq. And it was there that the 13th Hussars – with Private Archibald Roberts among their ranks

– took part in one of the greatest cavalry charges of the Great War, one to rival the Charge of the Light Brigade.

For Archibald – or Archie as he was known – this was the moment he had dreamed of. When he would make his first magnificent charge at the enemy. When his many months of training as a cavalryman – and his bravery – would be put to the ultimate test.

A dense and blinding dust storm was blowing over the desert sands close to the River Tigris in Mesopotamia as he came under enemy shell and rifle fire from concealed trenches on broken ground ahead of him.

Amid this murderous onslaught, he heard the order 'draw swords – charge' and, with an almighty cheer, found himself sweeping forward at great pace to confront, and hopefully rout, the hidden Turkish soldiers threatening his life.

Archie and the 13th soared across a low trench, or 'water-cut' where a hundred or so Turks initially dropped their weapons and threw up their hands in surrender, only to then pick up their rifles and fire into the backs of the cavalrymen.

As he galloped on, he and his fellow soldiers were met by a 'blaze' of rifle and machine gun fire and bombs from a network of secret trenches which killed or wounded many officers and men who were thrown from dying or injured horses.

Seeing there was no way forward, and to prevent a greater bloodbath, the 13th Hussars' commanding officer, Lieutenant-Colonel James Jardine Richardson, ordered his three attacking squadrons to withdraw, dismount and occupy a nearby trench.

There, Archie, knowing he was lucky to be alive and unhurt, remained until nightfall. As the Turks retreated during the night, he helped in the rescue of wounded and missing officers and men stranded on the sands in front of the enemy positions.

For Archie and so many others riding with him, the Fight at Lajj, on the morning of March 5, 1917 turned out to be a brutal and bloody introduction to cavalry warfare in the Middle East – and a taste of what was to come in the next 20 months or so.

Sadly, the immense courage of the 13th Hussars that day is not celebrated in the same way as their Crimean counterparts.

Partly because of the horrors and loss of life in so many battles across the world, and partly because so little was known or reported about the war in Mesopotamia.

Three of their officers and 22 other ranks were killed in the charge – or fight – at Lajj. An officer and four other ranks died of wounds. Five officers and 50 NCOs and men were wounded, many of them seriously. Fifty-four of the charging horses were killed and 36 wounded.

The devastating casualties suffered by the 200-year-old regiment were greater than those they sustained – formerly as the 13th Light Dragoons – 63 years earlier in the ill-fated Charge of the Light Brigade, on October 25, 1854.

In the celebrated book, *The Thirteenth Hussars in the Great War*, author Sir Henry Mortimer Durand said that, for Englishmen, the Charge of the Light Brigade would always be 'one of the most splendid deeds' in history, while the actions at Lajj would remain 'almost unknown'.

But, said Durand, 'to the 13th it will always be one of the regiment's great days, for the level sands by the Tigris saw that morning in the dust storm a death ride just as brave and devoted as the one which has become immortal'.

In the months to come, the regiment fought 'sword in hand' at Tekrit, Kulawand and at Tuz Kermatli. In their 'final onslaught' at Hadraniya, in October 1918, officers and men not only charged their enemy in the face of heavy gun fire across open sands, but climbed a steep cliff to fight on foot with bayonets.

Archie, one of eight children of Charles and Eliza (nee Bryant) Roberts, enlisted in the 13th Hussars on December 12, 1915 after working as a horseman on a farm in Devon. He was one of at least three brothers to fight in the Great War.

His eldest brother, John Francis Bryant Roberts, served as a private in the 9th Devons – and survived. Another older brother, Sidney, a rifleman in the Queen's Westminster Rifles, died of wounds sustained in the Battle of Langemarck on August 17, 1917, at the age of 28.

Archie undertook months of basic Army and specialist military training to sharpen his skills as a cavalryman – learning to cope with the shocking sights and sounds of battle and how to respond quickly and effectively to commands and maintain close riding formation with fellow soldiers.

He joined the 13th Hussars in Mesopotamia in September 1916, almost two months after the regiment first arrived in Basra. The 13th had moved to the Middle East after a frustrating 20 months in France where they were frequently 'inactive' amid gruelling trench warfare.

Archie was encamped at Makina Masus, on the outskirts of Basra, until November 3 that year before undertaking a 123-mile long march over ten days to the town of Amarah on the River Tigris, via Gurmat Ali, Qurnah and Ezra's Tomb, believed to be the burial place of the biblical figure.

After two weeks at 'No 1 Marching Post' at Amarah, his regiment journeyed another 93 miles in ten days to Arab Village on the Tigris, arriving there on December 6 via Suliman, Ali Gharbi, near Kut, and Sheikh Sa'ad.

There, the 13th remained encamped until December 13 when they marched to a large ravine called the Dujailah Depression and, the following day, at the head of the 7th Cavalry Brigade, crossed the River Hai (or Shatt-al-Hai), a branch of the Tigris.

The regiment's war diary records that they encountered 'opposition' on a large mound or embankment which was shelled by British artillery before two of the 13th Hussars' squadrons 'galloped round' the hostile area only to find the enemy were retiring.

When 'hostile cavalry' were found to be holding a nearby position, officers and men of A and B Squadrons left their horses in a river bed, 'took up positions' in a ravine and remained there until ordered to rejoin the brigade, at which point two of their ranks were wounded and a horse killed by enemy fire.

During the next two days, Archie and his men came under sniper and shell fire as they took part in patrol and reconnaissance missions, and headed for Bassouia. On December 17, close to their camp there, a regiment patrol became surrounded by '300 hostile horsemen'.

As artillery fire was opened on the horsemen, the 13th went out in support of the patrol. Now 'reinforced by a platoon of infantry', they were able to beat off their attackers. The regiment 'endeavoured' to chase down up to 1,500 enemy cavalrymen, but could not close on them.

As they 'slowly returned to camp' at Bassouia, they found themselves fighting a 'rear-guard action', exchanging rifle and machine gun fire with a mixed force of Turks and Arabs, action which resulted in three men being wounded, two horses being killed and four injured.

Archie and his men came under heavy shell fire on December 20 as they marched to the Hussaini bend of the Tigris where the British infantry attempted – and failed – to cross the river in the face of the barrage from 'strongly entrenched' Turks.

He ended the year, and began 1917, encamped at Arab Village. Heavy rain turned large areas of ground into a quagmire, making it 'exceptionally heavy going for horses' and providing new and unwelcome challenges in marching and carrying out reconnaissance work in the desert.

The regiment reached Hai Town, where the Turks had surrendered, on January 11. Food supplies were short. There were grocery rations but, for a while, the 13th Hussars had to 'subsist on the country' and, the war diary records, there was 'great difficulty' in cooking food because of a lack of pots.

Three days later, having reached Fort Suliman, they went to the assistance of the 14th Lancers who were 'being seriously engaged by Arabs'. The enemy were forced to retire after being 'severely punished' by artillery, machine gun and rifle fire.

Archie and his men again came under heavy shell and rifle fire after leaving Bassouia at the end of January. From a protective ravine, the 13th Hussars attempted to send out patrols but were 'unable to advance'. One man was wounded, six horses were killed and nine injured in the action.

A popular and courageous officer, Lieutenant John Francis Munster was killed in a 'sharp fight' on February 4, 1917, while 'gallantly leading' a squadron across open ground. One other rank was also killed in the attack and two officers and eight men were wounded.

There was an historic and poignant moment 28 days later – the recapture of Kut where, in December 1915, a siege of the British garrison by the Turkish army led to a humiliating surrender in April 1916, and the loss of thousands of lives.

Durand, in *The Thirteenth Hussars in the Great War*, said the 'maze of trenches which had resisted so many onslaughts were carried with a rush, and sweeping on rapidly, the British troops replaced the British flag on the walls of Kut'. The regiment played their part in the victory. Although 'unable to storm entrenchments held by a resolute enemy, they did much to cover and facilitate the operations of the infantry and guns and they did all that mounted men could do to harass the retreat'.

As Archie and his men pursued the Turks on horseback on February 25, they dismounted and attacked the enemy rear-guard on the north bank of the Tigris. The 13th Hussars suffered heavy losses, with two men killed and one officer and 33 other ranks wounded. The pursuit of the Turks, now in full retreat, continued the following day. The regiment captured 300 prisoners and six field guns in an area littered with abandoned small arms ammunition, rifles, trench mortars, shells and equipment-laden carts.

The 13th Hussars arrived in Lajj amid reports that a Turkish convoy, with a 'small escort of infantry' had been spotted retiring in the direction of Baghdad. As scattered enemy troops opened fire on another regiment, two advancing squadrons of the 13th Hussars came under attack from Turkish soldiers in concealed positions.

Within minutes, and before they could get into 'formation order', a shell burst near Archie and his men and rifle fire erupted from hidden trenches. No enemy guns or infantry were then visible, 'nothing but the convoy and its escort in the distance'. But they were evidently there, and it was 'impossible to say in what strength'.

As pilots in reconnaissance aeroplanes had not reported large numbers of enemy troops, it was decided that the 13th Hussars should ride them down and, if possible, 'gallop the convoy'. As the regiment drew swords and advanced at a trot, it immediately became clear that they had in front of them not only scattered bands of Turks, but hidden enemy infantry with machine and artillery guns.

The order was given to charge, and the 'eager horsemen swept forward with a cheer'. A first low trench was taken at a gallop and scores of Turks defending it 'threw up their hands'. But as the regiment galloped on, the surrendering soldiers suddenly picked up their rifles and 'fired into our men from behind, while in front the charging lines were met by a blaze of musketry which emptied many saddles', said Durand. 'Many brave men pressed on to the edge of farther trenches, and even in places over them, but they found they could do little against infantry in such numbers and on such ground. Lt-Col Richardson (later wounded by a Turkish bullet) saw that the attempt to ride through was hopeless ... and withdrew them some distance until they were in comparative safety.'

One officer, Lieutenant Harold Constantin Dillon Fitz-Gibbon, described the charge as a 'damned fine effort, but rather a mad one'. He added: 'We had been given wrong information by aeroplanes and ran our heads against the most beautiful trenches full of Turks I have ever seen. The old Turk just sat back and waited for us and by God he let us have it. The noise was something impossible to describe; how the devil we any of us ever got out of it I still do not know.'

Colour-Sergeant Frederick Spanton had a remarkable escape from death. 'After a few minutes, we were galloping towards the enemy with drawn swords, at a fair pace. After we crossed the first trench my horse was apparently hit and pitched over, causing me to be thrown. I landed between the lines of Turks and remained quiet, waiting to see what would happen next,' he said.

'The Turks had now turned about, and were firing over me into the rear of the squadrons. The regiment changed direction to the right, and passed out of my view; the Turks got out of the trenches and continued to send a hail of bullets after the disappearing squadrons. I watched this as I lay on the ground, weighing my chances of re-joining the regiment.

'The Turks in front of me were now retiring, and moving to the left of the trench, and I thought if I remained quiet they would all probably pass me by unnoticed, and then I could get back to my squadron again. But no such luck: as the tail-end of

159

the Turks passed by, one fellow stopped when he saw me, and raising his rifle to his shoulder he fired point blank – but missed – the bullet not coming so near as the one that had cut the belt of my haversack a few minutes before.

'This man, evidently disgusted with his bad shooting, walked hurriedly away, so once again I thought my chances of getting back were good; but a group of three men coming along a little later came to see who I was, and lugged me off to a dug-out. I had hurt my knee rather badly when I was thrown, and couldn't get along over fast; this annoyed the Turks, as we were still under a heavy fire from the British machine guns, so they jabbed me in the back with the butt of a rifle as a signal to hurry,' said Colour-Sgt Spanton, who was taken prisoner.

2nd Lieutenant E F Pinnington was hit by a rifle bullet a few yards from the Turkish trench. 'As I stood there dazed amid the dust, I saw another squadron come galloping up. It was a sight I shall not readily forget,' he said. 'The leader to the fore with sword aloft, the line of panting horses, the grim eager faces of the men, the flashing swords – I thought of Lady Butler's (or Elizabeth Thompson's) painting *Floreat Etona*, and marvelled at seeing the living parallel.' The leader of that squadron was Captain William Henry Eve, who was among those killed in the charge. The other two officers who died were 2nd Lieutenants Geoffrey Lynch-Staunton – initially taken prisoner and then killed – and Ernest Victor Rolfe, both of whom had 'not seen a shot fired before that day'.

On March 11, the day Baghdad was captured from the Turks after a two-year campaign, the 13th Hussars became the first cavalry regiment to enter the city. The regiment, believed to have been 'specially selected' for this honour as a 'reward' for their actions at Lajj, were also asked to form part of the garrison there.

Archie and his men later marched to the city of Baqubah, on the Diyala River, and then to Serai and Deltawa. On April 9, while the regiment were making a reconnaissance of Deli Abbas, they encountered thousands of soldiers of Turkey's 13th Army Corps who had marched down from the hills during the night.

They took up a defensive position on a long, low mound and, with the help of their Hotchkiss machine guns, inflicted heavy losses on the enemy owing to 'their eagerness to surround and annihilate what they took to be an isolated regiment', Lance-Corporal George W Bowie recalled in Durand's book. 'In this action – and while the remainder of the 7th Cavalry Brigade and the 6th Cavalry Brigade were deployed for action – Lt FitzGibbon, although wounded, succeeded in getting all our Hotchkiss guns safely out of action, when we were in danger of envelopment and were forced to retire amidst a perfect hail of lead and shell.'

Now began, said Lance-Cpl Bowie, 'what proved to be one of the hardest fights in which the cavalry had yet been engaged, the enemy trying their hardest to effect an enveloping movement by forced marches. This ... we were only able to defeat by a most stubborn rear-guard action, which we had to maintain until the arrival of the main force.'

The two cavalry brigades were involved in fierce fighting the whole day. The Turks attacked with 'increased violence' the following morning but were eventually routed after a timely intervention by the British infantry, with hundreds of dead and wounded Turkish soldiers found abandoned on the battle-field.

Archie and the 13th Hussars moved to their summer camp, at Chaldari, near Baghdad, in May. On the 16th of that month, the regiment were ordered to march with the 7th Cavalry Brigade to Kazimain to find and deal with a band of Arabs who had slaughtered a British survey party including three officers.

'We attacked them and inflicted heavy casualties ... at the same time driving them before us on to General (Alexander) Cobbe's column which had marched down from Samarrah. This column exacted a terrible revenge for these murders, and literally mowed them down with machine gun fire,' Lance-Cpl Bowie recorded.

The 13th Hussars remained at Chaldari throughout the summer of 1917. As temperatures reached more than 120 degrees Fahrenheit, many of their number were plagued by sickness. In July, 18 men were evacuated to hospital, with 15 more taken to hospital in August. By the end of September, they were again on the move, this time marching to Balad Ruz.

They were soon involved in a skirmish with a Turkish cavalry patrol on the outskirts of the oasis town of Mandali, on the old Persian border, where they bivouacked until October 18. Later, in marching to Kizil-Robat, the regiment attacked and routed enemy soldiers, capturing the village and taking a dozen prisoners, after a 'severe day's fighting'.

Gruelling day and night marches to Sadiyeh, Istabulat and Samarrah, eventually brought them to Turkish-held Tekrit, on the Tigris, where, on the afternoon of November 5, 1917, the 13th Hussars launched a bold assault on the enemy. With a squadron of the 13th Lancers, they were ordered to charge the Turkish army and 'to do as much damage as possible to the enemy'. Under a 'moving curtain of fire from the artillery', the 13th Hussars drew swords and 'charged straight into the enemy's trenches, passing through our own infantry on the way who cheered us madly', Lance-Cpl Bowie recorded. 'We took their first and penetrated into their second line of defences, where we dispersed a considerable number of their reinforcements who were being massed for a counter-attack, inflicting on them heavy losses.

'An incident which enraged us beyond measure was the tactic the Turks resorted to on this and previous occasions when we had attacked them in a similar manner. Immediately on us charging their front line, they would throw down their arms and cry for quarter, which on us lifting our swords and granting, thus leaving them to surrender to our supports while we charged on to their second line, they would deliberately regain their rifles and fire into our backs. On realising this treachery again, we wheeled about and literally cut our way through this treacherous mass.'

One officer and six NCOs and men of the 13th Hussars were killed in this brutal attack and more than 20 were wounded. Among those who died, in hand-to-hand combat, was Captain Stephen Owen Robinson, commander of B Squadron. Thirty-one horses were killed and 13 injured. The war diary reported that, by 8pm that day, 'all the wounded had been collected'.

Meanwhile, battered and defeated, the Turkish army, believed to have suffered 2,000 casualties in combined cavalry and British infantry attacks, evacuated Tekrit during the night.

The 13th Hussars ended the year encamped at Sadiyeh, where they remained until April 16, 1918. Eleven days after their welcome respite came to an end, they were in action again, this time charging Turkish troops near Kulawand with the 21st and 22nd Cavalry regiments – and while temporarily attached to the 6th Cavalry Brigade. The enemy were found to be holding a position on the Tuz-Kilfri road. 'Although we had no support within 20 miles of us, it was decided to attack them at once. We drew our swords and trotted into the plain where ten squadrons were formed into an extended line in the formation of a scythe,' Lance-Cpl Bowie recalled.

'As we rode on at this pace, Turks started running down the road while others fired on us. The Turks showed some of their old spirit in the stand they made, but the sudden flash of our swords in the sun which made a wide arc of light, seemed to take the heart out of them and their fire was wild and high, and our casualties few. Our artillery kept up a creeping barrage on the village as we attacked, and our line maintained this pace until within some 500 yards of the enemy, when we lowered our swords and charged into them. Our aeroplanes which took part in the action flew very low and increased the enemy's confusion with bombs and machine gun fire. Over 150 Turks were killed and 538 prisoners taken.'

Three men were wounded in heavy shell fire as the 13th Hussars marched on Kirkuk in early May. 'We galloped forward and dismounted for action against the enemy holding trenches just outside (the town). They were so strongly entrenched, we were unable to advance, but hotly engaged them until dusk when we were ordered to withdraw,' recorded Lance-Cpl Bowie. When the regiment entered the town the following morning, 'no resistance was encountered'. A number of large hospitals were discovered, one containing more than 350 patients. The local population were 'starving' and the bodies of 'horribly mutilated' Turkish soldiers were found in the streets.

On May 10, as the regiment marched on Guk Tappah, a

village hidden from view by high ground, they came under heavy mountain, machine gun and rifle fire. Officers and men dismounted and engaged the enemy for almost seven hours until ordered to withdraw. They were shelled with 'increasing violence' as they retired to Daraman, with six men being wounded and 12 horses killed. The 13th Hussars returned to Kirkuk the following day and then embarked on a series of exacting marches to their summer camp at Chaldari.

They covered 150 miles in ten days, travelling via Taza, Daur, Samarrah and Baqubah. The journey not only took its toll on the officers and men, but also on the horses, at least two of which had to be destroyed because of exhaustion. 'This proved a very trying time for us, the little water which we were able to obtain before leaving the springs being very brackish and salty, which combined with the intense heat, produced a thirst which was … unendurable,' Lance-Cpl Bowie recalled. 'These arduous marches, coming on top of our very recent hard fighting, tested our endurance to the utmost, several of our men falling out of their saddles from sheer weakness from want of food and rest.'

They remained at Chaldari until October 10, with 93 officers and men being admitted to hospital in August and September. They then embarked on a 200-mile march over 14 days to a position four miles from Fathah Gorge, where retreating Turks had abandoned their defences, and on to the Zab River. In pursuing the enemy, Archie and his men came up against a formidable and dangerous ford opposite Hadraniya, about 15 miles above Shergat. It was there, Durand wrote in his book, the 'Turks were to make a real stand' and where the 13th Hussars would fight their final battle of the war, on and off horseback.

The treacherous ford crossed three Tigris channels, one of which was almost 5ft deep, with a strong current. A brigade of cavalry under General Robert Cassells succeeded in crossing the water on October 26, 1918 and galloped forward to seize a gorge five miles downstream, near the Turks who were 'retreating upon him'.

By the following morning, Cassells had taken up a strong

position blocking the road to Mosul. It was a daring move, said Durand, for the general had only three 'weak regiments of cavalry' and a battery of horse artillery against a superior and desperate enemy force who made repeated, but ultimately unsuccessful, infantry and field gun attacks on his defences.

Support, in the shape of the 13th Hussars and other regiments of the 7th Cavalry Brigade, arrived on the evening of October 28. After a 70-mile march in 36 hours, it was nearly dark when the 13th Hussars crossed the Hadraniya ford. Difficult to negotiate in daylight, it 'became positively dangerous after dusk', said General Charles Norton, commander of the 7th Cavalry Brigade.

'A number of men, particularly those leading pack horses, got into difficulties and were carried downstream. Hampered as they were by their ammunition and other equipment, their situation was precarious, but most managed to scramble out on one bank or another.' Twenty-one men drowned in the crossing, including a lance-corporal and two privates of the 13th Hussars.

The Turks were holding a range of hills, at the southern extremity of which was the Hadraniya Bluff. At 8.15am on October 29, the 13th Hussars were ordered to lead an attack on enemy positions. Emerging from the cover of a river bed, they galloped across open ground in front of the Bluff in the teeth of a storm of machine gun fire.

When an officer commanding the leading squadron fell severely wounded, his men halted under the cover of Cemetery Hill where they were soon joined by the remainder of the regiment. At 1.20pm, the 13th Hussars emerged into the flat, open ground again, under the protection of artillery and Vickers machine gun fire, and galloped for the Bluff amid a hail of bullets.

'During this phase of the attack, although these galloping squadrons were absolutely exposed for 500 yards to the fire of 12 machine guns and 1,000 infantry, at ranges from 500-1,500 yards, not a single man was hit, and only one or two horses,' said General Norton. 'On reaching the foot of the Bluff, the 13th Hussars lost no time in dismounting and forming for attack. Having fixed bayonets, they swarmed up the almost precipitous hill, gallantly led by their commanding officer.'

As the supporting bombardment lifted, Lt-Col Richardson and his men 'charged over the crest, shot or bayoneted such Turks as still confronted them in the trenches, and then rapidly forming line to the right, swept along the crest to deal with the Turks who were still holding their position at the north end of the hill', said General Norton.

As soon as their attack had 'gained the crest', two supporting regiments captured enemy guns and cut off the Turkish infantry's retreat. Seeing there was no escape, the enemy forces surrendered. Almost 1,000 prisoners, two mountain guns and 12 machine guns were captured and the hills were strewn with a large number of Turkish dead and wounded.

In a letter to Sir Robert-Baden Powell, a Lieutenant-General in the British Army who once served in the 13th Hussars, Lt-Col Richardson said his regiment's 'performance' had been described by General Norton and other commanding officers and eye-witnesses as the 'finest thing they have ever seen. I myself agree that not only as a spectacle but in its complete and immediate success it is the finest performance put up by the regiment during the war. But as a test of discipline and tenacity, I would put Lajj first. There we were on the verge of annihilation and yet managed to put up a fighting front to the enemy,' said Lt-Col Richardson.

In his report on the 'storming of the cliff and plateau near Hadraniya', he said the 13th Hussars attacked in two waves, with A and D Squadrons in the first and B and C in the second. 'The first wave reached the foot of the Bluff with only one casualty (a man who fell in jumping a deepish nullah which lay across part of our course) and dismounted to climb the almost precipitous cliff side, the footing on which was made the worse by the loose rolling gravel surface. How the men scaled that cliff carrying their Hotchkiss guns and ammunition bags will always remain a marvel to me.

'Meantime, the second wave had reached the hill, also without casualties, and taken position on the right of the first. As we appeared on the crest fire broke on us from all sides, but the morale of the Turks had been so severely shaken by the artillery that our casualties were very slight, and by bringing our right forward we were soon able to bring enfilade fire on the trenches to our front, and at 1.45pm the first white flag was hoisted. The other trenches did not take long to follow their example, and in less than half an hour after leaving Cemetery Hill, we were in complete possession of the plateau.'

The fight, said Lt-Col Richardson, was 'short and sharp and the victory complete'. The 13th Hussars suffered few losses because of the 'excellent shooting' from the supporting artillery and Vickers guns. Sergeant Robert Edward Holloway was one of two men killed in the attack. One died from wounds received in action and at least five were wounded. From that day forward the Bluff at Hadraniya became known as Richardson's Bluff.

An 'eye-witness' to the charge said the Bluff was a 'veritable inferno' before the 13th Hussars set off on their path of glory, with high explosives bursting in black clouds and shrapnel in 'fleece-like puffs' hurling death on the Turks. 'One continuous and awful roar swept the threatened area. Deafened by the noise and rendered dizzy by the concussion, Turks in the advanced trenches on the crest of the hill could be seen getting up and running in a drunken manner to the rear, some caught by bullets ... others disappeared in the burst of a high explosive shell.'

And then, he said, the Hussars advanced. 'It was a glorious sight. The first line led by their gallant colonel, in perfect order, as if on a drill parade, swept round the edge of Cemetery Hill. The pace increased – on they went with a loud, inspiring cheer. Then, equally steady, followed the second line. The enemy's machine guns rattled furiously, ours replied viciously. On, on went the Hussars. Then, to our horror, we saw a check, and we realised that straight across the front of the Hussars, between them and the Bluff, lay a nullah.

'What is going to happen? Is it too wide? Can they cross it? A little crowding, a horse down. Then a cheer rose to our lips as we saw the colonel thread his way across, and then, on his heels, scrambling, hustling, thrusting, scarcely checking, the first line crossed and went on. By this time the onlookers on Cemetery Hill were mad with excitement. Quite oblivious of the bullets still whistling over them, they were standing up wildly cheering on the gallant Hussars. Now they had reached the foot of the Bluff. So close was it to us, that we could distinguish individuals.

'Off they get (with bayonets fixed). Up the hill they scrambled, with their colonel still at their head. The barrage lifts beautifully in time, and the Hussars clear the crest and, spreading like a fan, on they go. A machine gun is rushed, then a Hussar was seen to fall. Bayonet work begins. "By God, they are counter-attacking," bursts from the Brigade Major's lips, as a party of Turks drive back a troop of the Hussars. But, steady as rocks, the Hussars meet the new attack – a few shots and then the bayonet. On our left, there is a thunder of hoofs ... the 13th and 14th Lancers are hurrying forward in support, lance in rest ready for the pursuit. This is the final act in the drama, and then all sobriety is forgotten. Our helmets fly in the air as we cheer and cheer again, as on all sides white flags of surrender are raised by the defeated Turks.'

On November 1, 1918, news reached Archie and his men of an armistice with Turkey. The war was over. The 13th Hussars bivouacked at Mosul for most of that month and into December. They were encamped there on December 10, when Archie was discharged after 'serving with honour' and becoming 'disabled'.

Durand recorded that the regiment were 'perhaps fortunate' in that they did not come to Mesopotamia until 1916, when the first, and most trying, half of the campaign was over. 'They had no part in the earlier fighting, when the British force was small and its difficulties great. They were spared the troubles and sufferings endured by the troops who conquered the lower part of the country. They did not march up with (General Charles) Townshend to the bloody field of Ctesiphon, or share in the desperate efforts to break through to his relief when he was shut up in Kut.

'When they landed at Basra, all that was over ... The 13th came in on the turn of the tide, and though they had before them two years of hard work and hard fighting, they were never to know the bitterness of defeat. Nevertheless, the work was severe and the issue of the fighting was often doubtful. That it uniformly ended in success, and eventually in complete triumph, was proof of very high qualities in the men who led, and the men who followed.'

They 'gained much honour at a heavy cost'. Of their officers, eight were killed in action or died on service in Mesopotamia, two were disabled and taken prisoner and 14 were wounded. Ninety other ranks were killed and 176 wounded.

Archie, whose regimental number was 32933, was discharged after being wounded in service in Mesopotamia. No longer 'physically fit for war service', he was awarded a Silver Badge (number B58167) to indicate he had been honourably discharged, and a 'King's Certificate of Discharge'. He also received the Victory and British War Medals.

He was born in the village of Washford Pyne in Mid-Devon on July 28, 1894 and attended Stoodleigh Manor Church of England School in 1900. At the time of the 1901 Census, he was six years old and living with his family at Slade Farm, Washfield, where his father was working as a dairyman. At the time of the 1911 Census, Archie, aged 17, was employed as a waggoner by farmer Herbert Dunn, at Fillbrook Farm, Butterleigh, near Cullompton. He later worked for Percy Thomas, as a horseman and farm hand at Yellowford Farm, Thorverton.

Archie, who returned to agricultural work after the war, married 19-year-old Edith Mary Batten at Thorverton Parish Church on February 4, 1922. Archie was aged 25 and living at Berry's Bridge Thorverton at the time of his marriage. They had six children – Doris, Arthur, John, Peggy, Michael and Edna. Archie died from cerebral thrombosis at his home at 1, Bullen Close, Thorverton, on November 8, 1968, aged 74. Edith, the daughter of William John and Mary Batten, died on February 26, 1984, aged 80.

Notes

- A memorial tablet honouring the officers, NCOs and men of the 13th Hussars who died in the Great War was dedicated at All Saints Garrison Church, Aldershot on August 2, 1920.

- The last survivor of the Charge of the Light Brigade in 1854 was Sergeant-Major Edwin Hughes, who died in 1927, aged 96. Born in Wrexham, he enlisted in the 13th Light Dragoons (who later became the 13th Hussars) in 1852. A total of 670 cavalrymen took part in the attack in which more than 150 men and 300 horses were killed.

- Lt FitzGibbon, later promoted to captain, was killed by Kurdish soldiers in a 'frontier affray' in Southern Kurdistan on January 13, 1922. He was 31.

16

FRANK — SHOT IN THE HEAD IN FIERCE FIGHTING IN PALESTINE

W as this where his life would end – on a barren, dusty battlefield on the outskirts of Jerusalem? The bullet struck him in the head, knocking him unconscious. Surrounded by hundreds of dead and wounded soldiers, he collapsed on the steep and rocky ground, a 'casualty' in fierce fighting against the Turks at the hilltop village of Beit ur al-Foka.

It was December 3, 1917 and Private Frank Roberts' chances of survival seemed less than slim. Barely alive, he was carried to safety when his battalion, the 16th Devons, captured the village in a daring night-time attack and then withdrew from it after facing wave after wave of desperate counter-strikes from the Turks.

But this was the day Frank, of Witheridge, Devon cheated death. Emergency first aid treatment – carried out by fellow soldiers and medical staff – saved his life. Eventually transferred to a hospital in Cairo, Egypt, he recovered sufficiently from his 'serious gunshot wound' to continue service in the Army.

He had been wounded in an attack on a village which had once been the site of the town of Upper Beth-Horon. Mentioned in the Bible, in the books of Joshua, Samuel, Kings and Chronicles, Upper Beth-Horon was said to have been rebuilt and fortified by the legendary King Solomon during his reign over ancient Israel.

According to the Bible, it was in this area – close to where Frank fought that day – that Joshua, who led the Israelites to the Promised Land after the death of Moses, had clashed with the Canaanites and Amorites and issued a successful cry for the sun to 'stand still' to enable his army to take vengeance on their enemies.

The harsh, mountainous landscape at Beit ur al-Foka – now known as Foqa or Fauqa – was a perilous place to do battle. The 16th Devons had to fight on and around uneven, rocky ground and deep and steep ravines, or wadis, where enemy troops could hide in large numbers and snipe – and throw bombs at – advancing soldiers without being seen.

It was at 1am on December 3 that the battalion launched their assault from the upper part of a ravine, the Wadi Zait. In the next two hours, Frank and his men had to climb and scramble all their way to the village. They entered Beit ur al-Foka with all guns blazing and were involved in fierce bombing exchanges and hand-to-hand fighting.

The 16th Devons captured up to 60 prisoners and three machine guns as they drove the Turks out of the village. But before they could consolidate their position, they were hit by wave after wave of counter attacks. And as they used bombs, rifles and bayonets to help keep the enemy at bay, they were running short of ammunition.

In the face of unrelenting rifle fire, more bombs and small arms ammunition were rushed to the 16th Devons by 'carrying parties' from the Royal Scots Fusiliers and the 10th (Irish) Division. But these could only be conveyed in small numbers because of the difficulty of the terrain and the severity of the counter-attacks, and were utilised almost as quickly as they arrived.

The enormity of the task facing the 16th Devons in defending their hard-won positions in Beit ur al-Foka – and staying alive – could not have been clearer as night gave way to daylight. The Turks, holding commanding hill-top positions on three sides of the battalion, were now directing devastating machine gun fire at them.

The Turks were not only entrenched in deep ravines, out of

sight of artillery and rifle fire, but on the nearby Zeitun Ridge, which towered over the hill at Beit ur al-Foka, the flanking Kareina Ridge and another hill, from where they were able to fire repeatedly, and destructively, at the front, side and rear of the 16th Devons.

Surging in large numbers up the steep face of protective ravines, the Turks launched attack after attack. Now, barely able to withstand the assaults, and with casualties mounting, the battalion were forced to withdraw just after 1pm, an exhausting ten hours after Frank and his men had first stormed into the village of mud and stone houses.

The evacuation, conducted under cover of artillery fire, was successful. But more than 80 officers, NCOs and men were killed. Nine officers and more than 130 other ranks were wounded, some of whom were taken prisoner. Survivors were evacuated to a bivouac at Beit Likia (or Liqya), near Ramallah, on the outskirts of Jerusalem.

It was – and would remain – the bloodiest day in the history of the 16th Devons. Among those killed in action were five young men from Torrington, Devon and the nearby village of Langtree – Acting Corporal John T Burrows, Lance-Corporal Henry Frain, and Privates Thomas Henry Adams, Albert Ernest Luxton and Rodney Ayre.

Frank would almost certainly have known a number of those who died. From villages and rural hamlets close to his home in Devon, they included 21-year-old Private Robert Kent Kingdom, of Carscombe, Stoodleigh, 31-year-old Private George Galling, of Lapford, and 22-year-old Private William Nott, Meshaw's only casualty of the Great War.

Some of those who died were buried where they fell in Beit ur al-Foka. More than 70 were buried at the Jerusalem War Cemetery, close to the Mount of Olives on the outskirts of the city. Fourteen, with no known grave, are remembered on the Jerusalem Memorial, within the war cemetery. One – Lance-Cpl Henry Frain – has a grave at Ramleh War Cemetery, near Tel Aviv.

Among those captured by the Turks was Captain S R E Snow. Taken to the Turkish Divisional HQ near Ramallah, he was treated in hospital and imprisoned in Constantinople before being moved to a prisoner of war camp in Anatolia. Also captured was Sergeant Ernest J Ivey, of Black Torrington, Devon, whose experiences in captivity were published in *The Western Times* in December 1918.

On arriving home, he told the newspaper that, while 'surrounded by very superior forces of the Turks' on December 3, 1917, four of the 16th Devons' officers, one sergeant-major, five sergeants and 25 men were taken prisoner. Sgt Ivey was shot in the thigh. His kit, money, books and clothing were taken from him, 'leaving him in the dirty suit he was wearing'.

His wound was treated in a primitive Turkish hospital where he remained for six weeks before being sent to work at Kelebek, on the projected German railway to Baghdad. 'Here he was a ganger of about 20 men for about three months, receiving about 25 piastres (about 10d) per day, the other men having to be satisfied with 11-18,' reported *The Western Times*.

'The prisoners lived chiefly on boiled wheat, rye bread, some goats' meat, peas and haricot beans. Their last year's Christmas dinner consisted of boiled wheat.' Sgt Ivey suffered an attack of malaria fever in August 1918. While in a convalescent camp, he was examined and selected as a prisoner for exchange. He was sent to Smyrna and then to Alexandria in Egypt where British authorities sent him home via Italy and France.

Six days after the fighting at Beit ur al-Foka, Jerusalem was captured. On December 11, 1917, Field Marshall Edmund Henry Hynman Allenby, the Commander of Britain's Egyptian Expeditionary Force, entered the city on foot as a mark of respect for its holy status – and became the first Christian in many centuries to control Jerusalem.

Frank was born in Rackenford on April 13, 1892, a year of political turmoil in which the Conservative Prime Minister Robert Cecil, the Marquess of Salisbury lost a vote of no confidence in his government and was succeeded days later by 82-year-old Liberal William Ewart Gladstone, who served as Prime Minister on four separate occasions.

Frank was born in the same year as J R R Tolkien, author of *The Lord of the Rings*, British actor Basil Rathbone, actress

Margaret Rutherford, and Arthur 'Bomber' Harris, who was in charge of the RAF's Bomber Command in the 1939-45 War. 1892 also saw the inaugural publication of *The Adventures of Sherlock Holmes* by Arthur Conan Doyle.

Frank was the eldest son of Thomas and Mary Ann (nee Morrish) Roberts who had 10 children, two of whom died in infancy. In 1911, Frank was a farrier on his father's Newland Farm at Witheridge in Devon. He was one of three brothers to serve his country in the war. His younger brother, Albert, died from wounds in France in October 1915, aged just 19.

While still working for his father, Frank enlisted in the Royal 1st Devon Yeomanry on January 20, 1912, when he was three months away from his 20th birthday. Over the next two years, he received training at the East Devon village of Rousdon, at the Army's Hamilton Camp, near Stonehenge, and at Bovey Tracey in Devon.

The Devon and Exeter Gazette in May 1912 reported that the regiment's annual training was to take place in a 'spacious field' to the east of Rousdon Mansion – at the invitation of Sir Wilfred Peek, the 3rd Baronet of Rousdon, who went on to serve as a Major with the Royal 1st Devon Yeomanry in the Great War. The newspaper said the training would begin on May 28, 1912 and continue for 15 days. 'It is expected that between 300 and 400 officers and men (including Frank) … will be under canvas. Most of the regiment's work will be carried out on a long stretch of common land at (nearby) Shapwick,' it added.

When Britain declared war on Germany in August 1914, the headquarters for the regiment – then under the command of the 2nd South Western Mounted Brigade – was at 9, Dix's Field in Exeter, with A Squadron based in Thorverton, B Squadron at Ottery St Mary, C Squadron at Totnes and D Squadron at Bodmin.

The 2nd South Western Mounted Brigade – including the Royal 1st Devon Yeomanry – were mobilised on August 4 that year and moved to Colchester in Essex under the command of Brigadier-General R Hoare, a brother of Colonel Wilson Hoare, of Westward Ho!, Devon. Frank and his men were based in St Osyth, a village five miles west of Clacton-on-Sea.

It was here, on the east coast, that the Yeomen of Devon and Cornwall were transformed into an impressive cavalry regiment. But in September 1915, as they were about to go to war for the first time, their destiny was to be 'dismounted', to fight on foot. As a symbol of the change, they wore a broken spur as their insignia.

It was in that month that Frank and the Royal 1st Devon Yeomanry left St Osyth for Liverpool to board *RMS Olympic*, an ocean liner converted to a troop ship, for a voyage to Turkey's war-torn Gallipoli peninsula. The vessel sailed on September 25 to Mudros, on the Greek island of Lemnos, arriving on October 1, and then on to Suvla Bay, on the Aegean coast of Gallipoli.

The *Olympic* was famous as the sister ship of *RMS Titanic*, the passenger liner which sank with the loss of more than 1,500 lives in April 1912 after striking an iceberg on her maiden voyage to New York. Another sister ship, *RMS Britannic*, sank in November 1916, with the loss of 30 lives after striking an underwater mine.

The *Olympic* – carrying 7,000 soldiers and a large quantity of munitions – narrowly averted a potential catastrophe when a German U-boat fired two torpedoes at the vessel as she made her way to Gallipoli. Both torpedoes missed their target by small margins, one passing just ahead of the ship and the second almost shaving the stern.

Frank and the Royal 1st Devon Yeomanry landed in Gallipoli, on October 9, 1915, just two days before plans to evacuate the peninsula – where British, Australia and New Zealand forces had suffered devastating casualties in offensives against the Turks and been decimated by dysentery and other illnesses – were hatched.

Their arrival was hampered by appalling weather. Attached to the 11th (Northern) Infantry Division, they moved into a bivouac in the area of Karakol Dagh, and were given the unenviable task of building and reinforcing dug-outs in soil comprising sand and stone. In the trenches, Frank and his men were in constant danger from snipers and had little or no respite from enemy shell-fire.

The regiment suffered their first casualty on October 26,

17 days after their arrival in Gallipoli, when a man was severely wounded in a shell attack. Five days after taking over front-line trenches at Jephson's Post in Suvla Bay, one of their men was killed – Private Frederick William Davey, of Winkleigh, Devon, who was shot in the head while on sentry duty.

On November 11, 1915, the regiment suffered a major blow when Captain Edward 'Teddy' Hain was killed and two men were wounded by an enemy shell in a dug-out. The only son of a shipping magnate and former MP for St Ives in Cornwall, he was an outstanding and gallant officer greatly respected by men of all ranks.

Just a few days before his death, 28-year-old Captain Hain sent a moving letter to his parents. 'In the trenches, life is very monotonous,' he said. 'You feel very shut in, as you see little but earth walls and sandbags except when looking through a loophole (a hole cut into steel plates to protect soldiers from snipers and to help them fire more safely at the enemy) ... I have never been fitter or more cheery, only a little more appreciative of the comforts of home.'

In the letter, published in *The Western Times* in November 1915, he added: 'It really is an odd existence, and yesterday morning, while bringing my squadron back from the trenches before daylight to the dug-outs, it felt like coming home.'

Four days later, and now attached to the 2nd Mounted Division, which had been fighting in Gallipoli since April 1915 under the command of Major-General William Peyton, the regiment moved into support trenches near Lala Baba, a hill between the southern side of Suvla Bay and the Salt Lake, before returning to the front line.

Gallipoli was hit by a devastating storm and blizzard at the end of November that led to the deaths of 200 British soldiers from frostbite and exposure and left 10,000 others 'unfit for service' because of sickness. Torrential rain lasting for 24 hours was followed by a hard frost and heavy blizzard. Trenches were flooded and turned into raging torrents and many were later filled with snow.

Officers and men of the Royal 1st Devon Yeomanry were forced to move to open ground in biting winds and snow. Many suffered from severe frost bite after being 'half drowned' in the downpours, and then having to endure the snow and bitter cold without warm clothing, kit, waterproof sheets and equipment which had been washed away in the floods.

On December 19, the regiment were evacuated to the island of Imbros, in the Aegean Sea, as part of the mass evacuation of British forces from Gallipoli before Christmas. After two days, Frank and his men sailed to Mudros and on December 30 arrived in Alexandria in Egypt. From there they were transported by railway to the Sidi-Bishr Camp, on the outskirts of the city.

In the 72 days they spent in Gallipoli, 11 officers and men of the Royal 1st Devon Yeomanry were killed in action. More than a dozen died from wounds or from sickness. Among those killed in action was Corporal Francis Frederick Yeandle, of Bidwell Barton, Thorverton, who died when a shell burst over him on November 25.

In Egypt, in February 1916, the 2nd South Western Mounted Brigade – comprising the Royal 1st Devon Yeomanry, the Royal North Devon Yeomanry and the West Somerset Yeomanry – were incorporated into the 2nd Dismounted Brigade, and found themselves serving alongside the 1st Fife and Forfar Yeomanry, the Lovat Scouts and Highland Mounted Brigade Signal Troop.

As part of the 2nd Dismounted Brigade, Frank and his men served in the Western Frontier Force which, in a 15-month campaign, fought the German and Turkish-backed Sanussi religious sect in skirmishes in Wadi Senba, Wadi Majid, Halazin and Agagia. The brigade's tasks included patrolling the Kharga Oasis, west of the Nile valley.

A major re-organisation of Yeomanry forces on January 4, 1917, led to Frank becoming part of a new infantry unit – the 16th (Royal 1st Devon and Royal North Devon Yeomanry) Battalion of the Devonshire Regiment. Formed at the Moascar military camp, near the town of Ismalia in north-eastern Egypt, the battalion later became part of the 229th Brigade of the 74th (Yeomanry) Division.

After the amalgamation, the 16th Devons moved to the Suez Canal – the critical 120-mile long waterway connecting the Red

Sea to the Mediterranean – and helped British forces to defend a substantial part of it on the eastern bank, including military railways and trenches, at El Ferdan, Toussom and Serapeum.

Based at El Arish on the Sinai Peninsula in early March that year, the battalion joined the 229th Brigade on a long march to Kahn Yunis, Palestine at the end of the month, via El Burj, Sheikh Zuweid and Rafa where, two months earlier, British forces were involved in a battle to win control of the peninsula.

The 16th Devons were defending an outpost near In Seirat in the days before a British attack on Turkish-held Gaza in April 1917. They helped form the 'reserve' for the assault on the enemy fortress and were not called into action. However, a senior officer and 16 men of the 229th Brigade were wounded when they came under heavy shell fire.

As spring turned to summer in the desert, the Turks were not the only enemy facing the battalion. Frank and his men were plagued by flies, lice and scorpions. Sickness spread in the heat, with even the tiniest of scratches becoming infected. They were also plagued by hot wind (or Khamsin) storms, carrying vast quantities of sand and dust at speeds of up to 90mph.

As British forces prepared for a third and decisive attack on Gaza, the 16th Devons helped to patrol the area of No Man's Land in front of the Turkish defences. They killed four of the enemy in an engagement on the night of May 31 and June 1, and inflicted further casualties in another skirmish the following night.

In November, in the aftermath of the Third Battle of Gaza, the battalion took part in fighting in Sheria, with some of their men helping the 74th Yeomanry Division's 230th Brigade as they defended field guns captured from the enemy. The 16th Devons left Gaza on November 22 and arrived in Latron, in the Ayalon Valley six days before the attack on Beit ur al-Foka.

An insight into the 'trying ordeal' faced by the Devons in fighting to free Palestine from Turkish rule, was given in a letter written by Private Arthur William Grater of the 5th Battalion of the Devonshire Regiment, and sent to his family home in Highampton, near Holsworthy, Devon. 'There was much hard fighting,' he said in the letter, published in *The Western Times* in February 1918.

The battalion had seemed to face 'nothing but marching, with barely time for food. We had no bread ration for a month and when we found water we did not drink it, fearing we should fail to find some further on.' The fighting, he said, had been 'incessant and the Turks know how to use machine guns ... They put bullets amongst us like peas and it is remarkable the escapes some fellows had. I was fortunate up to November 28 (1917) when ... a shell found me and a piece entered my back. By good luck it came out further down. I think I was very lucky. I had another bullet through the flesh of my right arm.

'This happened about five miles west of the Holy City. It took six days to get to hospital. The roads are bad and we had to travel in stretchers on the backs of a camel for some miles. Just imagine the pleasure – it would make an excellent see-saw for the children. At present, I am in hospital in Cairo, and am getting on fine, out of bed and able to get about, so I shall not be long now before I am discharged, and return to my unit. Don't worry about me as I am A1. Keep smiling.' Pte Grater was killed in action in France on September 27, 1918. He was just 21.

What happened to Frank after he was helped from the battlefield on December 3, 1917 and transferred to hospital in Cairo? It is not known when he returned to his battalion. But his service records reveal that, when the 16th Devons were transferred to France in the spring of 1918, he travelled with them to Marseilles.

He moved to Kantara, on the eastern side of the Suez Canal, at the end of April and boarded *HMT Leasowe Castle* on the last day of the month. The troop ship – perhaps fortunate to be still in service after being torpedoed in a U-boat attack off Gibraltar in 1917 – sailed at 2pm on May 1 and arrived in Marseille on May 7.

Just 20 days later the same vessel, while carrying 3,000 troops from Alexandria to Marseilles, was sunk by a torpedo. More than 100 men, including the ship's captain, were killed. Among those on board were officers, NCOs and men of the

Warwickshire Yeomanry, the South Nottinghamshire Hussars and the Buckinghamshire and Berkshire Yeomanry.

On reaching Marseilles, Frank and his men marched to a rest camp before travelling by train to Noyelles, on the Somme, arriving in billets in Favieres on May 11. Over the next nine days, the battalion underwent rigorous physical exercise and training in bayonet fighting, battlefield tactics and dealing with gas attacks.

The 16th Devons journeyed by train to Ligny-Saint-Flochel on May 20 and marched to billets at Sus-Saint-Leger. There, they continued training before marching on May 25 to billets in Liencourt where, over the next 30 days, they took part in 'tactical schemes' with tanks and practised their shooting skills on local ranges.

They journeyed to the village of Witternesse in northern France on June 26, moving three days later to Le Foret, where two companies were attached to trench digging working parties. They were in the village of Guarbecque on July 11. Twelve days later, they were in front line trenches, in the 'Amusoires section' between St Venant and Robecq.

But Frank would not be joining them in the front line. On July 20, 1918, while at Guarbecque, he was transferred to the Labour Corps. His injury meant he was no longer suitable for the demands of fighting in the trenches. In his new role, he helped with digging and other physical duties, unloading supplies and other similar work.

On the front line, the 16th Devons came under heavy attack on the morning of July 24, from high explosive and gas shells. Early the next day, they fought off a German raiding party, inflicting 'about 20 casualties'. On August 6, as it became clear that the enemy were withdrawing from their trenches, one company ventured out and captured a German and a machine gun.

The war diary shows that, in early September 1918 they were involved in a major attack on the Somme village of Moislains which resulted in devastating casualties. The battalion's task was to provide two companies – A and B – to carry out 'clearing up' work in Moislains, which was reported to be evacuated by the enemy. But the Germans were still holding the village 'in force'.

The two companies came under heavy shell and gas fire as they launched an attack. Captain Joseph Oscar Muntz, (who later died of his wounds) and three 2nd lieutenants were wounded. Almost 50 NCOs and men were killed and 140 wounded in the attack and in subsequent heavy artillery and gas fire, making it the second blackest day in the battalion's history.

Among those who died on September 2, 1918 was 19-year-old Private John William Entwistle, of Helmshore, Lancashire. The officer who found his body – recovering from it for his family a treasured Sunday school card – told his mother that John was of a 'wonderfully bright and willing disposition, and a splendid soldier'.

Another soldier killed at Moislains while 'gallantly charging the enemy', was Lance-Corporal William Lock, of Parracombe, near Lynton, Devon. He was an only son, and it was the second tragedy his mother had had to endure that year, for her 61-year-old husband, William, died after falling from a loft at his farm in March 1918.

Frank, officially listed as '20% disabled', returned to England on September 5, 1918. Serving with the 448 Agricultural Company of the Labour Corps, he worked on farms during the final two months of the war, and beyond. He was discharged on April 29, 1919, after completing more than seven years' service with the Royal 1st Devon Yeomanry, 16th Devons and Labour Corps.

The cause of his discharge – under King's Regulations, paragraph 392 (xvia) – was that he was 'surplus to military requirements (having suffered impairment since entry into the service)'. A holder of the Silver War Badge, awarded to men honourably discharged after service at home or overseas, he received a weekly pension of 5/6 (five shillings and six pence).

The Labour Corps did not always get the recognition they deserved for their important work in the war. But, in his Somme and Lys River despatch in January 1919, Field Marshall Sir

Douglas Haig, Commander in Chief of the British Army in France and Flanders, praised the Corps for rising to the many challenges they faced.

'The British labour companies were composed entirely of men medically unfit for active operations, and more than half their number owe their incapacity to wounds or sickness incurred while serving with fighting units. The men of the Corps, however, made light of their disabilities', he said. 'Many companies worked for months on end under shell fire, long marches were willingly undertaken, and the essential work entrusted to them was cheerfully performed often under conditions entailing all the hardship and strain without the excitement of actual fighting.

'The successive British advances imposed upon all ranks daily increasing work and responsibilities. It is to the credit of the Corps and of the excellent system of command and administration developed during the earlier part of the year that the Labour Companies have invariably answered all demands made upon them.'

After the war, Frank returned to Witheridge to work with his father. He married Alice May Bending at Cadeleigh Parish Church on January 3, 1921. He was 28 at the time and Alice, the daughter of Mark and Elizabeth Bending, was 24. They lived at Cuckoo Farm, West Anstey and had three daughters – Doris Beatrice May, Ivy Rita and Vera Mary. Ivy and Vera married two brothers in a double wedding at Molland Parish Church in February 1945. The sisters married Herbert John and Reginald James Bucknell, three years after they were bridesmaids at Doris Beatrice May's wedding to Wilfred Hunkin at the same church.

Frank worked as a farmer until his retirement. He spent his final years at 45, West Street, South Molton and died from congestive heart failure and chronic bronchitis at the town's Cottage Hospital on September 17, 1970, aged 78. Alice died 19 years later, aged 93.

Frank received the British War and Victory Medals and the 1915 Star. His regimental number with the Royal 1st Devon Yeomanry and 16th Devons was 2043. His regimental number with the 448 Agricultural Company of the Labour Corps was 571290. His Silver War Badge number was B343098.

Note

- A memorial to the 124 officers, NCOs and men of the Royal 1ˢᵗ Devon Yeomanry who fell in the Great War, was unveiled and dedicated at Exeter Cathedral on May 25, 1924. The memorial, crafted by Herbert Reed, of St Sidwell's Studio, Exeter, was unveiled by Viscount Hambleden, the last commanding officer of the regiment.

17

JOHN FRANCIS BRYANT — HOW HE FACED 70 DAYS OF HELL ON THE SOMME

It was a year he would never forget. He had survived the killing fields of the Somme, fighting in battles that claimed the lives of hundreds of his fellow soldiers. He had witnessed barely imaginable savagery and carnage, the stuff of nightmares. He had seen ordinary men do extraordinary things in extreme conditions – showing immense valour in the face of the greatest adversity.

1916 was the most challenging year in the life of Private John Francis Bryant Roberts. He fought with the 9th Battalion of the Devonshire Regiment at Mametz on the first day of the Battle of the Somme on July 1 when so many of the officers and men he served with were mown down by German machine gun fire. Close to him that day was his cousin, Corporal Samuel 'Sam' Roberts, of the 8th Devons, who was among the many thousands killed in the offensive.

In the next 70 days, John and the 9th Devons were involved in some of the fiercest and bloodiest engagements on the Somme – the Battle of Bazentin, attacks on Caterpillar Wood, the Battle of Delville Wood and the Battle of Guillemont. The latter, four-day offensive included a remarkably bold and courageous attack by the battalion on the tiny but strategically important village of Ginchy in early September 1916.

The assault on key German defensive positions in the village, which almost wiped out the 9th Devons, was heralded in *The Western Times* in April 1919. The newspaper reported that, pounded with shrapnel, the battalion led the attack on Ginchy. 'All through the day they struggled to get to the village ... the German artillery was deadly and put up such a barrage that it was impossible to get through it.'

Very soon 'walking wounded' were seen struggling their way to dressing stations and tales spread of 'what seemed to be the impossible task which had been set them'. This, said *The Western Times*, was not at a time when men could be 'thrown recklessly into the furnace. Every man had to be saved if possible, and the officers so directed operations as to minimise as much as they could the chances of casualties. Yet they were heavy – terribly heavy.'

The 9th Devons' losses were catastrophic, with more than 300 officers and other ranks killed or wounded. They later retired to Montauban. 'In view of the way in which they had suffered and the numbers to which they were reduced, it was thought that the (battalion) could be taken out of the line to reorganise. It came rather as a surprise, therefore, when ... the next evening orders were again received for them to try another attack on Ginchy.'

The advance was hugely problematic with the ground, in many places being 'waist deep in mud'. The 9th Devons spent the night in Dead Man's Trench, 'so called because in it the Germans had previously burned hundreds of their dead'. At this time, the British artillery was 'not what it might have been', and dozens of 2nd Gordon Highlanders who were holding the line were being hit 'by our own shells' as they retired.

Casualties mounted as the Germans opened a 'furious bombardment' on the trench. Among those killed and wounded by shell fire was the 'single remaining machine gun team'. Amid continuing artillery barrages, the 9th Devons came under heavy machine gun fire but, undaunted, many officers and men successfully entered the village. There, they met resistance from machine guns and snipers tasked with holding up the advance.

There was 'furious hand-in-hand fighting in the streets', the bayonet being the 'weapon chiefly used by the men', while officers fought with trench sticks and their revolvers. Two officers were killed and three wounded as they clashed with the enemy among bomb-wrecked houses in Ginchy. Amid the mayhem, a sergeant courageously charged and killed two Germans manning a machine gun – and captured the weapon.

One officer – a Lieutenant Pitts – had a 'remarkable experience,' *The Western Times* recalled. 'After being hit (and wounded) in the back, he was placed for safety in a shell hole, and just afterwards another shell burst near him and he was buried where he lay. He was reported as wounded and missing and four hours afterwards was discovered and dug out by (men from the Border Regiment) who had come into the line.'

As night fell, 'the enemy concentrated all (its) artillery on the village, and it became impossible to live in it. There were only about 50 of the 9th Devons left by his time, and they had no officers. Still they were reluctant to yield what they had won, although in the end they had to do so and fall back to their original front line where the Border Regiment took over from them.'

The incredible challenges encountered and overcome by the battalion in entering and capturing Ginchy, if only for a brief period, truly emerged in the days ahead. For it ultimately took an entire Irish Division (the 16th) to take and successfully hold the village and this was only achieved after 'long, hard and costly fighting'.

The 9th Devons' war diary for the attacks on Ginchy between September 4 and 7, 1916, revealed that over those four days, four officers were killed and 18 wounded, with one being reported missing, believed killed. A total of 405 other ranks were killed or wounded. The bravery and sacrifice shown by the battalion led to the commanding officer, Lieutenant-Colonel Henry Innes Storey, being awarded the Distinguished Service Order.

The battle marked the end of a sustained and brutal period of fighting for John who had first joined the 9th Devons in France on October 7, 1915. It was the last major offensive in which he would be involved in the Great War. He was discharged from service after being wounded – and regarded as 'no longer physically fit for war service' – on March 12, 1917. It is not known how or when he was wounded.

John was one of three brothers to fight in the war. His younger brother, Sidney, a rifleman in the Queen's Westminster Rifles, died of wounds sustained in the Battle of Langemarck on August 17, 1917, at the age of 28. Another younger brother, Archibald, or 'Archie', served with the 13th Hussars, surviving two of the great cavalry charges of the war.

John was born at 20 Acres Farm in Puddington, Devon on September 14, 1883. He was the eldest son of Charles (Charlie) and Eliza (nee Bryant) Roberts, who had eight children. Queen Victoria ruled over the British Empire and Liberal statesman William Ewart Gladstone was Prime Minister when John was born. Clement Atlee, who became Prime Minister after the Second World War, Kahlil Gibran, the Lebanese novelist, poet and painter, and the American actor Douglas Fairbanks, were also born in 1883.

The year was one of tragedy and triumph, with nearly 200 children dying in a stampede at the end of a variety show at the Victoria Hall, Sunderland and Thomas Edison's first electric lighting system using overhead wires being unveiled in America. Two classic children's novels were published in 1883 – *The Adventures of Pinocchio* and Robert Louis Stevenson's *Treasure Island*.

In 1891, John was living with his family at Down Cottage, Cruwys Morchard, where his father was an agricultural worker. In 1901, John was employed as a 'domestic worker' at Palfrys Farm, Cove, Tiverton, which was run by Cruwys Morchard-born John B Hill, who lived there with his wife, Elizabeth and two young children.

In August 1901, while working at Palfrys Farm, John Francis Bryant Roberts, aged 17, joined the 4th Battalion of the Devonshire Regiment in Exeter. At 5ft 1ins tall, he was 1½ inches below regulation height, but was 'physically fit' and he signed up for six years' service. He was discharged as a private in April 1903, buying himself out for £1.

He married Edith Mabel Chorley, daughter of William and Fanny Chorley, at Washfield, Devon on April 16, 1906. They had six sons and two daughters, four of whom were born before John went to war. He was a carter in 1911 and living in North Cadbury, near Bath. He enlisted in the 9th Devons in January 1915, nine months before he went to the Western Front.

John was among 300 NCOs and men drafted into the battalion after they suffered heavy losses at the Battle of Loos in September 1915. The new arrivals were inspected by Lt-Col Storey at Le Preol, near Bethune, on October 9. The 9th Devons marched to Ferme du Roi the following day and were in trenches at Cambrin on October 14 and 15 where two men were wounded, one by a sniper.

One man was killed by shell fire, one shot dead by a sniper and four others were wounded when the battalion were in trenches at Givenchy between October 20 and 23. They spent the last week of the month in billets in Ferme du Roi, carrying out 'attack practice' and bombing, machine-gunning and wiring practice, before returning to trenches knee deep in mud after heavy rain in early November.

Enemy shell fire killed three men and wounded 12 others between November 10 and 14. John and the 9th Devons left Givenchy on the 16th, moving to billets in Essars and Bellerive and eventually marching to Festubert. Rifle fire, shrapnel and trench mortars killed one man and wounded an officer and nine others between November 24 and 27, as they worked on the outskirts of the village on repairing damaged and water-logged trenches.

A lance-corporal was killed by a German sniper and four men were wounded by shell fire on December 1 – John's final day in the trenches in the run-up to Christmas. The battalion marched to Essars, Busnettes and Lillers before moving by train to Saleux in the Somme area and marching to billets in Ailly-sur-Somme. They spent the rest of the month there, undergoing rifle, musketry, field engineering and other training.

During January 1916, the 9th Devons were trained in railway

and road building and mining, working with the 2nd Highland Field Company of the Royal Engineers, who provided invaluable technical support for British infantry and other fighting units, and later – at the village of Puchevillers – with the Royal Engineers' 112th Railway Construction Company, who played a pivotal role in ensuring the smooth movement of men, munitions and supplies in France.

A rugby match involving 'as many officers and men as could be spared' was played against the 1st Devons at Montigny on February 2. Three days later the battalion marched to Meaulte with 260 men from 1 and 2 Companies forming a garrison at the village of Becordel, near Albert. There, working parties were formed to carry out 'mining fatigues' work in the Tambour, on the front line opposite the village of Fricourt.

Four officers and 220 men carried out this exhausting work which involved moving large quantities of sand bags filled with wet mud from sites where the British were busily building tunnels to plant underground explosive charges or mines beneath enemy front lines. The mines in the Tambour area were among a total of 19 detonated in a huge explosion on July 1, 1916 as the Battle of the Somme got underway.

Becordel was heavily shelled by the Germans on February 22. As the artillery fire continued and the British retaliated, all men of the garrison were ordered to take shelter in cellars. In the bombardment, which continued for 5½ hours, nine men were wounded by a shell as they passed through a railway arch north of the village on their way to the Queen's Redoubt. Another man died from wounds received in the Tambour area. 'Several parties of the enemy attempted to cross into our line … but were driven back by our rifle and Lewis gun fire,' the war diary recorded.

One man was killed and two wounded by shell fire and rifle grenades on February 28 as the 9th Devons took over trenches opposite Fricourt from the 8th Battalion of the Devonshire Regiment. The following day, enemy soldiers attempting to raid these trenches were successfully driven off by 'rifle and Lewis gun fire'. An hour-long bombardment of the front line took its toll, killing one man and wounding 13 others.

Shell fire and rifle grenades killed three men and wounded 26 others in March 1916 in attacks on Fricourt, Becordel and Meaulte. An officer – 2nd Lieutenant H P Cole – died after being shot in the head by a sniper at Tambour on April 3. The battalion moved to Bray three days later, and took over trenches at Mametz. Shell and trench mortar fire, rifle grenades and German snipers claimed the lives of four more men during the month and wounded 34 others.

In early May 1916, John and the 9th Devons were working with the Royal Engineers at Grovetown Camp and at Bray-sur-Somme, near Mametz. They marched to bivouacs in Bois des Tailles and Treux Wood for training and work on improving trenches. In June, in the run up to the Battle of the Somme, the battalion continued training at Bois des Tailles and spent a week in the trenches in Mametz, between the 12th and 19th.

On the night of June 30, John was on the eve of his first major action of the war – the 'Big Push', designed to crush the German resistance on the Western Front. The 9th Devons were to help lead the attack on Mametz on the first day of the Battle of the Somme. By the early hours of July 1, 12 officers and 753 men of the battalion were in assembly trenches, waiting to go 'over the top'. A further 12 officers and 308 other ranks were kept 'in reserve'.

What was going through John's mind in those final tense hours and minutes before the attack? His thoughts must have drifted to his life back home, his wife of ten years Edith, his (then) three sons, nine-year-old Charles Francis, seven-year-old William John and four-year-old Sydney George, and his 15-month-old daughter, Ellen. Would he see them again? Or would his life end here, on the grim battlefields of France, at the age of 32?

The 9th Devons, attached to the 20th Infantry Brigade of the British Army's 7th Division, started their dramatic assault at 7.27am on July 1, three minutes before the enormous pre-attack barrage on enemy lines came to a halt. They were cut down in huge numbers by machine gun and artillery fire as they advanced along Rose (or Death) Alley below the village of Mametz.

In his report on the attack, Brigadier-General Cyril John Deverell, Commander of the 20th Infantry Brigade, said that on reaching the front line, in the area of Mansel Copse, the 9th Devons 'came under a heavy artillery and machine gun barrage, and suffered severely'. The leading companies lost all their officers 'soon after entering hostile trenches'.

Having to pass over trenches 'completely wrecked beyond recognition by shell fire', they became 'somewhat disorganised'. But in the face of fierce fire, they continued to open fire on the enemy 'in front of and behind them'. Brig-Gen Deverell said: 'They undoubtedly did great service in keeping the enemy engaged, and in clearing the trenches, and sent back many prisoners.'

Against all the odds, and despite devastating losses, a group of 9th and 8th Devons reached their objective – the western end of Mametz. The 9th suffered 480 casualties between July 1 and 3. Eight officers and more than 150 NCOs and men were killed, the vast majority mown down by German machine gunners who had survived the pre-attack bombardment. Nine officers and 267 men were wounded and dozens more were listed as 'missing in action'.

John survived the carnage to fight another day. On July 2 and 3 his battalion 'consolidated their position' in the trenches and carried out the unenviable task of collecting dead comrades, including his cousin Sam, from the battlefield for burial at Mansel Copse (which became known as the Devonshire Cemetery), as well as recovering abandoned 'bombs, ammunition and stores'.

The 9th Devons moved back to the Citadel, a British Army base near Bray-sur-Somme, arriving there at 1am on July 4. After attending the funeral service for their fellow soldiers at Mansel Copse, they marched to billets in Ribemont, near Albert, staying there until July 11 when they moved into trenches in Marlboro Wood and Caterpillar Valley, via Meaulte and Fricourt.

Two men were killed and two officers and 20 others wounded when they came under heavy shell fire in Caterpillar Valley on July 12. The following morning, the battalion received orders to support the 8th Devons and the 2nd Borders in an attack on

German defensive positions in nearby Caterpillar Wood in the early hours of July 14.

The war diary reveals that the 9th Devons were 'placed at the disposal of the 22nd Infantry Brigade' for the attack, but were 'not used'. However, amid fierce enemy shell fire, four of their men were killed, and three officers and 50 NCOs and men were wounded. The battalion were still in Caterpillar Valley on the night of July 15 and 16 when they endured a gas shell attack.

They moved to a new position on the night of July 19 and 20, north of Bazentin-le-Grand Wood to support attacking companies of the 8th Devons and 2nd Gordon Highlanders. Heavily shelled during an enemy bombardment, the 9th Devons suffered 'only a few casualties owing to the fact that the men had dug themselves in well', the war diary recorded.

At 5.10am on the 20th, the battalion's No 1 Company were sent to support the 2nd Gordons after they made an urgent request for reinforcements. The company's commanding officer, 2nd Lieutenant Launcelot Sulyarde Robert Cary, was killed in the advance as they came under heavy machine gun and rifle fire, with many men forced to take cover in shell holes.

Later that evening, the 9th Devons moved to a bivouac near the village of Dernancourt. The following day, they were transported by train from Mericourt to the village of Hangest-sur-Somme and later marched to Ailly-sur-Somme where they stayed for the next 18 days, taking part in rifle, grenade and bombing practice – with disastrous results.

Five men were wounded – one later dying of his wounds – when a No 5 Mills grenade (named after engineer and designer William Mills) accidentally exploded prematurely at a bombing practice on August 2. One private died and another was wounded the following day when another explosive device 'burst' prematurely. A private was wounded on August 7 in an 'accidental discharge of a rifle during loading practice' and an officer, 2nd Lieutenant A S Robinson, was 'accidentally wounded' during a Lewis gun demonstration on August 10.

The 9th Devons were transported by train from Vignacourt to Mericourt two days later and marched to billets in the village of Buire where they continued training until September 2,

1916. After the gruelling attack on Ginchy, they moved by train from Albert to Airaines, near Amiens, and marched to billets in Bettencourt.

They later moved to Longpre-les-Corps-Saints and then to trenches near Nieppe. On the night of September 30-October 1, a party of two officers, 16 other ranks and two sappers launched a daring and successful raid on a German machine gun house which led to the killing of up to 25 Germans and the apparent destruction of an enemy bomb store.

A report by Captain J C E Inchbald, said the raiding party – equipped with Mills grenades, knobkerries, or trench clubs, bombs and incendiary devices – left their base at 9.05pm on September 30. Four sections of a 'Bangalore torpedo', an explosive device usually packed in metal tubes, were 'laid' just before 10pm when a planned bombardment on the enemy got underway.

'At this point the first hitch occurred,' said Captain Inchbald. 'Just previously to the artillery fire, the Germans in the machine house were heard to fix bayonets. They were clearly well on the alert and must have spotted the torpedo party. When the artillery fire opened, the Germans threw about eight bombs … and one of these burst by the torpedo and exploded it, before the party could explode it properly themselves.

'What followed was somewhat confused. Our shells were unfortunately dropping a bit short and several were actually falling on the machine gun house. The first shell that dropped on the house sent out … about eight Germans who advanced with fixed bayonets. This (group) was successfully bombed and not one could have lived.'

A second group of seven Germans emerged, again with fixed bayonets, and 'ran back towards their trench'. They were 'accounted for' by an officer and three men from the raiding party who had made their way to the machine gun house before being bombed back. However, they were 'able to throw their bombs right among this second (group) of Germans and apparently killed the lot'.

Captain Inchbald said: 'One man – a sapper – got into the German trench and shot down a German with his revolver. All this time the raiding party was in the middle of our barrage as our shells were still falling on the machine gun house. The officers accordingly decided to withdraw. In doing so, the incendiary bombs were thrown at the house which was completely demolished.'

Soldiers sent to look for wounded members of the raiding party found and brought back two men. Three others were reported missing, but two of them returned at dawn on October 2 after laying low in No Man's Land, 'uncertain which was the hostile line and which was ours', according to the battalion's war diary.

Captain Inchbald said 16 Germans were 'killed for certain' and another nine were killed or 'put out of action'. He added: 'It is also thought a German bomb store was blown up in the house. The artillery barrage, which was magnificent, must have done severe damage. It is also certain two machine guns were knocked out by the trench mortars.'

An enemy patrol seen approaching wire entanglements in front of trenches manned by the 9th Devons, were driven off by Lewis machine gun fire on the night of October 3. Officers and men came under trench mortar and phosphorous bomb attack before they were relieved by the 2nd Gordon Highlanders on October 7 and moved into support areas.

The battalion spent the remainder of October in trenches at Le Touquet and in billets in Pont de Nieppe. Seven men were killed and 19 wounded during the month by snipers, trench mortar and shell fire. Two signallers were buried when a dug-out was 'blown in' on October 31. Only one of them could be rescued.

The 9th Devons spent much of November on the move in northern France – marching to Moolenacker, Wardrecques, Moulle, Tournehem-sur-la-Hem, Quelmes, Delettes, Lisbourg, Humieres, Doullens, Bertrancourt and Mailly-Maillet. By the end of the month, during which one man was killed and eight others wounded, they were in the trenches at Beaumont Hamel, on the Somme.

They were in these trenches, or in billets at Mailly-Maillet, throughout December and in the early days of January 1917. On

New Year's Day, the Germans captured Hope Post – near the Beaumont Hamel-Serre road and defended by the 9th Devons – in a surprise attack just hours after the battalion had taken 21 enemy prisoners.

Four days later, as the battalion moved to Bertrancourt, 50 of their men stayed in the trenches to retake Hope Post – and they managed to win it back at 6.20pm on January 5. Two men were killed in the operation. Three others were reported missing, 'believed killed', and two officers and nine other ranks were wounded.

The 9th Devons remained in Bertrancourt until January 15 when they returned to trenches amid heavy snow. Two men were killed and one wounded by shell fire before they left the front line on January 18. They later marched to Louvencourt and Beauquesne and moved to billets in Halloy-les-Pernois on the last day of the month.

There they stayed until February 16, 1917 when they moved to billets in Beauval on the Somme and later to Puchevillers before returning to Bertrancourt and then Mailly-Maillet. On March 2, the battalion moved into Brigade support at White City, near Beaumont Hamel. Three men were killed and six wounded when 'working parties' were attacked on March 11, and five more men were wounded on March 12 – the day John was discharged from service.

On his honourable discharge for wounds received in service, John was awarded the Silver War Badge, bearing the words: 'For King and Empire – Services Rendered'. John, whose regimental number with the 9th Devons was 15307, received Silver Badge number B81359. He was also awarded the British War and Victory Medals and the 1915 Star.

John and his wife, Edith had four more children between 1917 and 1925 – Herbert Henry, Arthur Ernest, Alfred Thomas and Elsie May. He had been married 23 years when he died in Somerset, aged 46, on December 4, 1929. He was buried at St Mary Magdalene Church cemetery in Sparkford, Somerset. Edith died in Sparkford on August 21, 1976, aged 87.

18

GEORGE — ARTILLERY
VETERAN OF TWO WARS

The bombardment was devastating – the worst Sergeant
George Henry Roberts had experienced in his 17 years
with the Royal Field Artillery. In just four hours, German
gunners fired 70,000 shells deep into British defences, killing
and maiming hundreds of soldiers.

Thirty-eight-year-old George, who had been engaged in
increasingly fierce combat in an area below the enemy-held
Vimy Ridge, near Arras in northern France for almost a month,
was at the sharp end of the blitz.

He was serving 'in the field' with A Battery of 112 Brigade
of the RFA when the barrage – one of the heaviest of the Great
War and preceding a German infantry attack – was launched in
the early hours of May 21, 1916.

The war diary said all four of 112 Brigade's batteries
were 'heavily shelled through the day, causing a great many
casualties'. Men came under attack from tear gas shells and
communication lines were 'continually cut by hostile fire'.

George, who survived the attack, had seen a gradual
escalation in enemy artillery fire since moving into the combat
area 27 days earlier.

Almost daily, his battery had been involved in disruptive
action, firing on enemy front lines, support and communication

trenches and German field guns, and also led 'retaliatory attacks' after trench mortar strikes on British infantrymen.

His battery regularly faced counter-artillery shell fire. The dangers George and his men encountered became all too real when the Germans scored a direct hit on one of their guns on May 3, 1916, killing one man and wounding another.

While war continued to rage on the surface, British and German tunnellers were engaged in a desperate battle underground, setting and blowing mines to destroy infantry positions and to thwart each other's tunnelling activities.

After British troops exploded a series of mines in front of German defences on the Vimy Ridge on May 15, the enemy retaliated with a heavy bombardment – but it was just a prelude to one of the most highly concentrated attacks ever experienced in the area.

A thick cloud of smoke and dust could be seen for miles as the Germans fired those 70,000 shells from 80 field gun batteries on May 21, obliterating trenches and forcing soldiers to fight for their lives with little or no visibility.

George's involvement in the war ended just three days after the attack on Vimy Ridge. He returned home on May 24, 1916, the day after a British counter-attack was halted by heavy German artillery and machine gun fire.

He had arrived in France with 112 Brigade on September 27, 1915, spending the early months 'covering trenches' at Le Bizet, a hamlet on the French-Belgian border, before moving to Villers au Bois in the run up to the Vimy Ridge offensive.

This had been his second campaign on the Western Front. His first was with the British Expeditionary Force (BEF) in a brutal four months in 1914 when he was a gunner with the 118 Battery of 26 Artillery Brigade.

He was 36 when he went to France in August that year. The oldest of John Roberts' grandsons to fight in the Great War, he was also the only one to have experience of armed conflict, having fought in the Second Boer War in South Africa 14 years earlier.

He was not involved in the BEF's first major action of the war, the Battle of Mons on August 23, 1914 when the British faced a formidable German army more than twice its size and with considerably greater artillery fire power.

But as the British were forced to retreat in the aftermath of the battle, he took part in fierce rear-guard actions against the German army as it relentlessly pursued British soldiers in the 'Great Retreat' from the Belgian city to the River Marne in France.

The two-week retreat was widely recognised as one of the most dramatic events of the war, with soldiers showing remarkable courage and endurance in fighting for their lives and marching up to 200 miles to escape the enemy.

On August 27, a section of George's 118 Battery and the 2nd Battalion of the Royal Munster Fusiliers became involved in one of the most extraordinary last stands in British military history, in the area of Oisny and Etreux.

With only two field guns, 40 men led by battery commander Major Abingdon Robert Bayly, fought with the Munsters for 12 hours as they halted the rapid advance of the German army – enabling tens of thousands of British soldiers to withdraw to safety.

When they were finally overwhelmed, in an orchard in Etreux, and forced to surrender, the Munsters had been decimated. About 120 of their officers and men were killed in action and of the hundreds taken prisoner, many were wounded.

Twelve men from 118 Battery were killed. Some were blown up when a shell disabled one of their two field guns. Others were shot when the remaining gun was about to fire on an enemy-occupied house. Major Bayly and 11 others were wounded and were among more than 20 captured.

Many of those killed – including seven from 118 Battery – were buried in the orchard where they had fired their final shots. Known today as the Etreux British Cemetery, it is dominated by a Celtic cross honouring those who died so courageously.

While George did not take part in this last stand, he was almost certainly among two sections of 118 Battery supporting the 1st Battalion of the Black Watch Regiment in a rear-guard action on 'high ground north of Etreux' that same day.

He took part in the follow-up Battles of the Marne and Aisne and in the First Battle of Ypres in October and November 1914, a 35-day offensive that resulted in more British casualties than suffered in the entire Second Boer War.

The Artillery had the most pivotal – and devastating – role on the battlefields of the Western Front. Used to destroy enemy trenches, to halt and break up infantry attacks and to disable 'rival' batteries, artillery guns killed and injured more soldiers than any other weapon during the war.

A team of up to 17 men, led by a sergeant or 'No 1' such as George, operated each field gun. A number of different shells were fired at the enemy, including those filled with high explosive material, shrapnel and poison gas.

Guns were transported by teams of horses or motorised vehicles. Manoeuvring them into safe, out of sight positions was a challenge in difficult terrain, particularly at Ypres where the landscape was transformed into a mud bath in the winter.

The Royal Artillery had up to 550,000 officers and men serving in France and Flanders, Gallipoli, Mesopotamia and other 'theatres of war'. Almost 50,000 were believed to have been killed or wounded between 1914 and 1918.

In the early stages of the war, the British Artillery was frequently outnumbered and out-gunned on the Western Front. A shortage of high-explosive shells caused controversy on the battlefields and a political storm at home.

The war diary for 26 Artillery Brigade for 1914 on two occasions indicated a looming crisis during the First Battle of Ypres. It recorded how, on October 30, there were orders from Divisional Artillery HQ to 'scrutinise ammunition' – on a day the brigade were heavily bombarded by the Germans. On November 4, the brigade were 'ordered to economise ammunition'.

The crisis was so serious in early 1915 that shells were 'rationed' on the British front line. It brought about the downfall of Herbert Asquith's Liberal government, the appointment of Lloyd George as head of a new Ministry of Munitions and the building of many new shell factories across the UK.

George Henry Roberts was born in Puddington, Devon in

1878. Baptised in the local church on September 15 that year, he was the eldest son of William and Eliza (nee Sage) Roberts and lived with his family in nearby Cruwys Morchard in his early years.

He served with the Exeter-based 1st Devon and Somerset Volunteers before joining the Royal Field Artillery in the city on June 13, 1899, at the age of 20. He enlisted in the 'golden age' of the British Empire.

The greatest global power the world had ever seen, the empire included countries from South Africa to India, Australia and New Zealand, and at its zenith covered almost a quarter of the world's entire land area.

He went to South Africa as a gunner in November 1899, a month after the start of the Second Boer War. He spent almost seven months in the Cape Colony as the British Army fought to relieve besieged garrisons.

The Boers invaded northern Natal, besieging the town of Ladysmith for 118 days. Thousands of Boer troops also invaded Cape Colony, many of them laying siege to the British garrison in Mafeking for a total of 217 days.

Although greatly outnumbered, the garrison withstood the siege. A second British garrison in Cape Colony, at Kimberley, was surrounded by thousands of Boer troops but it too survived a siege lasting 124 days.

He was among hundreds of soldiers from Devon who fought in South Africa. The 1st and 2nd Battalions of the Devonshire Regiment were involved in some of the most brutal clashes of the war, which ended in May 1902.

Crediton-born General Sir Redvers Henry Buller, who was awarded the Victoria Cross for gallantry fighting against the Zulus in 1879, was Commander-in-Chief of British forces in South Africa during the early part of the war.

And a senior officer from Exeter, Lieutenant-Colonel Robert George Kekewich, was feted as 'The Defender of Kimberley' when he was in command of the garrison in the town as it was besieged by the Boers between October 14, 1899 and February 15, 1900.

The 1st Battalion of the Devonshire Regiment are forever

remembered for their heroic bayonet charge in the Battle of Wagon Hill – a key area on the perimeter of the town of Ladysmith in Natal – in a blinding hail storm on January 6, 1900.

They routed Boers firing at them at close range from a well defended ridge. Three of the Devons' five officers and 14 other ranks were killed. Another 25 were wounded in an attack praised not only by the commander of the Ladysmith garrison, Sir George White, but also by Queen Victoria.

The 2nd Battalion of the Devonshire Regiment, who suffered heavy losses in the battle at Colenso, on the bank of the Tugela River in Natal in December 1899, were among the troops involved in the relief of Ladysmith on February 27, 1900.

George left South Africa on June 3, 1900. Just over three years later, on November 8, 1903, at the age of 25, he married Nora Maria Wilson, the daughter of a former colour sergeant in the Royal Irish Regiment, at the Roman Catholic Church of Our Most Holy Redeemer in Chelsea, London.

He and his wife were trained as tailors. Before joining the RFA, he had completed a six-year apprenticeship as a tailor for a family business at Thorverton in Devon. He continued his trade within the RFA and eventually qualified as a master tailor.

George and Nora had six children – one dying in infancy – between 1904 and 1915. Two of their daughters, Ena Bridilia Elizabeth and Hilda Lilian, were born in India, in Bareilly and Ranilet, when George served there with the RFA between December 1905 and March 1909.

He was posted to 16 Brigade of the RFA later that year. In 1911, he was based at the Royal Field Artillery Barracks in Woolwich. His wife was living in married quarters there with their then four children, Nora, Ena, Hilda and Ernest.

Appointed Assistant Bombardier in May that year, George joined 118 Battery of 26 Royal Artillery Brigade in 1914. He sailed with the British Expeditionary Force from Southampton to Boulogne in France on August 16, 1914 on *HMS Cardiganshire*, and was initially based in billets in Boue, in the Aisne region.

The war diary for 26 Brigade shows that on August 23, as the

Battle of Mons raged, he was in the village of Grand-Reng, just over 11 miles from the Belgian town. He later moved to Villers-Sire-Nicole, La Longueville and Fesmy-le-Sart as the 'Great Retreat' began.

He was promoted to Bombardier on August 27, the day of the rear-guard action at Etreux. The war diary did not record the heroics of 118's actions in supporting the Munsters. It only reported that two officers and 40 men were 'missing' – and that 'they did not re-join' battery bivouacs that night.

George marched to Vauxbuin, a village near Soissons, on August 31 and moved on to La Ferte-Milon, La Ferte-sous-Jouarre and Nesle before advancing with 26 Brigade to Puisseax in northern France on September 6.

His battery were 'in action' south of Bellot – during the Battle of the Marne – on September 8, 1914. They later advanced to Latilly, Bazoches-sur-Vesles and were 'in action' in Paissy in the early hours of September 14, as the First Battle of Aisne got under way.

It was here, at Aisne, that all hopes of a swift end to the war were dashed. The 16-day battle marked the finale of mobile warfare on the Western Front and the dawn of gruelling, internecine trench warfare which would continue until 1918.

George and his men 'engaged' with enemy artillery on September 14 at the Chemin des Dames, an area between the valleys of the rivers Aisne and Ailette. They came under heavy howitzer fire in the following days, and had one gun disabled and four men wounded in an attack on September 22.

The offensives took their toll on 26 Brigade. Including 116, 117 and 118 Batteries, and under the command of the British Army's 1st Division, 13 of their officers and men were killed (three from 118 Battery) in September, and 45 were wounded (seven from 118 Battery).

By the end of the month and through to October 13, 26 Brigade were in Pargnan, Aisne. One of 118 Battery's men was killed while two field guns were in entrenched positions to the west of the community.

Another man was killed on October 14 during a march to Loupeigne. Two days later, George and his men were on a train from Fere-en-Tardenois to the Flanders town of Hazebrouck in readiness for the First Battle of Ypres.

After marches to Poperinge and Elverdinge, 118 Battery were firing against the German infantry on October 21 near Langemarck. One officer was wounded in counter-attacks which led to field guns being withdrawn to Pilkem.

The following day, the battery launched an attack on German field guns near Mangelaare. They later withdrew to a position west of Pilkem in the face of a strong enemy fire before targeting the German infantry.

After two more days of fighting in this area, George and his men marched to the village of Zillebeke. Between October 27 and 29, 118 Battery fired on German trenches and field guns at Zuidhoek and Becalaere, with the help of aeroplane reconnaissance.

An officer was wounded in fierce exchanges on October 29 as the Germans launched an attack on British trenches. The following day, 11 men of 118 Battery were wounded as they came under heavy howitzer fire, the war diary reported.

As the battle raged on, the battery covered the retreat of British soldiers shelled out of their trenches at Zillebeke on October 31. Casualties continued to mount with three officers and men from 26 Brigade killed (one from 118 Battery) and 28 wounded.

Two of George's fellow soldiers were wounded on November 1 and 2 as they fired on enemy field guns and trenches near Zanvoorde. Another six were wounded and two men were listed as missing as they fired on enemy soldiers massing in a wood near Gheluvelt on November 3.

118 Battery were withdrawn to Dickebusch the following day and later marched to Hazebrouck and then Vlamertinghe, near Ypres. After carrying out further artillery attacks on enemy trenches and infantry, they moved to billets in Strazeele, in northern France, on November 21.

George left France on December 9, 1914 to return home. It would be more than nine months before he went back to the Western Front, this time with 112 Brigade, under the command of the British Army's 25th Division.

Promoted to Sergeant in July 1915, he sailed from Southampton to Le Havre, arriving in the French port at the end of September that year.

His A Battery defended trenches in the Le Bizet area from October 1 through to the end of January 1916. They then moved to a rest area near Caestre before marching to Berguette on March 10 and then to the small farming village of Averdoingt for training.

From April 25, 1916, George and his men were 'in the field' at Villers au Bois. In the following days, they fired on enemy front line, communication and support trenches and were regularly heavily shelled in German counter-attacks.

There was little respite from enemy fire in the run-up to the German attack at Vimy Ridge on May 21. Thousands of shells were fired at German lines during the month – with particular emphasis being put on destroying 'troublesome' trench mortar batteries.

When he finally left the battlefields of France and Flanders, he was posted to the home-based RFA's 5C Reserve Brigade on May 25, 1916. In early June that year, he was attached to the RFA's 326 (Territorial Force) Brigade.

George stayed with this brigade until he left the RFA on August 10, 1920, having completed 21 years and 59 days' service. He and his family lived in Littlemore in Oxfordshire for many years and he worked at the now closed Littlemore Hospital in his later years.

George – who was a qualified shoesmith as well as a master tailor in the RFA – died on November 18, 1946, aged 68, after accidentally falling from a bicycle. His wife, Nora, died in Littlemore on May 26, 1948, aged 69.

He was awarded medals from two wars. He received the Queen's South Africa Medal and Cape Colony Clasp for his service in the Boer War. For his service in the Great War, he was awarded the British War and Victory Medals and the 1914 Star. His RFA regimental number was 73.

Notes

- A statue of General Sir Redvers Henry Buller was unveiled in Exeter on September 6, 1905. He was among the many thousands attending the ceremony. After his death in 1908, he was buried in the churchyard of Crediton's Holy Cross Church. A memorial to the general was unveiled at the church on the third anniversary of his death, on June 2, 1911.

- Lt-Col (later Major-General) Robert George Kekewich died on November 5, 1914. He was buried in St Martin's Churchyard, Exminster. A memorial to the 'Defender of Kimberley' was unveiled in Exeter Cathedral.

19

WILLIAM JOHN — NAVAL STOKER WHO SURVIVED TORPEDO ATTACK

HMS *King Alfred* was close to completing her journey across the Atlantic – convoying food ships from Halifax in Nova Scotia, Canada to Glasgow – when, suddenly, she came under threat from a torpedo fired by a German U-boat.

Desperate, last-minute attempts to avoid the torpedo failed and the 14,000-ton armoured cruiser was struck on her port quarter, between the stern and midships, off Northern Ireland at 7.20am on April 11, 1918.

Her crew included Tiverton-born Stoker William John Roberts, who was just 18 years old. He had served on *King Alfred* for almost eight months when she came under attack 30 miles north of Malin Head, on the Inishowen Peninsula, County Donegal.

William survived the attack, but one of his fellow stokers, 30-year-old Nestor Wareing, of Wigan, Lancashire, was killed. He was the only casualty in the strike, the first and only attack on *King Alfred* during the Great War.

The 550ft long ship anchored in Belfast Lough, a large sea inlet on the east coast of Northern Ireland, later that day as divers examined the damage caused by the torpedo. On April

12, many of the 900 men on board helped to pump and bail water out of the vessel.

They later assisted with clearing away wreckage and with salvage operations before the vessel headed to Liverpool where, on April 30, the remains of Stoker I Class Wareing were recovered. He was later buried in Bootle Cemetery, on Merseyside.

King Alfred was successfully repaired and returned to service. But William did not return to the ship. He instead was transferred to *HMS Vivid*, the Navy barracks at Devonport, Plymouth before going on to serve in *HMS Bellona*, a Royal Navy 'mine layer'.

The submarine that attacked *King Alfred* was U-boat 86, commissioned in November 1917 and skippered by Hans Trenk. Between February and August 1918, the U-boat sank four other ships and damaged another off the British coast.

The Royal Navy log book for *King Alfred* – published on Naval-History.net – shows that on April 11, 1918, the ship was en-route from Halifax to Glasgow and was positioned off Rathlin Island in the early hours.

Zig-zagging – to avoid submarines – started at 5.10am and at 7.19am, the 'track' of a torpedo was sighted on the port beam. The ship 'went hard starboard' to try and avoid the missile but was struck on the port quarter a minute later, while the starboard engine was at 'full speed'.

Just after 9am, Oversay Island was sighted and many of the men on board were employed on 'shoring up damage' to the vessel. At 12.30pm, *King Alfred* 'parted company' from the convoy she was escorting, and anchored in Belfast Lough at 3.20pm.

Captain of the armoured cruiser was John Garnet Armstrong. Also on board at the time of the attack was Commander William John Persse, who received an 'expression of appreciation' from the Lords of the Admiralty for the part he played in saving the ship.

U-boat 86 torpedoed and sank the Swedish steamer *Mercia* 85 miles east of Peterhead on February 21, 1918. Seven days after attacking *King Alfred*, it sank the British steamer

Gregynog 16 miles south west of Hartland Point.

The U-boat torpedoed two vessels off Cornwall on August 17, the British steamer *Denebola* and the Danish steamer *Helene*. And it damaged the British steamer *Charity* in its final attack, off Hartland Point, on August 19, 1918.

Records for U-boat 86 – published by Uboat.net – show that it surrendered on November 24, 1918, 13 days after the end of the war. After grounding near Falmouth, the submarine, along with a number of other U-boats, was broken up 'in situ' in 1921.

King Alfred was one of seven ships attacked by U-boats on April 11, 1918. In that month alone, German submarines sank 39 ships and damaged 28 others. More than 1,600 vessels were attacked or struck mines in 1918, and more than 3,700 were sunk or damaged in the previous year.

The U-boat attacks – disrupting major trade routes around the British Isles and in the Mediterranean – wrought havoc, particularly between 1916 and 1918, and killed many thousands of men, women and children.

William joined the Royal Navy on May 25, 1917, eight days after his 18th birthday. He served as a Stoker II Class and was based at *HMS Vivid II*, the stokers and engine room artificers school, at Devonport, until August 8, 1917.

A day later, he joined *HMS King Alfred*. First launched in 1901, the Drake class armoured cruiser regularly escorted food ships in convoys from Dakar in Senegal, West Africa and Halifax in Nova Scotia to Britain in 1917 and 1918.

The ship had two four-cylinder triple expansion steam engines, powered by 43 Belleville boilers. Carrying up to 2,500 tons of coal, she could travel 12,500 miles, at a cruising speed of 14 knots, before needing to be refuelled.

As a stoker, regularly working in temperatures of more than 100 degrees under the ship's water line, William would have been at the greatest risk of death or serious injury when a torpedo was fired at the 35-gun *King Alfred*.

With furnaces roaring and acrid coal dust filling the air around him, he would have worked as a trimmer, bringing coal from the ship's bunkers to the boilers in wheelbarrows, or as a fireman, shovelling coal into the boiler fireboxes.

His was a back-breaking and frequently dangerous task without the threat of submarine attack – a hazard he and his fellow stokers had to live with every day they were at sea in warships and other vessels.

Thousands of stokers were killed or injured between 1914 and 1918. Of the 6,000 British officers and men killed in the Battle of Jutland, the largest naval confrontation of the Great War, a third of them were stokers.

Fourteen British and 11 German warships were sunk and many more were damaged in the battle which was fought over 36 hours in the North Sea, off Denmark's Jutland peninsula, between May 31 and June 1, 1916.

Hundreds of stokers were among the 1,266 crewmen who perished when the battlecruiser *HMS Queen Mary* exploded and sank after being twice hit by shell fire from the German warship *SMS Derfflinger*. Almost 400 stokers died when the battlecruiser *Indefatigable* exploded and sank after being hit by the German warship *Von der Tann*. More than 300 were killed when *HMS Invincible* was destroyed in the battle.

Another 500 stokers of all ranks – from 1st and 2nd class to leading stokers, petty officers and chief stokers – died when the armoured cruisers *HMS Black Prince*, *HMS Defence* and *HMS Shark* were sunk. And 200 were killed when the destroyers *HMS Tipperary*, *HMS Ardent*, *HMS Turbulent* and *HMS Fortune* were sunk, and the battlecruiser *HMS Lion* and the armoured cruiser *HMS Warrior* were badly damaged by shell fire.

When the armoured cruiser *HMS Drake* was torpedoed off Northern Ireland on October 2, 1917, 16 of the 18 crewmen killed were stokers. Ten of the 15 men who died when *HMS Cornwallis* was sunk in the Mediterranean in a torpedo attack in January 1917 were stokers. More than 30 of the 523 men who died when the British cruiser *HMS Hawke* was torpedoed in the North Sea on October 15, 1914 were stokers, all from Ulster.

A surviving stoker from *HMS Hawke* recalled: '*Those on deck for an instant immediately after the explosion saw the periscope of a submarine which showed above the water like a broomstick. The Hawke was holed above the engine room and commenced to cant over to starboard with alarming rapidity. Her plates were twisted and torn and a huge gap was rent in her side.*

'*An attempt to man the guns was made but owing to the extra acute list of the vessel it was found impossible to train them on the submerged craft. The horror of the situation was added to when a tank of oil fuel caught fire and the flames advanced with fatal rapidity. Seeing there was not the ghost of a chance of doing any good by remaining in what was obviously a death trap, I determined to make a dash for it. I scrambled precipitately up the iron ladder to the main deck. All this had happened in less time than it takes to tell.*'

Torpedoes and shells were not the only hazards on board a ship. In April 1914, at Chatham Dockyard, Kent, three stokers, including a petty officer, were killed after a boiler tube burst in the destroyer *HMS Albacore*. Four stokers were severely scalded by escaping steam after a boiler explosion on the French battleship *Gaulois* in Toulon harbour in January 1914. A 20-year-old stoker from Okehampton, Devon drowned in 1915 after being washed overboard while serving on *HMS Titania*. And a stoker serving on *HMS Galatea* was thrown overboard and died after stepping on a piece of galvanised iron on the deck of the ship in March 1915.

Although stokers faced a high risk of death or injury, a stoker born in Kingsbridge, Devon became one of the last surviving veterans of the Great War. 'Bill' Stone, who enlisted in the Royal Navy when he was 18 in September 1918, and trained in Plymouth, died in 1909 at the grand old age of 108. He served on *HMS Tiger* just after the war ended and served on the minesweeper *HMS Salamander* and the cruiser *HMS Newfoundland* in the Second World War.

William was born in Bolham, Tiverton on May 17, 1899. The second son of Walter and Helena (nee Cook) Roberts, he may well have been the only one of John Roberts's grandsons to have served in the Royal Navy during the Great War.

He was born in the same year as American gangster Al Capone, actors James Cagney, Humphrey Bogart, Charles Laughton and Fred Astaire, jazz musician Duke Ellington, film director Alfred Hitchcock, novelist C S Forester and playwright and composer Noel Coward.

1899 marked the start of the Second Boer War in which William's first cousin, George Henry Roberts, served with the Royal Field Artillery. It also saw the school leaving age for children in England and Wales raised from 11 to 12.

An extraordinary lifeboat launch from Porlock Weir to rescue the crew of a ship in distress in the Bristol Channel took place on January 12 and 13 that year. Lynmouth Lifeboat was called into action when the three-masted *Forrest Hall* hit trouble in hurricane-force winds.

The stormy weather prevented the lifeboat, *Louisa*, being launched from Lynmouth harbour. Instead, she was taken overland on a hazardous journey to Porlock Weir, with the help of a team of 15 horses and up to 100 'willing helpers'.

The 'stupendously difficult' trek, via 'one of the worst roads in the country', and in darkness, took nine hours to complete. The lifeboatmen then rowed through appalling weather to reach the *Forrest Hall*, and helped to navigate her to safer waters.

In 1901, William lived with his family – father William, a farm worker, mother Helena, and his four-year-old brother Sidney – at Horn Road, Kentisbeare in Devon. Educated at Cruwys Morchard School, he enlisted in the Navy while working as a farm labourer.

He joined *HMS King Alfred* at Devonport's No 8 Dock on August 9, 1917. Ammunition was loaded on to the ship between August 14 and 16 and coal on the following two days. Thirty-eight bags of coal were 'lost overboard' during this period.

The Royal Navy log book for the vessel shows that she left Plymouth on August 22 for Dakar along with the destroyers *HMS Lance* and *HMS Acheron*. The destroyers 'parted company' the following day and *King Alfred* arrived in Dakar on August 31, hours before a tornado and heavy rain.

Captain Armstrong joined the ship in Dakar on September 1, before she escorted a convoy to Plymouth on September 14, arriving in Devonport two weeks later. *King Alfred* led another convoy to and from Dakar in October.

She escorted ships to and from Sierre Leone in November and December 1917. Cargo brought back to the Westcountry in

December included gold bullion from South and West Africa and mail from 'naval and military authorities'.

William spent Christmas and early January in Devonport. He and the *King Alfred* led convoys to and from new destinations in January, February, March and April 1918 – Halifax, Nova Scotia to the River Clyde in Glasgow, Scotland.

On February 18, en route to the Clyde and a week away from Glasgow, the ship was taking in water in heavy seas in a Force 10 storm. Hand and motor pumps were used to help remove the water which damaged stores.

In the days before the submarine attack in April 1918, ships leaving Halifax with *King Alfred* included *RMS Carmania*, an armed merchant cruiser, *SS Megantic*, an ocean liner used as a troop ship and *SS Ceramic*, an ocean liner also used as a troop ship.

William spent 24 days at the Navy barracks at Devonport before joining *HMS Bellona*, on May 28, 1918. The scout cruiser was converted into a 'mine layer' – deploying explosive mines to protect British shipping – in 1917.

William, whose service number was K42894, was promoted to Stoker I Class on July 20, 1918. His Royal Navy service – for which he was paid a war gratuity – ended on March 12, 1919, when he was 19 years old. He was awarded the Victory and British War Medals.

After the war, *HMS King Alfred*, at one stage one of the mightiest cruisers in the British Navy, was sold for scrap. *HMS Bellona*, after placing hundreds of explosive mines during the war, was also broken up for scrap.

William returned to farm work, at Cove, near Tiverton. In May 1920, he and farmer Frederick Hill, of the Mid-Devon hamlet of Clayhanger were, according to a report in *The Western Times*, each fined 7s and 6d at the Tiverton County Sessions for riding bicycles without lights.

Sadly, I have been unable to find out what happened to William after 1920.

20

THOMAS — TWICE SAVED FROM FIGHTING IN THE WAR

He was the man who missed the war — not once, but twice. And for two different reasons. Just one day after Britain declared war on Germany, Thomas Roberts was found to be 'medically unfit' for service. When he was called up almost four years later, in 1918, the war was over when he was sent to Italy to serve with the 8th Devons.

His parents would be eternally grateful that he never ended up in the firing line. For Thomas's younger brother, 19-year-old Albert, died from wounds he sustained in France in October 1915. And his older brother, Frank, miraculously escaped death when he was shot in the head in fierce fighting in Palestine in 1917.

Thomas, while working on his father's farm in Witheridge, Devon, followed in Frank's footsteps in joining the Royal 1st Devon Yeomanry in February 1913, when he was 19. After a year and 169 days as a private in the territorial regiment's A Squadron, he was discharged on August 5, 1914 after being declared 'medically unfit' to serve.

His service records do not explain the rationale behind the decision. They only show that the discharge was approved in Exeter by Thomas's senior officer, Captain Wilfred Peek, the 3rd Baronet of Rousdon, who was Devon's High Sheriff in 1912 and who went on to fight with the regiment in Mesopotamia.

In the final stages of the war, and as Britain faced a shortage of soldiers on the front line, Thomas was called up in June 1918 to serve in the Royal Warwickshire Regiment. Initially posted to the 3rd Devons, he went to Italy in November that year, arriving several days after fighting had come to an end. Transferred to the 8th Devons on reaching the country, he remained in Italy until April 1919.

Although he never had to fire a shot in anger, Thomas was declared fit to go to war. When he was medically examined in Exeter in June 1918, he was listed under medical category A1 (i.e. that he was 'able to march, see to shoot, hear well and stand active service conditions' and was physically and mentally fit for 'despatching overseas' and training).

The reasons behind his discharge in 1914 may well have been resolved by the time he was called up. But after 1916, when conscription was introduced, there was huge controversy over the way that some rejected and discharged men said to be 'entirely unsuitable' for military service were being called up after medical re-examinations.

William Pringle, Liberal MP for Lanarkshire North West, told the House of Commons in 1917 that it was a scandal that re-examinations had been carried out in a 'harsh, cruel, unfair and wasteful way' with totally unfit men being drafted into the Army. He contended the 'halt, the blind, the mute, and the mad', were being called up.

He claimed the sick, wounded and maimed were being forced into the Army, some suffering from tuberculosis, valvular heart disease and epilepsy. Some men, he said, were 'sworn at and bullied by recruiting officers and marshalled like convicts' and had medical certificates outlining their conditions 'torn up in their faces'.

Philip Snowden, the Labour MP for Blackburn revealed the story of a man with no fingers on his right hand, and suffering from a rupture, who was passed for garrison duty abroad. 'The man was born like that … He has been quite unable to handle a rifle or to take part in the ordinary work of the Army,' he told Parliament in March 1917.

He outlined the tragic case of a young man with a history of suffering from pneumonia, pleurisy and congestion of the lungs, who was called up. He became seriously ill while on guard duty and had to walk two miles to a doctor and wait 2½ hours to be examined. He was admitted to hospital and died three days later.

'I really do not know why the War Office … appear to be so anxious to take men into the Army who can be no more than an expense to the country and certainly of no military value,' said Mr Snowden. 'The only explanation is that the War Office is obsessed by the idea of getting a paper army, and they think if they put these men on the strength that some useful purpose will be served.

'I am convinced, from the number of cases that have been brought to my own personal knowledge, that there must be at least a couple of hundred thousand, probably more, of men in the Army who are physically quite unfit for any military duty and who would be rendering far more useful and necessary service in this time of national crisis if they were permitted to go back to their occupation.'

Mr Ian MacPherson, Under-Secretary of State for War, said 'the Army we have at the present moment is a very large one indeed, recruited from all classes of the community'. About 1.5 million men had been examined in a comparatively short time and it would be 'exceedingly surprising if out of such a very large number of cases some mistakes had not been made'.

In the early stages of the war, many men had been rejected on 'the cursory inspection of recruiting sergeants'. It was calculated that re-examinations would secure 60,000 'A' recruits and 60,000 in lower categories. Many men were required for work behind the trenches, he said, and 'practically every man who was sufficiently fit to earn a living in a civil capacity could be usefully employed in the Army'.

An extraordinary letter, said to have been addressed to the deputy directors of medical services in 1915 by Lieutenant-General Sir Alfred Henry Keogh, the Director General of Army Medical Services during the Great War, was read at a Parliamentary Select Committee on Medical Re-examination hearing in July 1917 by the chairman, Edward Shortt, the Liberal MP for Newcastle.

The letter said: 'I want you to regard what I say as confidential. It is imperative for you to get as many men as possible, not fit for war service, put into the category as fit for garrison duty abroad. We have so many civilian medical men working with us that you will have to be very strong in your action as regards the acceptance of their opinion when they reject men as unfit for garrison duty abroad.'

The letter went on to say that only very severe disabilities should be regarded as rendering men unfit, and that all disabilities which in peace time they had been accustomed to consider should 'go to the wall'. It concluded: 'Take it upon yourself to overrule decisions which place men in categories unfit for garrison duty abroad ...'

Surgeon-General William George Birrell, Deputy Director of Medical Services of the British Army's Southern Command, appearing as a witness before the select committee, said he had never heard of that letter. Edward Shortt then read further correspondence sent by Lt-Gen Keogh to deputy directors in September 1916.

It stated: 'Please issue orders to Medical Boards in your command not to reject totally any man who can perform any kind of work without danger to himself or to others. Every man who can earn a livelihood in civil life can do something in the Army, and it is perfectly ridiculous this large number of rejections in each command. Will you please stop it at once?'

According to a report on the select committee hearing – published in *The Devon and Exeter Gazette* in July 1917 – Surgeon-General Birrell said that, in response to this particular plea from Lt-Gen Keogh, he sent a telegram instructing that no man must be rejected who was fit to do any work in the Army.

Military service tribunals in Devon, established in town and rural areas between 1916 and 1918 to hear formal requests for exemption from conscription into the Army, considered – and in numerous instances rejected – applications from men suffering from heart and other serious conditions and producing medical proof of their poor health.

Many of these rejections were upheld on appeal, including one from Yelverton grocer and postmaster Leonard Stone who, according to a report in *The Western Morning News* in July 1916, had asked for 'total exemption' after producing a certificate from his doctor that he was suffering from valvular heart disease.

An appeal by 23-year-old surveyor Reginald Worth against a decision by the Calstock tribunal to refuse him exemption, was told that he would be 'useless for the Army' because he was suffering from valvular heart disease which, according to *The Western Morning News* in September 1917 was 'certified by two eminent physicians'. Reginald's plea for a medical re-examination was refused.

South Molton Rural Tribunal, however, took pity on a Chulmleigh mother who applied for exemption on behalf of her son, William Henry Chard, 26, who suffered from heart disease. According to *The Western Times* in March 1916, she had lost one son in the war, another had been wounded and a third had been called up. She was told that her family had 'done very well' and her son was exempted.

Heart disease claimed many lives in the war. Thomas Roberts' cousin William Henry Kingdom, died from it while on service in Mesopotamia in 1916, although there was no evidence that he was suffering from it when he first joined the 1/4th Battalion of the Devonshire Regiment in 1914 and in the months leading up to his death.

Before the war, nearly 500 men a year were invalided from the Army because of valvular heart disease or heart strain, according to a report in *The Western Morning News and Mercury* in September 1923. During and after the war, there were accusations that, in some cases, Army service had brought about the deaths of soldiers with serious heart and other health problems.

In 1921, a Court of the House of Lords Pension Appeal Tribunal, sitting in Exeter, was told of a wheelwright from Heavitree who joined the Royal Engineers as a sapper in April 1915. Sent to France in August that year, the man – who was not named – was twice admitted to hospital suffering from rheumatism caused by lying in wet clothes.

A report in *The Western Times* said that, on one occasion, he was transferred to an Army base 'suffering from rheumatism all over the body'. He was kept there for 12 months before returning to England as 'unfit for further duty in France'. He was invalided out of the Army in February 1919.

He died from a cerebral haemorrhage in March 1921. His widow – appealing on behalf of herself and four dependant children for a pension – based her claim 'on the fact that death was brought about through service in the Army'. A surgeon, Mr C E Bell, gave evidence to the tribunal that death was 'clearly due to military service'.

The widow, according to the report in *The Western Times*, said her husband had 'never had a day's illness before serving in France'. His duties included 'fixing up wire entanglements' which involved lying 'about in the wet'. After he was invalided from the Army, he was unable to do a proper day's work. He complained of pains in the back and of giddiness, but he would never consult a doctor.

An inspector with the Exeter City Police told the hearing that the man – who, on being invalided out of the Army, had been granted a disability pension because of his rheumatism and valvular heart disease – was 'robust' when he joined the Army. He was a 'perfect wreck when he demobilised, and his condition rapidly deteriorated'.

In an important judgment, the court, told that the man had twice had his pension increased in 1920, found that his death was due to cerebral haemorrhage aggravated by military service. It also concluded he had a 'continuous medical history'. His widow was consequently informed that her appeal was successful.

Thomas was born at Blindwell, Rackenford on July 22, 1893. The second eldest son of Thomas and Mary Ann (nee Morrish) Roberts, he grew up on Newland Farm, Witheridge, working with his father and brothers, Frank and Albert. The 1911 Census return shows that, in the early part of the year, aged 17, he was working as a carter on the farm.

When he joined the Royal 1st Devon Yeomanry, he was examined on February 18, 1913 by a medical officer in

Witheridge who declared him fit for service, having found that 'he does not present any of the causes of rejection specified in the regulations'. The doctor said he could 'see at the required distance with either eye, his heart and lungs are healthy' and he had 'free use of his joints and limbs'.

Thomas, who joined the regiment's Thorverton-based A Squadron, underwent 17 days' training at the Army's Hamilton Camp on Salisbury Plain in May 1913 and 14 days' training in Bovey Tracey, Devon in May and June 1914. He was discharged on August 5, 1914 after being declared 'medically unfit' to continue serving.

He worked on his father's farm until called up by the Army in June 1918. He officially enlisted in the Royal Warwickshire Regiment in Exeter, a month short of his 25th birthday and was posted to the 3rd Devons at Devonport on June 28. He was posted to the British Expeditionary Force in Italy on November 6, 1918, serving as a private.

Thomas sailed from Southampton that day to Le Havre in France and arrived in Arquata, Italy just over a week later. He was transferred to the 8th Devons, joining the battalion at the end of the month. The battalion's fighting days were over by the time he arrived, thanks to an Armistice in early November ending the war with Austria-Hungary on the Italian front.

When the Armistice came into force, the 8th Devons were in Cisterna, about four miles east of Gradisca. They later moved to the town of Orgiano and here, Thomas remained with the battalion until the end of February, taking part in athletics events, 'educational training and occasional ceremonial and manual drill'.

He was transferred to the 1/7th Battalion of the Royal Warwickshire Regiment in February 1919 and returned to the UK for demobilisation in April that year. Of his total service of 325 days with the 3rd and 8th Devons and 1/7th Royal Warwickshires, he spent 165 days in Italy. He left with a specialist military qualification – musketry 1st class.

In the final months of the war, a new and deadly enemy emerged. An influenza, or 'Spanish Flu' pandemic killed between 20 and 50 million people worldwide in 1918 and 1919, including more than 200,000 in Britain. Many soldiers serving in France, Italy and elsewhere fell victim to the virus – and men returning home from the trenches were thought to be responsible for its spread across the UK.

Men from the 8th and 9th Devons were among the hundreds of thousands who died in Italy from the flu, including Private Fred Blackmore, aged 27, of Chudleigh. Tragedy struck an officer, 2nd Lieutenant P G Handford, when his wife died from pneumonia in Torbay and he was unable to attend her funeral because he was on active duty in Italy.

In Devon, many schools were closed for long periods during the flu outbreak. In some areas, to try and contain the virus, theatres, music halls, cinemas and other places of entertainment were placed 'out of bounds' to troops. In October 1918, sickness was said to be 'rampant' in Exeter and Plymouth, where dozens of fatalities were recorded over a period of weeks.

Among the victims in France was North Devon war hero Lieutenant George Raymond Dallas Moor, who was awarded the Victoria Cross for 'conspicuous gallantry' while fighting the Turks in the Dardanelles in 1915. Lt Moor, whose mother lived in Braunton, near Barnstaple, was described by senior officers as 'one of the bravest men of the war'.

The Rector of Rackenford, the Rev G J Lester died from flu in France a month after arriving there as an Army chaplain. Crediton Private Leslie Harold Stemson, of the 3rd Battalion the Machine Gun Corps, who survived the war in Mesopotamia, Egypt and France and being in a ship torpedoed by a German U-boat, died from pneumonia after suffering from flu in November 1918.

A report in *The Western Times* in February 1919 said the death of Exeter Corporal Harold Street, of the 7th Queen's Own Hussars, was a 'piquant illustration of the irony of fate'. He joined the Army in 1908, 'escaped all the perils of war and looked none the worse for his two years of hard fighting in Mesopotamia'. He then contracted double pneumonia, almost certainly caused by the flu, and died.

Thomas married Beatrice Mary Boundy at Rackenford Parish Church on January 3, 1923. A dairyman, living at Mill

Barton, George Nympton, in North Devon, he was 27 at the time. Beatrice, one of 13 children of Frederick and Cora Boundy, of Mogworthy Farm, Rackenford, was 26. Their wedding was recorded in *The Western Times* of January 12 that year. The newspaper reported that Beatrice was given away by her brother, Harvey. The bridesmaids were her sister, Phyllis and Thomas's sister, also called Beatrice. Thomas's brother, Reuben, was among the witnesses.

Thomas and Beatrice had a daughter, Joyce Mary Ann, who was born in George Nympton on June 15, 1923. She married Albert Cole in 1946. Thomas died from a brain haemorrhage and hypertension on April 4, 1966 at 51, High Street, North Tawton, aged 72. He left £3,378 in his will, with probate being granted to his brother, Reuben and solicitor, William James Hallett. Beatrice died in London in 1972, aged 76.

Thomas's regimental numbers were: Royal 1st Devon Yeomanry (2170); Devonshire and Royal Warwickshire Regiments (78753 and 55271). He received the British War and Victory Medals.

21

GEORGE BURNETT — ONE OF THE GREAT UNSUNG HEROES OF THE WAR

He was just 17 when he went quietly to war. There were no 'farewell' fanfares or cheering crowds for farm worker George Burnett Roberts when he sailed to France just before Christmas in 1915 to join the 'forgotten army' on the Western Front – the Army Service Corps.

George wasn't there to fight with a rifle and bayonet. Instead, as a dedicated and hard-working horse transport driver, he became one of the great unsung heroes of the war, playing a pivotal role in helping to keep the British Army on the move and able to sustain a long, hard and brutal campaign against the Germans.

He worked long hours, frequently in the face of enemy shell and other fire, to supply food for the infantry and cavalry and forage for the war horses. There was little glory in – or praise for – the tasks he performed behind the firing line. But they would prove to be as valuable as any cavalry or infantry charge in winning the war.

George was my grandfather. He survived the travails of France, hardly ever talking about his exploits. He occasionally spoke to my father, Sydney, about the awful things he had seen – from decomposing and mutilated bodies of British soldiers in mud and water-filled trenches to men who had become friends being killed or seriously wounded.

He told of how a horse-drawn wagon he was driving almost disappeared in a 'sea of mud' when a wheel was smashed by a large stone on the edge of a shell-damaged road. And of the day a shell exploded, killing three of his horses and wounding two men with whom he had been working, while he was taking a 'comfort break'.

He considered himself 'fortunate' to return home. 'He couldn't wait to get back to what he knew best, farming,' his son and my father told me. 'He believed the war took years off his life. He was only just over 20 when he came home but he looked so much older than his years. The war took its toll on him like so many others.'

George, a horse transport driver in the ASC, was attached to the British First Army which was heavily involved in many of the key offensives of the war, including the Battles of Arras in 1917 and 1918, attacks on the formidable German defences of the Hindenburg Line and the advances in Artois and Picardy in the days leading up to the Armistice.

Joining the Army Service Corps (ASC) was wrongly and unfairly dismissed by many as a 'soft option'. The ASC suffered huge losses between 1914 and 1919. Of the 280 officers and 8,187 warrant officers, NCOs and men who lost their lives, more than 1,000 were killed in action and more than 5,000 died from disease or in accidents.

Although operating behind the front or firing lines, men like George had to work under the constant threat of hostile fire. Their supply routes, depots and resting places of their horses were regularly targeted by the German artillery in attempts to disrupt and halt the progress of the British and Allied Forces' war machine.

Articles, letters and poems published in newspapers regularly referred to the 'excellent' and 'gallant 'work' performed by the men of the horse transport companies – and 'seldom or never mentioned' in official reports by many commanding officers, an omission which created much rancour among serving and former soldiers.

A 'military expert' writing in the *St Andrews Citizen* in March 1916, said no day ever passed without the ASC having to achieve, through intense effort, something 'closely allied to the miraculous'. He argued that their motto, *Nil Sine Labor* – Nothing Without Labour – could not have been more appropriate.

'There is of course, no branch of the Army that is useless, but there are certainly some branches whose usefulness in war time is of inestimable value. Among the latter, the ASC are entitled to a leading place,' he wrote. Their duties made them a 'sort of foster mother' to the forces. But very few understood the 'stupendously staggering proportions of the struggle' in which they were engaged.

'If the food and forage consumed by only the British force in France alone during the last six months had been required to be transported there on one day, and the only means of transport available had been ordinary ASC horse wagons, with a carrying capacity of 1.5 tons each, not less than 1.5 million wagons would have been needed, and the procession of vehicles, if stretched out in a straight line, would easily have reached from Aldershot to America.

'I have not bothered to calculate how many more wagons would have been needed if all the other supplies for the Expeditionary Force in France, such as ammunition, equipment, clothing, medical comforts etc. had had to be dispatched at the same time, nor the numbers of millions of men that would have had to be employed,' said the expert.

Versatility was the keynote of the ASC. When, occasionally and humorously, they were called the Corps of 'butchers, bakers and candlestick makers', there was a good deal of truth to this. All kinds of trades were found in their ranks. The ASC were a combination of infantry and cavalry, the supply and mechanical transport men being the infantry and the horse transport and remount men the cavalry.

Because of the peculiar blend of mounted and dismounted soldiers in the ASC, a 'rather uncomplimentary nickname' was sometimes bestowed on the Corps, Ally Sloper's Cavalry – Sloper being a red nosed and lazy fictional comic strip character, created by artist Charles H Ross for the British magazine, *Judy*.

The writer for the *St Andrews Citizen* believed the nickname may have been coined by the ASC's horse transport men. 'The ASC drivers are, above everything else, humorous and hard-working and, though they wear spurs, they are under no delusions about their being cavalry men. However, if they are not versed in the cavalryman's drill, they nevertheless know practically everything there is to know about horses. As for driving – well, they compare favourably with even the superbly clever riders in the Royal Horse Artillery.'

Although the ASC did not fight in the trenches, every one of their officers and men were, to a great degree, trained fighting soldiers. With many of their servicemen constantly coming under enemy fire, innumerable numbers being awarded Military Crosses and Distinguished Conduct Medals and being mentioned in despatches, their standard of gallantry rivalled that of any combatant unit.

A disabled ASC corporal admitted to Derby Royal Infirmary in 1916, told how a young girl – one of a school group visiting 'wounded soldiers' – seemed 'sadly disappointed' when, asking where he was injured, was advised that all his limbs were intact and he was 'merely suffering from chronic rheumatism'.

He said he had 'no lurid experiences' of bombing raids or 'other exciting incidents' that the girls from the school seemed to expect as 'regulation thrills'. But he had faced risks – such as sitting on top of ten tons of boxes of live ammunition on Christmas Day while nailing direction labels. 'A slight mishap then would have meant the city of Calais being blown sky-high.'

Cpl J Hymers recalled how a young ASC corporal had his head cut off by a bomb dropped on a barge by a German monoplane. And how a young member of the Corps died after falling off a ship. 'The poor fellow tried to save himself by swimming, but the heave of the ship against the side caught him and crushed him like an egg shell'.

Cpl Hymers argued that the 'fate, not only of armies, but of the whole future of civilisation' had depended on the efficiency of the ASC. This had been clearly demonstrated at key battles on the Western Front when the ASC had been so effective in 'rushing up necessary supplies' to the front line and keeping the British Army on the move.

The importance of the work done by men of the ASC was not always recognised, not just during the war but in the years leading up to it. An 'old boy' of the Corps recalled how, in October 1899, the ship *Braemar Castle* left Southampton Docks, with 1,500 officers and men of the ASC on board, for service in the Second Boer War in South Africa.

'There were no bands, cheering crowds or other distractions to keep the thoughts busy, such as occurred when other troops were being embarked – the boat just left the dockside and all was quiet,' he wrote in *The Bedfordshire Times and Independent* in December 1912.

In times of war, the man on the street was 'struck with the graphic accounts' of battles and 'in his mind's eye appeared the surging lines of infantry charging with bayonets fixed, of gunners working like demons around their death-dealing pieces and of the wild "hurrah" of the cavalry as they rushed into their opponents'.

Who, he asked, gave a thought to the hard-worked soldiers of the ASC? 'Not a solitary individual.' Yet, it was not charges of cavalry, or rushes of infantry that wholly won a campaign. The man on the road behind the firing line, very often the hardest working and the last to get any rest, was 'as valuable to the cause as the man in the act of pressing the trigger'.

In 1914, the ASC had 500 officers and 6,000 warrant officers, NCOs and men. By the end of the war, they had 11,406 officers and more than 311,000 warrant officers, NCOs and men. The Horse Transport section was the largest element. The ASC became the Royal Army Service Corps in late 1918, an honour bestowed on it by King George V.

Although the ASC were frequently dubbed the 'forgotten army' by many among their ranks, and by those who championed their cause at home, Field Marshall Sir Douglas Haig, Commander in Chief of the British Army in France and Flanders, praised the Corp's work in his despatch from the Arras front in January 1918.

'The long period of active fighting, combined with the

magnitude of our operations, has once more placed a heavy strain upon the personnel of the Army Service Corps and of the Administrative Services and Departments generally. The difficulties of supply have been increased by the unavoidable congestion of the areas in which operations were taking place, as well as by the inevitable deterioration of roads and by long-distance shelling and bombing by the enemy,' he wrote.

'In spite of all difficulties the Army Service Corps have never failed to meet the needs of our troops in food, ammunition, material and stores of all kinds. Particularly good work has been done by the Motor Transport drivers, who have shown the greatest gallantry and devotion to duty in getting forward the requisites of the Army under heavy shell fire and during long hours of exposure.'

A tribute in prose to the way the men of the ASC quietly slipped off to war, and continued working with a 'never-say-die' attitude while other soldiers rested, was penned by a man serving in the mechanical transport section and eventually published in *The Hartland and West Country Chronicle* in 1916.

> *There's a handful of men in the Army*
> *Who seldom shoulder a gun,*
> *And it's little that's known about them,*
> *When everything's said and done;*
> *And they try to escape any notice*
> *As they quietly slip off to war.*
> *For they never expect a send-off*
> *In the Army Service Corps.*
>
> *They don't aim at capturing prisoners,*
> *Or of taking the enemy's flag;*
> *But they serve in a humble vocation,*
> *For the sake of the grand old flag.*
> *Amid the inferno of battle,*
> *And in spite of the cannon's roar,*
> *They keep on quietly working*
> *In the Army Service Corps.*

When the foe-man's heavy gun fire
Has scattered and smashed their supplies,
They take good grips on their upper lips
And with 'never say die' in their eyes,
They hustle around and square things up,
And put them in order once more;
For they don't know the meaning of quitting
In the Army Service Corps.

When their fellow soldiers are resting,
Awaiting a new day's dawn –
They are desperately heaving and straining
With muscle, sinew and brawn,
For they must deliver the rations,
Although they are weary and sore –
They are ripping good men that can stick it
In the Army Service Corps.

And when the war is over,
And peace once more doth reign;
This handful of men come silently
Back to their homes again –
And they try to escape any notice
As they quickly slip ashore –
But it's a way they have of doing things
In the Army Service Corps.

George, the eldest son of Benjamin and Elizabeth (nee Burnett) Roberts, was born at Edgeworthy Cottage, Cruwys Morchard on March 8, 1898. When the Census was carried out in 1901, he was three years old and living with his parents, two older sisters, Amelia and Ella, and younger brother, Edwin Buller, at Edgeworthy Cottage, on Edgeworthy Farm.

During the 1911 Census, George, then aged 13, was working as a 'farm lad' at Edgeworthy Farm, for farmer William Lake, who lived with his wife, Jeanette and their one-year-old son, Herbert John. George's parents and his younger brother were living on the neighbouring Higher Edgeworthy Farm, where his father worked as a waggoner.

He joined the ASC as a private in 1915 and arrived in France on December 18 that year. Attached to the British First Army for the duration of the war, he was at Fromelles in Northern France on July 1916 when thousands of British and Australian soldiers were killed in an attack on German forces.

George was with the First Army, commanded by General Sir Henry Horne, when it fought in the two-month long Arras Offensive in 1917 – including the Battle of Vimy Ridge and the Battles of the Scarpe. Tens of thousands of Allied soldiers were killed in the offensive, which started encouragingly with British-led forces making significant advances before becoming embroiled in attritional trench warfare.

He also had a pivotal supporting role in keeping the First Army fed when it:

- Tackled a major German offensive in Flanders, in the Battles of the Lys – at Estaires, Hazebrouck and Bethune – in April 1918;

- Had a leading role in the Battles of Arras in August and September 1918, successfully breaking German defences on the Drocourt-Queant Line;

- Attacked and successfully broke through the heavily fortified German Hindenburg Line, the enemy's last line of defences;

- Advanced in Artois and Picardy, liberating the Belgian town of Mons (where the British Expeditionary Force fought its first major battle in 1914) on November 11, 1918, Armistice Day

On his return home, George worked with his father at Yeo Barton Farm, Mariansleigh. On December 4, 1920, at the age of 22, he married Lilian Ellen Arscott at Crediton Register Office. Lilian, the daughter of farmer Charles Henry and Alice Arscott, was aged 20 and lived at New House, Thelbridge before her wedding.

George and Lilian, who had two sons, including my father, Sydney George, and two daughters, moved to Home Farm, Newton St Cyres – the home of Quicke family – in the late 1930s. There, George was employed as head cowman and farm bailiff until his death in 1948, aged 50. He died from heart failure due to coronary thrombosis.

The cause of his death on September 15, 1948 was certified by coroner W Rackwood Cocks after a post-mortem, but there was no inquest. George was buried at Newton St Cyres Churchyard. Lilian died ten years later, on April 4, 1958, aged 57 and was buried with her husband. Close to their last resting place is the grave of their daughter, Margaret Ellen, who died in 1943, aged 21.

George left £278 17s 1d to Lilian in his will. Nine days after his death, an advertisement seeking a new head cowman at Home Farm – to look after its machine-milked dairy shorthorn herd, record calf rearing and carry out general management duties – with a 'good cottage' to live in, was published in *The Western Morning News*.

After his war service, George received the British War and Victory Medals and 1915 Star. His regimental number was T1/3714 (T for Horse Transport and 1 for British First Army).

Note

- Many hundreds of thousands of horses sent to France between 1914 and 1918 were killed or destroyed. The losses would have been devastating to the men looking after them – including George. As the losses grew, Britain could no longer supply the Army's needs, so animals were shipped in from Canada and the US.

22

BEN — THE ONLY ONE OF THREE BROTHERS TO COME HOME

He was one of three young brothers from the North Devon village of Rackenford to go to war. And William Ben Roberts, who served as a sapper and lance-corporal in the Royal Engineers on the Western Front, was the only one who made it home.

The last of the three to enlist, he went to France at the end of 1915. By September the following year, he was the last one standing. His brother Sam was killed on the first day of the Battle of the Somme in 1916 and his brother Frank was killed by a shrapnel bomb two months later.

Ben, as he was known, played a pivotal role in keeping the British Army on the move – a monumental task in war-torn France and Flanders which would not have been possible without the vital work of the Royal Engineers.

The scale and scope of the challenges they faced were huge, ranging from digging attacking tunnels under enemy lines, to building bridges, laying and clearing minefields, repairing field defences and maintaining essential infrastructure.

'Without engineers, there would have been no supply to the armies, because the Royal Engineers (RE) maintained the railways, roads, water supply, bridges and transport,' military historian Chris Baker declares on The Long, Long Trail website.

'There would have been no communications, because the RE maintained the telephones, wireless and other signalling equipment. There would have been little cover for the infantry and no positions for the artillery, because the RE designed and built the front-line fortifications.

'It fell to the technically skilled Royal Engineers to develop responses to chemical and underground warfare. And finally, without the RE the infantry and artillery would have soon been powerless, as they maintained the guns and other weapons.'

Their work earned them the highest accolades from Field Marshall Sir Douglas Haig, Commander in Chief of the British Army in France and Flanders, who, in his despatch from the Western Front in January 1919, praised 'all branches of the Royal Engineers' for showing the 'greatest energy and skill in the discharge of their different tasks'.

On many occasions, particularly in the building of bridges under fire and in the removal of mines, they had shown 'courage of the highest order', he said. They built 700 road bridges – and many more pontoon and footbridges – in the advance across the Western Front. Many of these were constructed under heavy shell and machine-gun fire.

In early 1916, Haig said the 'systematic destruction of roads, railways and bridges' by the enemy made 'unprecedented demands upon the Royal Engineers'. The bridging of the Somme at Brie was a clear example of the obstacles with which troops were met and of the 'rapidity with which those obstacles were overcome'.

Six gaps had to be bridged across the canal and river, some of them of 'considerable width and over a swift flowing stream'. The work was started on the morning of March 18, 1916 and carried out night and day. By 10pm on the same day, footbridges for infantrymen were completed. Crossings for horse transport and cavalry were finished by 5am on March 20 and eight days later, heavy bridges capable of taking all forms of traffic had been built.

In his report from the Arras front in January 1918, Haig said the prolonged period of active fighting and the vast amount of work involved in different offensives, had thrown a 'peculiarly heavy burden' on the Royal Engineers, both before and during operations. 'The Field, Signal, Army Troops and Tramway Companies, together with Pioneer and Labour Battalions, from home and overseas, have played an increasingly important part, not only in the preparation for our offensives, but also during the latter stages of the battles. The courage and enduring self-sacrifice displayed by all ranks, whether in the organisation of captured positions or in the maintenance of forward communications under heavy shell fire, are deserving of the highest praise.'

Tunnelling companies, who built attack tunnels to enable mines to be exploded under German defences, faced some of the greatest hazards on the Western Front. Manned by experienced coal miners in the ranks of the Royal Engineers, Haig said they possessed 'in the highest degree the qualities of courage, perseverance, and self-sacrifice' and 'worked with great courage and cheerfulness under conditions of much hardship and danger'. The Tunnellers' discovery and safe disposal of more than 14,000 German mines and traps, totalling over 540 tons of explosives, in the final three months of the war, illustrated the size of the challenges they faced.

Because of the demands on their expertise, the number of officers and men serving in the Royal Engineers increased from just over 25,000 in August 1914 to almost 300,000 in 1917. They were awarded 15,000 honours during the war, including 16 Victoria Crosses, and suffered almost 100,000 casualties.

A memorial to the 18,000 officers and men of the Royal Engineers who were killed in action or died from wounds or sickness between 1914 and 1919 was unveiled at the School of Military Engineering in Chatham, Kent, on July 19, 1922 by Prince Arthur, Duke of Connaught and Strathearn.

Queen Victoria's last surviving son, he paid tribute to the work of the Royal Engineers, describing them as both 'gallant soldiers' and 'very fine workmen' who saw service in every theatre of war across the world and took part in every major action.

In a ceremony witnessed by thousands, the memorial was dedicated by the Rt Rev John Reginald Harmer, the Bishop of

Rochester. He had a Devon connection in that, after retiring from his post in 1930, he lived for a while in Instow, dying there in 1944, aged 87.

Ben, born in Rackenford on March 3, 1892, and baptised at Tiverton Cove Church, was the son of John and Elizabeth Roberts, of Blindwell Cottage, Rackenford. At the time of the 1901 Census, he lived with his family in the village, at Windsor Cottage.

In 1911, at the age of 18, he was working as an apprentice baker for 47-year-old Henry Herbert Churchill, who was running the bakery and grocer's shop in West Street, Witheridge with the help of his wife Bessie and family.

The Western Times in October 1915 reported that Ben had joined the Royal Engineers and, as part of Lord Herbert Kitchener's vast volunteer army, was about to be 'sent across' to France to serve his King and country.

The same newspaper, on February 8, 1918, recorded that Ben, now promoted to lance-corporal, had returned 'home from Flanders for a few days after a year at the Front, and is looking fit and well'.

He continued his training as a baker when the war was over. On May 2, 1927, at the age of 35, he married 37-year-old Flora Bray, the youngest daughter of John and Harriet Bray, at Knowstone Parish Church.

They ran a popular and busy bakery, Post Office and village store at Rose Cottage in the village for many years. They had a son, Anthony John, who, later lived in Melbourne Road in Wimbledon, London.

Ben and Flora found themselves at the centre of a legal dispute in 1944 when, at the Devon Assize, Exeter, Knowstone's Vicar, the Rev George Henry Butcher, sought an injunction to restrain them from using a school playground adjoining their shop.

The court was told that the couple thought they had a perfect right to use the playground for their vehicles. But when it became cut up and potentially dangerous, the vicar complained and started legal proceedings to resolve ownership of the land.

It emerged that, when the school was built in 1859, the

owners conveyed, via two sets of deeds, to the then vicar and his successors land upon which it had been built as well as additional land for use as the only playground.

Details of this transfer became forgotten over the succeeding years, particularly when Rose Cottage was sold to Ben and Flora's predecessors – and only became clear when the Rev Butcher traced the deeds for the school and playground.

In a settlement announced before the court – and published in *The Western Morning News* in February 1944 – it was agreed that the couple could use the playground for lorry deliveries of flour for baking bread twice a week.

Ben died as a result of acute heart failure and hypertension at Woodburn Cross Bungalow in East Anstey, Devon on September 10, 1969, aged 77. Flora died in July 1957, aged 67. Living at Rosecroft, Knowstone at the time of her death, she left £1,812 7s and 4d in her will to Ben, who had by then retired as a baker.

His war service is remembered on the granite war memorial on the outskirts of Rackenford. He was awarded the British War and Victory Medals. His regimental number was 282397.

Note

• Plymouth-born Acting Major Arnold Horace Santo Waters was among the 16 who received the Victoria Cross, for his bravery at Ors, in France. With his field company, he was 'bridging' the Oise-Sambre Canal under heavy artillery and machine gun fire on November 4, 1918 when he heard that all his officers had been killed or wounded in the attack. He personally supervised the completion of the bridge, working on cork floats while under fire from point blank range. The shooting was so intense that it 'seemed impossible that he could escape being killed', said the citation for his award, and the success of the operation was 'entirely due to his valour and example'.

23

SAMUEL AND SIDNEY — NEW TRAGEDY STRIKES 20 YEARS AFTER THE WAR

The immortal words of *For the Fallen*, Robert Laurence Binyon's evocative tribute to the men killed in the early battles of the Great War, echoed through the parish church as villagers said their final farewells to a popular and greatly respected veteran soldier.

> *They went with songs to the battle, they were young,*
> *Straight of limb, true of eye, steady and aglow.*
> *They were staunch to the end against odds uncounted,*
> *They fell with their faces to the foe.*
>
> *They shall grow not old, as we that are left grow old:*
> *Age shall not weary them, nor the years condemn.*
> *At the going down of the sun and in the morning*
> *We will remember them.*

The Rector, the Rev Robert Geoffrey Cruwys, read Binyon's poem – regularly quoted at Remembrance Day Services across the United Kingdom – at the conclusion of the funeral for Samuel Roberts, of Mudford Gate, Cruwys Morchard.

Samuel, or Sam as he was known by family and friends, died

in a mental hospital in 1938, aged just 39. He was a survivor of the Great War, but there are no known records to indicate which regiment he was with, where he served or for how long.

His name appears on an impressive tablet erected in the porch of the Church of the Holy Cross in Cruwys Morchard in honour of 54 men from the parish who served in the war. It shows that he took up arms in 1917, when he was 18.

The only other mention of his involvement in the war was a brief and undefined reference to it in reports of his well-attended funeral, published in *The Western Times* and *The Devon and Exeter Gazette* in December 1938.

A 'road labourer' for Devon Council Council's Highways Department for a number of years, he played a pivotal role in supporting families in his community who had been devastated by losses in the war.

For a number of years, Samuel was an 'active member' of the local committee of the United Services Fund (USF), which was founded by the government in 1919 to help families of men who were killed or disabled in the war.

The fund, incorporated by a royal charter, was established to administer a portion of the £6 million profits accumulated by Army, Navy and RAF canteens during the war, to aid ex-servicemen and widows of men who lost their lives and children and dependants of ex-servicemen.

Samuel won high praise from leading Royal British Legion members for his dedication while serving on the USF committee of what was then the Cruwys Morchard section of the Cheriton Fitzpaine branch of the RBL.

He was one of three sons – the others being John and Sidney – of farm worker Samuel and Maria (nee Morrish) Roberts. They would see all three of their sons go to war. And like many families around them, they faced more than their fair share of tragedy.

When Samuel was just 16 years old and working on a farm in his home village, his older brother, John, known to his family and friends as Jack, died from injuries sustained on a French battlefield on May 30, 1915 at the age of 20.

Jack, who had been a private in the 2nd Battalion of the

Devonshire Regiment, is remembered on the Cruwys Morchard War Memorial. Sidney survived and, like Samuel, went on to marry and have children.

Samuel was born in Cruwys Morchard on March 14, 1899. In 1901, he lived with his family at Edbury Farm, Poughill, Devon. He attended Cruwys Morchard and Oakford Church of England Schools and, in 1911, lived with his parents at Higher Furze Farm, Penny Moor, Cruwys Morchard.

At the age of 23, he married Ada Evelyn Boundy, of West Mogworthy Farm, Rackenford in Cruwys Morchard on November 8, 1922. Samuel and Ada, while living at Edgeworthy Cottage, in the village, had a daughter, Phyllis Gwendoline, who was baptised on October 12, 1924.

Ada was the daughter of Frederick and Cora Boundy. Ada's sister, Beatrice Mary, married Samuel's cousin, Thomas Roberts – of Newland Farm Witheridge, who served with the 8th Devons in Italy – in January the following year.

Samuel's all-too-short life ended at the Devon Mental Hospital in Exminster on September 28, 1938. His death certificate indicated that he died from chronic bronchitis, but a post-mortem carried out on him was 'indefinite'.

The hymns *O Valiant Hearts, Through all the Changing Scenes of Life* and *Abide With Me* were sung at Samuel's funeral at the Parish Church of the Holy Cross in Cruwys Morchard on October 3, 1933. The organist, the rector's wife, played Chopin's *March Funebre*.

His grave was 'beautifully lined with moss and flowers' and floral tributes included wreaths from the Cheriton Fitzpaine branch of the Royal British Legion and workmates from Devon County Council's Highways Department.

The mourners included Samuel's widow, Ada Evelyn, their daughter, Phyllis, his mother and his brother, Sidney. Also there were his widow's parents, Frederick and Cora Boundy, and many other relatives and friends.

Ada Evelyn died in Devon in 1994, aged 92.

The war had just ended when Samuel's brother Sidney, married Emily Chidgey at Bampton Parish Church in Devon on January 1, 1919. He was 27 and Emily 24. They would go on to have three daughters – Irene and twins Gwendoline Mary and Florence Emily. They lived at Langford Green, Cullompton for many years.

There are no known records of Sidney's war service, although it is believed he was in the Royal Engineers. Again, he is listed among those who served in the war on the tablet in the porch of the Church of the Holy Cross in Cruwys Morchard. It shows that he was among the very first to go to war, in 1914. He was still a 'soldier' when he married.

Born in Cheriton Fitzpaine, Devon he was baptised in the parish church there on January 3, 1892. In 1901, he was living with his family in Poughill, Devon. In 1911, he was working as a waggoner on Andrew Crang's Northcote Farm in Cruwys Morchard.

Sidney died in Cullompton, Devon in 1949, aged 58. Emily, the daughter of William and Keziah Chidgey, died in Taunton in 1967, aged 73.

Notes

- When Samuel and Sidney's father died in 1933, tributes were paid to him in *The Western Times*. The newspaper described Samuel Snr as an 'old native of Cruwys Morchard' and added: 'He was of a cheery disposition and was a special favourite with the children of the village.' Born in Moor Cottage, Cruwys Morchard, he was said to have been 'one of 17 children' of John and Mary Roberts (it is believed that this should have read one of a family of 17, including his parents). 'He was brought up on 13s a week in the "good old days".' For many years he worked as head carter at Cruwys Cross and latterly at Ford Barton, and won many prizes as a ploughman, reported *The Western Times*.

- The Rev Robert Geoffrey Cruwys, who conducted Samuel's funeral service, played cricket for Devon and Knightshayes for many years. Born in the family manor, Cruwys Morchard House, in Cruwys Morchard, which took the name from the Cruwys family, he died in 1951.

24

ARCHIE, HARRY AND WALTER —
THE SANDFORD SURVIVORS

He was just 18 when he was called up to serve in the Great War in May 1917. A pillar of his village community, Archibald – or Archie – Roberts was a local preacher and 'Band of Hope' worker 'of great promise' at his Congregational Church, a key employee at an agricultural merchant, and the son of a remarkable craftsman and 'Jack of all trades'.

One of three brothers from Sandford in Devon who joined 'His Majesty's Forces', he was among more than 200 men from the parish who were in 'active service' between 1914 and 1918. Thirty-eight of those men never came home, many losing their lives in France, Gallipoli, Palestine, Mesopotamia, Salonica, Belgium and in hospitals at home and abroad.

Archie and his brothers, Henry (or Harry) and Walter Roberts, survived the war. There are few clues to their involvement. Archie and Henry are named in a Sandford Roll of Honour, and Henry is listed on a special plaque displayed at St Swithun's Parish Church, Sandford which was created to encourage people to pray for local soldiers and sailors serving their King and country.

Newspaper reports in early 1917 of meetings of Crediton Rural Tribunal – one of many established across the country to hear applications for exemption from conscription into the British Army – include brief mentions of Archie and Walter. But details of regiments they were in, and where they served and when remain a mystery.

Archie, Henry and Walter were the sons of Henry and Mary Roberts, who lived near Sandford Mill. An old book of accounts kept by their father, details of which are published in the book, *A Parish Patchwork*, by Daphne Munday, reveal that he was a man of many talents, able to make and repair most things.

Tasks he completed included making coffins, doors, hen coops, animal houses and troughs, making and hanging gates, threshing corn and mending threshing machines, tilling and harvesting potatoes, pruning and felling trees, dung spreading, cutting up firewood, painting and decorating houses, and sheep shearing and dipping.

Henry Snr, who described himself as a carpenter, shepherd and farm labourer in Census returns between 1891 and 1911, kept a record of his children's birthdays in his account book. He also noted that Archie obtained 'exemption from school' in 1911, when he was aged 11 or 12, almost certainly to assist his father at work.

Archie was born in Sandford on December 14, 1898. He became a stalwart of Sandford Congregational Church, attending the Sunday school from infancy, becoming a member of the choir and a valued local preacher. In early 1917, the church pastor, the Rev Edwin Tully, said Archie 'gave promise of great usefulness'.

His work with the Band of Hope – a temperance organisation which had millions of members in the early 1900s – was widely praised. Established to help prevent working-class children from drinking alcohol and to encourage them to take part in musical activities and outings, the organisation was one of the most successful Christian movements ever launched in the UK.

The first hint that Archie would be called-up for war service came in February 1917. *The Western Times* reported that, at a meeting of the Crediton Rural Tribunal, he had been given three months to complete his work for Sandford agricultural merchant, Mr M Wright, before joining 'His Majesty's Forces'.

In May that year, the newspaper reported that, at the end of an evening service at Sandford Congregational Church, Archie was given a special 'farewell message' by the pastor. The large congregation joined in wishing him well and sang with great emotion the hymn *God be with you till we meet again*.

Archie returned to Sandford after the war. In April 1919, he was a bearer at the funeral in the village of Mrs Elizabeth Densem, whose son, John, was killed in action in 1918. Born in Sandford, John emigrated to New Zealand as a young man, joined that country's forces in 1915, and was a lieutenant in the New Zealand Rifle Brigade when he died.

Archie married Lily Mary Darch, who was born in Chulmleigh, Devon in 1900, at Sandford Congregational Church on November 4, 1922. They were married for more than 50 years and had three children. The church continued to play an important part in Archie's life. In 1970, he was awarded a certificate to mark more than 50 years' service to the church.

Archie died on June 16, 1979, aged 80. Lily, the daughter of Walter John and Mary Ann Darch, died in Exeter on October 4, 1979, at the age of 79.

Henry (or Harry), Archie's brother, was born in Cruwys Morchard on February 8, 1888, and baptised in the parish church on April 1 that year. In 1911, he was working as a groom for coachman Thomas Crabb, at Creedy Stables, Sandford. It is not known when he went to war, but it is understood that he was among the first in the parish to volunteer for service.

He is the only Roberts listed on an unusual and poignant plaque at the village's St Swithun's Parish Church. Including the words 'of your duty, pray for our sailors and soldiers', it contains the names of dozens of men from Sandford who fought and, in some cases died, on the Western Front and in many other theatres of war.

He married Georgina Mary Snell in 1914. The daughter of George and Mary Ann Snell, she was born in Thelbridge in 1892 and died as a young mother of two in 1925. Henry married Georgina's younger sister, Sarah Annie, in 1930 and they had a son. Henry died in 1964, aged 75. Sarah died in Exeter in 1969, aged 70.

Walter, born in Sandford on January 1, 1897, worked as a cow boy for farmer Herbert Lake at Combe Lancey, Sandford after leaving school. Herbert, the last tenant farmer at Combe Lancey, was also a great stalwart of the local Congregational Church, completing more than 60 years' service as its secretary, a post he held until his death in 1966.

Local records offer no indications that Walter served in the war. Unlike his brothers, Archie and Henry, he was not among the 202 men from Sandford listed in parish registers as joining the Armed Forces between 1914 and 1918.

The only intimation that he was involved in the war effort was contained in a report of a meeting of the Crediton Rural Tribunal, published in *The Western Times* in February 1917. It said that Herbert Lake was 'willing to accept' a 'substitute' worker at Combe Lancey for 20-year-old Walter – clearly suggesting that he had been called-up.

Walter was 30-years-old when he married 31-year-old Crediton-born dress maker Louisa Mary Steer at the High Street Meeting Room in her home town on December 11, 1926. He died at Westwood Farm, Crediton on June 24, 1963, aged 66. He left £411 5s in his will to his widow. Louisa, the daughter of James and Louisa Steer, died in 1966, aged 70.

Notes

- Archie, Henry and Walter's mother, Mary, died on January 13, 1933, aged 73. A report of her funeral, in which she was described as a 'much respected resident' was published in *The Devon and Exeter Gazette* seven days later. Their father, Henry, died on June 1, 1937, aged 78. He and Mary were buried in St Swithun's Churchyard.

- John Roberts, the brother of Archie, Harry and Walter, died after being involved in a road accident on September 14, 1939, aged 53. A road worker for Devon County Council, John, of Bagland Cottages, Copplestone, near Crediton, died from injuries sustained in a collision with a car while cycling home from Crediton.

- John married Jane Vodden in July 1909. His brother-in-law, Private Henry Vodden, who served in the 9th Devons, was killed in action on the Western Front on September 6, 1916, aged 22. Born in Woolfardisworthy, Devon, he was the son of John and Sarah Ann Vodden. He is remembered on the Thiepval Memorial and on the Morchard Bishop War Memorial in Devon.

Part Four

THE GRANDSONS-IN-LAW WHO SURVIVED — AND A GREAT NEPHEW KILLED IN ACTION

25

WILFRED BANTING — WOUNDED IN COURAGEOUS ATTACK NEAR KUT

It was a courageous and harrowing sight they would never forget. Hundreds of Sikh soldiers attacking a forbidding network of Turkish trenches in Mesopotamia – and being mown down by unrelenting machine gun and artillery fire.

Just two days after witnessing this massacre, brothers Wilfred John and Albert Cecil Banting were poised to launch a new assault on the same deadly defences on the Hai Salient, south of the town of Kut.

It was on February 3, 1917 that their battalion, the 1/4th Devons, and the 1/2nd Ghurkhas were ordered to storm the trenches. 'It was the sight of a lifetime to see the line of platoons walking over through a very hell,' observed one of their fellow soldiers.

The attack was a spectacular success, with two lines of Turkish trenches captured that day. But the Devons paid a heavy price for their triumph. Four of their officers and 63 NCOs and men were killed and six officers and 149 other ranks were wounded.

Taunton-born Sergeant William Ridler was awarded the Distinguished Conduct Medal for 'conspicuous gallantry and devotion to duty' for taking charge of one company of the 1/4th Devons when all their officers had fallen.

A Lance-Corporal Marshall showed remarkable courage when he encountered five Turks. The first he 'laid out' with his rifle butt, smashing his weapon in the act. Undeterred, he picked up another rifle, shot three more and bayonetted the last man.

Six of those killed were born in, or lived in or near Axminster in Devon, all serving with the 1/4th Devons – brothers Private Leslie Walter and Private Reginald Robert Sprague, Sergeant Leonard William Lethaby, Sergeant Frederick Perham, Private Frederick William Coote, and Private Fred Woodman.

Another six of those killed were born in or lived in Tiverton, again all serving with the 1/4th Devons – Sergeant Francis John Drew, Corporal Albert Barrington, Private William David Bastone, Private Herbert Darch, Private Harry Manley, and Private William John Tucker.

Also among those who lost their lives that day were Private John Bowden, of Cruwys Morchard, Sergeant John Eales of Cullompton, and Sergeant John Gollop and Private William Rowsell Alford, of Uffculme.

Wilfred and Albert were both wounded in the attack. They were listed as casualties in a 'roll of honour' published in *The Western Times* in March 1917. They survived their injuries, and the war.

Wilfred followed in his father's footsteps by becoming a gardener and went on to marry John Roberts' grand-daughter Florence Beatrice Kingdom, of Tiverton, Devon. She lost two brothers in the war – William Henry and Walter Kingdom.

William was a corporal in the 1/4th Devons when he died from heart disease in Mesopotamia in May 1916, at the age of 26. Walter was killed in action in the aftermath of the Battle of Epehy in September 1918, aged 20.

Wilfred, born in Headley, Surrey in 1895, was the son of George and Agnes Mary Banting. He was just eight when his mother died. His father remarried and Wilfred and his family moved to Whitehall Cottage in Ashley, Tiverton, where, in 1911, Wilfred was working as a grocer's assistant.

It is not known when he went to war, or when he joined the 1/4th Devons. He was in front line trenches near Kut on February 1 and 2, 1917 before taking part in the attack on Turkish defences the following day.

Two companies of the 1/4th Devons – A and C – and the 1/2nd Ghurkhas led the assault, going over the top at 10.30am on February 3, and dashing 30 yards before laying down in open ground under cover of an intense bombardment.

The assault continued at 10.38am, with men advancing in eight waves and at intervals of 30 paces. They moved so quickly that they found themselves under heavy fire from the British artillery.

2nd Lieutenant C K Dodd, in command of A Company of the 1/4th Devons, reported in the battalion's war diary how his men were 'hindered by our own artillery' as they approached the enemy trenches and had to wave warning discs to halt the barrage.

'We did not exactly halt in front of the Turkish trench, but had to slow down,' he wrote. 'As soon as the barrage lifted we went right on to the second trench and I took all my men into the nullah (or ravine) beyond.'

He said his original orders were to take the first trench and consolidate, to allow B and D Companies to 'go over and take the second'. But, explained 2nd Lt Dodd, 'everybody was determined to go on'.

Lieutenant F A Thoday, in command of D Company of the 1/4th Devons, said the final three waves of soldiers 'went straight over the first trench without stopping and stopped at the second for a little while and cleared it'.

He recorded in the war diary that 'we went on, over the nullah and into the open. Between the nullah and the Turkish trench, we came under fire from our own artillery. Here, we sustained over 50% of our casualties.'

But 'there was no stopping the men' and about 40 of them charged into a Turkish trench. 'The Turks were still in their dug-outs when our men got there and we inflicted heavy losses before they could get out,' said Lt Thoday.

The bravery of the 1/4th Devons and other battalions involved in the attack – all attached to the 37th Brigade of the 14th Indian Division – earned them the highest praise from senior British Army officers.

In a telegram sent to the 37th Brigade, General R G Egerton, Commander of the 14th Division, offered his 'most since congratulations on their success and thanked all ranks for their 'admirable gallantry and untiring efforts'.

A letter sent to the 1/4th Devons by Brigadier-General O W Carey, commander of the 37th Brigade, also congratulated the battalion on the way they had distinguished themselves in the assault on the enemy trenches.

He praised the 36th and 45th Sikh Regiments for their 'determined and gallant assault against the Turkish positions on the west bank of the Hai' on February 1. 'The two regiments advanced under a heavy enfilade fire from guns and machine guns from both flanks.

'Although many men fell as soon they left our trenches, each succeeding wave pressed on until they finally gained the enemy's position. They were unfortunately unable to maintain themselves and had to fall back, but the spirit of the survivors was in no way impaired and reflects the greatest credit on these two regiments,' wrote Brig-Gen Carey.

The 1/4th Devons, along with the Ghurkhas and 62 Punjabis, attacked the same position just 48 hours later 'with great gallantry and determination' despite having seen 'their trenches full of wounded Sikhs two days before.

'They captured three lines of enemy trenches and maintained themselves there all day against several counter-attacks. When withdrawn next day they were still ready to continue the offensive. The severity of the fighting during these two attacks may be judged by the casualties suffered, the losses being over 50% of the total strength of the regiments engaged.'

Although, as C T Atkinson observed in the book, *The Devonshire Regiment 1914–1918*, the 'brilliant success' of the attack 'cost the 1/4th Devons dear', it proved decisive in defeating the enemy on the Hai Salient.

Wilfred, who continued to serve in the battalion until October 1919, married Florence Beatrice Kingdom at St Paul's

Parish Church in Tiverton on June 11, 1921. Living at Upton Pyne, he was 27 on his wedding day.

Florence, the daughter of George and Lucy Kingdom (the eldest daughter of John Roberts) was 26. Born in Tiverton on March 12, 1895, she lived in Bushment Cottage, Westexe for many years, and attended Tiverton Heathcote School.

In 1911, at the age of 16, she worked as a domestic housemaid at the Ailsa Terrace, Tiverton home of retired surgeon Allan Edward Mahood, who lived with his wife, Caroline, and their 11-year-old son, Allan Stanley.

Wilfred, who was head gardener at Shobrooke Park, Crediton in the early 1930s – succeeding his father – died in Wincanton, Somerset in 1962, aged 67. Florence died on September 4, 1980, aged 85.

Wilfred's brother, Albert, worked as a junior railway clerk before enlisting in the Army in April 1914. He was posted to India with the 1/4th Devons in July 1916 before arriving in Basra, Mesopotamia in August that year.

He was among hundreds of soldiers treated for dysentery in the summer of 1916. Shot and seriously wounded in the attack of February 3, 1917, he was treated in hospital for three weeks before re-joining his battalion in March that year.

Albert, who served in the 1/4th Devons for five years, married Elsie May Roberts in 1925. He died in Monmouthshire in 1964, aged 67. Elsie, born in Poughill, Devon, died in Wales in 1987, aged 87.

Wilfred received the Victory and British War Medals. His service numbers were 3233 and 201337. Albert also received the Victory and British War Medals. His service numbers were 2124 and 200514.

WILLIAM WESTERN — A BLACKSMITH IN HUGE ASC 'TIN TOWN'

When he first walked into a 'tin town' on the outskirts of Avonmouth, blacksmith William Western could not have imagined the vital role it – and he – would play in keeping the British Army on the move in the Great War.

He had never seen anything like it before. A vast new township constructed on once rich pasture land with miles of corrugated iron roofs on hundreds of wooden buildings dominating the landscape.

This, the Shirehampton Remount Depot, at which hundreds of thousands of horses were handled and trained for the British Army overseas, would be his base, his 'home', for the next four years.

William – the husband of John Roberts' grand-daughter Lily Ann – had joined the Army Service Corps (ASC) as a shoeing smith in early 1915, when he was aged 32 and a father of five children.

Among more than 1,500 officers and men serving at Shirehampton, he was part of a large team of agricultural craftsmen making and fitting horse shoes in more than a dozen 90ft long lean-to 'shoeing sheds'.

The depot, spread over more than 100 acres, could

accommodate 5,000 or more horses and mules at any one time, the vast majority being shipped regularly to Avonmouth from America and Canada.

When it was first established in September 1914, men from the paramilitary group, the Legion of Frontiersmen, helped to train many of the wild horses brought to Shirehampton, breaking them in in true cowboy style.

The Western Daily Press reported in October 1914 how the Frontiersmen's distinctive uniform – khaki shirts, breeches, leggings and slouch, wide-brimmed hats – had 'attracted a good deal of attention' in the streets of Avonmouth and Bristol.

They included within their ranks 'some of the finest riders in the world, and men who can not only master any mount, but who understand a horse in every detail of its life and possibilities', said the newspaper.

A correspondent for *The Western Daily Press*, who visited the depot, said there was 'an air of abandon in these Frontiersmen which is foreign to the usual British "Tommy" and which smacks of the woolly west and the cowboys we see in the cinema drama'.

The 'battle royal' often conducted at the depot – 'between the skill of a kind-hearted, but iron-willed (Frontiersman) rider and a recalcitrant horse' – was, he contended, 'one of the finest sights the world can provide'.

He added: 'One pauses in wonderment at the mere spectacle of a young Frontiersmen astride a rearing and plunging horse, which bucks and jumps, side-slips and feints, in a manner which would astound many a clever circus equestrian.'

The correspondent witnessed the breaking-in of a large horse, led into a paddock by three men. A bridle and saddle were 'whipped upon him' before a tall Canadian Frontiersman rough-rider 'sprang' on to the horse's back.

The animal plunged, side-stepped and reared. 'As he pawed the air with his fore-feet, the great horse dashed here and there, but to no effect … It was bronco-busting in all truth, and a finer exhibition of real horsemanship it would be difficult to imagine.'

The correspondent visited the depot within weeks of its opening as 'enterprising contractors', under War office directions, were 'fast converting meadow after meadow into one great township of wooden structures with corrugated iron roofs'.

With 'rank after rank of stables' being erected, he said the once picturesque and wooded valley was being 'completely transformed from a scheme of sleepy rural life into one of bustling military activity'.

In its early months, the depot was staffed by officers and civilian personnel. William, who had the rank of private, enlisted in the ASC in February 1915 just as the depot was being changed into a military unit.

He was working there in September that year when King George V and Queen Mary toured the depot for an hour during a 'surprise visit' to Bristol during which they also met wounded soldiers at local military hospitals.

Shirehampton was one of the four largest remount depots in England. Out of almost 350,000 horses and mules that passed through its gates in four years, almost 320,000 were shipped from Canada and America. More than 6,700 came from Ireland, with another 9,000 purchased from within the UK or received from other remount depots.

Between 1915 and 1918, it sent almost 4,000 officers and men to France, Italy and Egypt to reinforce the remount service overseas and 1,000 were transferred to combatant units. About 6,000 recruits were trained at the depot, which was commanded by Colonel D C Carter and which also accommodated 2,300 civilians.

The first horses – 600 from Canada – arrived at Shirehampton on October 24, 1914. The largest number of animals landed at Avonmouth in one day and transferred to the depot was 2,953, and the greatest number of horses and mules accommodated at Shirehampton at any one time was 7,244.

After a voyage of 14-21 days across the Atlantic, the horses and mules spent two to three weeks at the depot where, *The Western Daily Press* reported, the objective was to 'get them as fit and as clean as possible, and then pass them on to reserve units at home for further training of a few months, before being sent to the various fronts'.

The depot had a veterinary hospital that could treat up to 200 animals at any one time. Disinfecting baths installed to treat horses with mange were found to be 'wonderfully successful' and were pivotal in ensuring that very few animals fell victim to the skin disease overseas.

Each ship sailing from Canada and America could carry up to 1,000 horses and mules. Their arrival at Avonmouth became a common occurrence with vessels even being unloaded at the port on Christmas Day between 1914 and 1917. Losses of animals during the voyages were reduced to a 'negligible quantity' as loading and care practices improved.

The depot – which repatriated more than 13,000 horses from France after the Armistice in 1918 – closed in October 1919. It disappeared almost as quickly as it materialised after the entire depot was sold at a three-day auction ordered by the Ministry of Munitions and held at the end of January 1920.

The huge swathe of corrugated iron and wooden buildings, stretching from Shirehampton railway station to Penpole Point, were among more than 900 lots offered at the auction, which was conducted by Geo. Nicholls, Young, Hunt and Co., of Demerara House, Colston Avenue, Bristol.

The lots included 63 50-stall stables, 33 saddle rooms, eight forage barns, the 13 shoeing sheds, 14 pay offices, 13 Alwyn (canvas) huts, 21 latrines, eight oil stores, four drying rooms, a pharmacy store, mess kitchen, bread and meat store, 18 brick and iron built incinerators, seven corn crushers, six chaff cutters, 52 pairs of bellows and 68 stoves.

The Bristol Corporation – now Bristol City Council – were major buyers, purchasing by private treaty the old officers' quarters. Many of the buildings it acquired were converted to homes. The Military Institute, at Pembroke Vale, Shirehampton, at which the auction was held, was purchased by Bristol University.

Just over a week after the auction, which realised about £25,000, work started on dismantling the depot. 'Already some of the structures have disappeared while others are now only mere skeletons,' *The Western Daily Press* reported in February

1920. Some were being transported to South Wales and the Midlands.

In March that year, the Ministry of Munitions ordered the sale of the depot's equipment and furniture, including 495 trestle and other folding tables, 400 dining room forms and stools, 2,200 sets of bedstead boards, 2,000 brooms and large quantities of enamel and ironware and china.

The auction, conducted by Edward T Parker and Co., of Stephen Street, Bristol, comprised more than 1,400 lots that also included 780 basins, 50 frying pans, 564 'feed tins', 1,700 galvanised buckets and pails, 76 large coal boxes, 164 corn bins, 50 fire extinguishers, 585 garden forks, 900 hoes, 968 garden rakes and 11 weighing machines.

In early May 1920, *The Western Daily Press* reported that 'the depot is gradually disappearing. Many of the buildings have been pulled down and only the concrete floors remain to mark the spot where they once stood.' Two months later, the depot had been completely dismantled.

In January 1921, the newspaper reported that a number of former depot huts had been converted to bungalows on the high ground to the north-east of Shirehampton railway station. 'They command splendid views across the river of Pill, Portbury and Portishead, with the Channel away in the distance.'

William was born in Frogwell, between Cruwys Morchard and Tiverton, in September 1882. The son of John and Frances Jane Western, he enlisted in the ASC at Woolwich. He was awarded a good conduct badge at Shirehampton in June 1917. His service records show that he was 'admonished' and forfeited a day's pay for being absent while on active service between midnight on March 27, 1916 and 11.15pm the following day.

He and Lily Ann – the daughter of William and Eliza (nee Sage) Roberts and sister of George Henry Roberts, who served in the Second Boer and First World Wars – married in Puddington, Devon, on March 18, 1906.

They had five children in eight years, William John, Rowland George, Wilfred, Winnifred and Albert Edward. Lily Ann and her four sons and daughter lived at 3 Peppers Court, Church Street, Tiverton while William served in the ASC.

William, whose service number was TS/6024, died in Tiverton in December 1954 at the age of 71. Lily Ann, born in Cruwys Morchard in 1882, and baptised in the village on Christmas Eve that year, died in 1957, aged 74.

27

WILLIAM JAMES — KILLED IN FIRST BATTLE OF YPRES

He had endured a true baptism of fire on the Western Front – fighting in some of the bloodiest battles of the war, testing his endurance to the limit on a series of punishing marches across France and Flanders and living through thunderous, earth-shattering, and seemingly endless, artillery attacks.

Just a day after arriving in Belgium in August 1914 with the 1st Battalion of the Coldstream Guards, Sergeant William James Roberts found himself caught up in the Great Mons Retreat, marching more than 200 miles in 13 days to escape a rampaging German army after their first encounter with the British Expeditionary Force in the opening battle of the war.

He fought in the gruelling Battles of Marne and Aisne, experiencing hand-to-hand combat and the dawn of brutal trench warfare. Of all the horrors he faced from day to day, perhaps the most difficult for him to withstand was the seemingly constant threat from and noise of field and siege artillery in action on the battlefields.

The deep boom of the shells being fired, the shriek of them moving through the air and the loud explosions resulting from them bursting over 'vast areas of struggle', created an 'incessant and deafening roar', Lieutenant-Colonel Sir John Ross of Bladensburg said in his book *The Coldstream Guards 1914–1918*.

'The large high explosive shells striking the earth scattered death around them and excavated huge craters some 15ft to 20ft wide by 10ft deep. Never before had war been so awe-inspiring, never had weapons been so destructive. It was a veritable pandemonium upon earth, as if hell had been let loose among men. But our troops took it all with calm and stoical indifference,' he wrote.

William had been on the Western Front for just over 70 days when he was killed by a shell in the First Battle of Ypres in October 1914. Fighting with his battalion at Langemarck at the time of his death, his body was never found. A great nephew of John Roberts – and cousin to his many grandsons serving King and country – he was just 25.

Official records state that William was killed on October 25 that year. However, it is believed he was among dozens of soldiers reported 'missing in action' between October 21 and 24 and that his death was only recorded on the 25th when his battalion left the battlefield at Langemarck to move to the village of Zillebeke, near Ypres.

William, born in Thelbridge, Devon on August 14, 1889 was one of five children of Mark and Ellen Augusta Roberts. As a child, he lived at Little Edgeworthy Cottage, Cruwys Morchard and later at Mount Pleasant, Templeton. He joined the Coldstream Guards before the war. In 1911, aged 21, he was based at their Caterham Barracks in Surrey.

In that year, his parents and his brothers, Mark Jnr and Alfred, were living at Farthing Park Farm, Morchard Bishop. There, his father – the son of John Roberts' brother, James – was farming 100 acres. Twenty-eight years later, in 1939, my parents, Sydney George and Sarah Helena Roberts bought the farm and lived and worked there until their retirement in 1975.

Just two weeks after the start of the war, William and the 1st Coldstream Guards left their Blenheim Barracks in Aldershot on the night of August 12-13, and embarked on *SS Dunvegan Castle*, an 18-year-old screw steamer, at Southampton to sail to Le Havre, arriving at the French port on the morning of August 14.

They later journeyed by train to La Nouvion and marched to the village of Boue, near Etreux, Cartignies and Vieux Reng before crossing the French border to Rouveroy in Belgium on August 23 as the Battle of Mons raged. The following day, the battalion helped to cover the retirement of British soldiers from the town as the Great Retreat began.

In 13 days, William and his men undertook a challenging march, estimated at over 200 miles, through Maubeuge to La Longueville and then on to Dompierre, Fesmy-le-Sart, Etreux, Janqueuse, St Gobain, Pinon, La Ferte-Milon, Chambry, Jouarre, Coulommiers and Nesles, about 12 miles south of Boulogne.

Commenting on the difficulties they faced, Lt-Col Sir John Ross said in his book: 'There was much fighting on the road, in overpowering heat and dust, and water was often scarce; the hours were long, there was little time for sleep, and the weight of the packs and ammunition added in no small degree to the men's troubles. During this time food was short.'

A Devonshire corporal serving in the 2nd Coldstream Guards told a friend that British soldiers had 'saved France from disaster' in the retreat. 'We kept the whole German army in check until France was able to get her army in position. Mind you, we retired back only 20 miles from Paris,' Corporal F Drew told Charles Rowe, of Chulmleigh in a letter published in *The Devon and Exeter Gazette* in December 1914.

As the retreat came to an end, William and the 1st Coldstream Guards fought in the Battle of the Marne which halted the German advance into France and marked the beginning of four years of trench warfare on the Western Front. William and his men came under heavy rifle and shrapnel fire near the village of Voinsles in an attack in which five soldiers were killed and four officers and 33 other ranks were wounded.

He marched with his battalion – attached to the 1st (Guards) Brigade of the 1st Division of the British Army – to Le Temple on September 7. The following day, in a valley near Bassevelle, four stretcher bearers were killed and 12 others, including a medical officer, were wounded when they came under heavy shell fire.

The 1st Coldstream Guards suffered devastating losses less than a week later, in the Battle of Aisne, when they acted as advanced guard in an attack on a heavily defended sugar factory near the hamlet of Troyon. Almost 80 officers and men were killed, more than 220 were wounded and almost 90 were captured by the enemy.

Many were cut down by heavy rifle and artillery fire. The battalion's commanding officer, Lieutenant-Colonel John Ponsonby was badly wounded in an assault on the nearby village of Cerny-en-Laonnois. He narrowly avoided capture after being brought back to safety by his own men in a daring night-time rescue mission.

He and his men (three officers and about 40 NCOs and men, mostly Coldstreamers) had been 'absolutely surrounded by the enemy', Lt-Col Sir John Ross said in his book. 'A German battalion marched into the Cerny close to them, without seeing them. Sentries were posted still closer to them, but they were not found out. Towards midnight they began their adventurous journey back to their own lines ... It was pitch dark, and raining and blowing hard. They succeeded in getting back without any casualties.'

A corporal in William's battalion spoke of how he was wounded by a dum-dum bullet on the first day of the Battle of Aisne when he returned to his parents' home in Wrafton, near Braunton, Devon. Corporal A J Williams told *The North Devon Journal* that he and his men advanced on German lines in the face of heavy artillery fire. Given the task of capturing an enemy battery, they sheltered in a walled garden before being forced to retreat to a road where many men lay wounded. In attempting to defend their 'perilous' position, all the men in his unit were shot or injured by rifle and artillery fire.

Cpl Williams told the newspaper in a report published in December 1914, that he was struck by a dum-dum bullet (designed to expand on impact) which left an exit wound four inches long and two inches wide. He lay on the ground for three hours until he was able to walk a mile to a field ambulance for medical assistance. He suffered septic poisoning and underwent a life-saving operation at the Queen Alexandra Military Hospital in London before returning to the home of his parents, Mr and Mrs Thomas Williams, of Heanton Hill, Wrafton.

The 1st Coldstream Guards suffered another 20 casualties on September 18 and 19 amid a heavy bombardment of their trenches at Troyon Ridge. 'The Germans never ventured to attack our position with infantry and there was no foe to be seen, no-one upon whom our men could concentrate their own fire, and the strain upon them was all the more severe. All they could do was to lie concealed under cover, to hold on tenaciously to their trenches, to watch the movements of the enemy wherever he could be seen, and to keep themselves ready to repulse any effort to dislodge them. This they did, and in one place where the trench was destroyed they clung to it to the end', wrote Lt-Col Sir John Ross.

They marched to Oeuilly the next day and on September 23 were back in front line trenches, near Verneuil, where they suffered dozens of casualties in a series of enemy bombardments. As the month drew to a close, William and his men were sent to a ridge overlooking Troyon, near the sugar factory where they had recently lost so many of their fellow soldiers. They were just 200 yards away from the Germans' entrenched positions. The space between the battalion and the enemy was swept by fire and 'strewn with dead men and horses'.

A party of 50 men, led by 2nd Lieutenant Merton Beckwith-Smith, launched an attack on newly-dug German trenches on the night of October 4-5. The first trench reached was found to be empty but for the bodies of 15 German soldiers believed to have been killed by shell fire and snipers, according to the battalion's war diary. 2nd Lt Beckwith-Smith was shot in the arm as he led a bayonet charge on the second trench. About 20 German soldiers were killed in this attack. The raiding party suffered seven casualties.

William and his battalion finally left Troyon on October 15 and marched to Blanzy and Fismes before journeying to Hazebrouck by train. They marched to Poperinghe, near Ypres on October 20, and then to Pilkelm the following day, in preparation for the Battle of Langemarck. 'Progress was slow, alternate short marches and long halts delayed the troops; everywhere they met and were obstructed by hundreds of forlorn refugees, some old and even bedridden people struggling to escape from the Germans,' recorded Lt-Col Sir John Ross.

Langemarck, at which the battalion suffered almost 200 casualties, was one of a series of battles in the First Ypres offensive which continued for more than a month, from October 19 to November 22, 1914. The offensive, frequently fought in heavy rain which turned battlefields into a quagmire, ended in stalemate and internecine entrenched warfare, with the British suffering almost 60,000 casualties.

In his letter to Charles Rowe, of Chulmleigh, Cpl F Drew, of the 2nd Coldstream Guards, said Ypres was 'like hell on earth'. He told of how 15,000 British soldiers 'drove back a great army of 75,000 Germans. There were bullets and shells, and the roar of the great French guns, and our own, and those 100Ib shells of the Germans, what we call "Jack Johnsons" which make a hole in the ground big enough to bury two horses. But what a sight. I never wish to see another battle of this kind and have so many comrades shot by one's side.'

William is remembered on the Ypres (Menin Gate) Memorial, on Panel 11. He is also one of 24 men commemorated on the War Memorial at Morchard Bishop. He was awarded the 1914 Star with clasp (2/2839 – given to those who served under fire) and the British War and Victory Medals. His service number was 7907.

Note

- As a young boy growing up in Morchard Bishop, one of my favourite places to sit in the village was opposite the local war memorial. I was fascinated by the names on the monument, and one in particular. He shared my surname and I often wondered who he was, where he lived and how he died in the war. It seemed William Roberts would forever remain a mystery when I left home at 16 to start a new life as a trainee newspaper reporter in Cornwall. More than 40 years later, the mystery was solved when it emerged that William was a great nephew of John Roberts, and was the first of his family to die in the war.

Part Five

DEVON'S TRIBUTES TO ITS FALLEN HEROES

28

MEMORIAL TO THOUSANDS
WHO DIED IN WAR

'There is no parish in the county and indeed there are very few homes
where vacant chairs do not stand as silent witnesses to gallant Jack
Tars (seamen of the Merchant or Royal Navy) or khaki-clad warriors'

The Devon and Exeter Gazette – June 7, 1919

The terrible toll of the Great War on Devon was not immediately obvious when the Armistice, or cease fire, came into effect on the 11th hour of the 11th day of the 11th month – on November 11, 1918. The war officially ended more than six months later – on June 28, 1919 when the Allies and the Germans signed a peace treaty in the Hall of Mirrors at the vast and historic Palace of Versailles, near Paris.

It took another two years to establish the number of servicemen and women from Devon killed in the war. The final figure was a staggering 11,601. The names of all those who lost their lives were listed in a 396-page Roll of Honour. A memorial to the county's fallen heroes, a magnificent 30-ft high cross made from the finest Dartmoor granite, was unveiled before a huge crowd in Exeter on May 16, 1921 by the Prince of Wales – later to become King George VI.

'The ceremony touched the souls of those present to their very depths,' reported *The Western Times*. 'Behind the mask of placid countenances fierce struggles ensued between heart-breaking emotions stirred up by vivid memories, and that English instinct of calmness and self-control. While the visible ceremony proceeded, an unseen battle swayed in the hearts of men and women who mourned. And deep sighs here and silent weeping there told their tales of mental anguish.'

A tear trickled down the Prince's 'bronzed cheek' said the newspaper as a battle of emotions – pride, gratitude, affection and sympathy – surged within him and the many thousands attending the unveiling of the memorial on St Mary's Green, close to the west front of Exeter Cathedral. He was, according to *The Western Times*, 'weeping for the mothers and sisters and sweethearts of rustic sons of the soil'.

Sir Herbert Russell, writing in *The Western Morning News and Mercury* the day after the unveiling, said the area around the cathedral was 'a wonderful picture of teeming humanity, vividly splashed with colour. The nestling, gabled old houses seemed to palpitate with eager countenances in every window; even the battlements of the hoary cathedral and of the Church of St Mary Major bore their ensconced clusters of spectators.'

A special service to dedicate the memorial was 'rich, sonorous, and altogether beautiful'. The very simplicity of the ceremony was profoundly moving, said Sir Herbert, who added: 'When the Prince laid a superb wreath against the sun-touched pinnacle after drawing asunder the two Union Jacks which had draped it, I am positive many an eye moistened and many a throat grew painful to the rising of a lump within it.'

The memorial, hewn from an old granite quarry at Haytor, was designed by Sir Edwin Lutyens, the celebrated architect of the Thiepval Memorial in France, The Cenotaph in Whitehall, London, Castle Drogo in the Devon village of Drewsteignton, and New Delhi in India. It was inscribed with the words: 'The county of Devon – to her glorious dead – 1914–1919 – *Te Deum Laudamus* (Thee, O God, we praise)'.

The Prince said it was a 'great honour' to unveil the Devon County War Memorial and to join in paying tribute to the gallant sons of Devon who gave their lives to their King and their country since 1914. 'I think that the magnitude of the

Great War, and what the British effort and sacrifice was, is brought home by the fact that the Devonshire Regiment alone sent 50,000 men overseas – that is over double the whole of the British forces at the Battle of Waterloo, and the regiment's casualties were well over double what there were at that ancient battle.'

Devon's Lord Lieutenant, Earl Hugh Fortescue, said at the unveiling: 'Our men fought on every front, and on every sea the world over. We praise God for their steadfastness and courage and for the victory which they helped to win. Their graves are far away, but we trust their names will be kept in everlasting remembrance in their native county as an example of duty done and as an inspiration in service to the State.' The cross commemorated men and women of all ranks – sailors, soldiers, merchant seamen, minesweepers, hospital workers.

The names of those who lost their lives were recorded alphabetically and parish by parish in the Roll of Honour. The book, listing the names of the fallen, regiment or ship they served in and the date and place of their deaths, was put in a copper casket and placed under the memorial. Two duplicates were presented to the Dean of Exeter, the Very Rev Henry Reginald Gamble, for preservation in the archives of the cathedral, and to Sir Henry Yarde Buller Lopes, chairman of Devon County Council, to be placed among the county records.

Two years earlier, on June 6, 1919, a special memorial service for Devon's war dead was held at Exeter Cathedral and attended by more than 3,000 people. The Dean of Exeter told the congregation that all those who died were 'martyrs – witnesses to what they believed to be the cause of justice and of right and, therefore, the cause of God, by their ready obedience to the cause of duty, their courage, their endurance, their self-sacrifice'.

There was, he said, 'cherished in many a Devonshire home, in many a hall or manor, in many a poor man's cottage, in many a quiet parsonage, the recollection of one, almost a boy, or sometimes more than one, a young artisan or labourer, or undergraduate or clerk, who went when the call came, whose cheery letters were read and re-read, but whose face they would see no more. One by one they would be remembered.'

Time, said the Dean, would fail to tell all of the gallant deeds done by Devon men in the war. He mentioned one striking instance out of many – the heroic last stand of the 2nd Battalion of the Devonshire Regiment at Bois de Buttes in France on May 27, 1918. On that day, the battalion were surrounded and repeatedly attacked by the advancing German army but against all odds defended their line – saving the lives of countless British soldiers gathering south west of the Aisne. In the face of relentless assault, the commanding officer, his 28 officers and 552 men refused to surrender and fought to the end.

The Dean said Devon would never forget the bravery of these men – and the courage of so many in the face of overwhelming odds. They were 'men of Devon ... bone of their bone, and flesh of their flesh, nourished among their own hills and vales, lovers of their streams and meadows and rugged shores, who died ... with a vision before their eyes of the old fields of home far away'. The memory of those men would live on in 'innumerable hearts'.

The Western Times, reporting on what was widely acclaimed as a 'beautiful and impressive service', said: 'There are few if any families from whom the war has not exacted terrible toll. Of the 3,000 people for whom seating accommodation had been provided for the service, there was probably no-one who was not mourning a relative or close friend. This fact invested the service with a unique solemnity and touching significance.'

The Exeter and Plymouth Gazette said, 'in all probability, it was the most representative united Devonshire service ever held in the Mother Church (the cathedral), for Devonians came from every district. All classes and all creeds, rich and poor alike, were there.' They were paying tribute to the men of Devon who, 'from mansion and cottage, from city and country, from parsonage and manse ... had upheld Britain's honour on many a terrible field of battle. In France and Flanders, in Mesopotamia and India, Italy and Salonica, Gallipoli and Palestine, they fought, and in many instances died.'

29

HOW CITIES, TOWNS AND VILLAGES HONOURED THEIR WAR DEAD

They were there to say their final goodbyes. To honour fathers, husbands, sons, brothers, uncles, cousins and friends who had died in the Great War. They included babes in arms and toddlers who never got to see their dads, young wives made widows all too soon and parents mourning sons who had been in the bloom of youth.

Villages, towns and cities across Devon unveiled hundreds of memorials – ranging from granite crosses to stained glass windows and clock towers to village halls and institutes – between 1919 and 1930 to commemorate the thousands of men from the county who died on the battlefields, in hospitals and at sea.

The people of Plymouth turned out in their thousands to watch the Secretary of State for War, Edward George Villiers Stanley, the 17th Earl of Derby, unveil an impressive memorial at the entrance to the city's famous Hoe on May 19, 1923. Among the crowds were hundreds of relatives of soldiers and sailors who never came home.

They included a little boy called Fred Selby, who was wearing the medals of a father he never knew. He was just ten months old when his daddy was killed. Close to him was another young boy clinging on to a Military Medal awarded posthumously to his father for 'bravery on the field', *The Western Morning News and Mercury* reported two days after the ceremony.

Plymouth had more men fighting in the war than any other city or town in Devon. Thirty thousand served in the Army and Navy between 1914 and 1918 and 2,000 did not make it home, Lord Derby told the huge crowds before unveiling the Cornish granite memorial, featuring a bronze female figure holding aloft a wreath of laurels.

Lord Derby said the memorial would forever honour the men of Plymouth who made the ultimate sacrifice. He also hoped it would act as a 'deterrent to war in the future'. Its very presence would, he said, be a constant and graphic reminder to future generations that conflict could be waged only at a very heavy price.

Perhaps the most impressive of Devon's monuments to the fallen was erected in Exeter, in the city's Northernhay Gardens. Designed by Newton Abbot-born sculptor John Angel, who devoted nearly four years of his life to creating the masterpiece, it was unveiled by Earl Beatty, the First Sea Lord and Admiral of the Fleet, on July 24, 1923.

The Western Times described the critically-acclaimed 31ft high memorial – crowned by a spectacular bronze 'Victory' figure and featuring four seated statues representing the sailor, soldier, nurse and prisoner of war – as 'exquisite' and believed that, as a work of art, it had to be 'considered as one of the finest in the country'.

In unveiling the memorial, commemorating almost 1,000 men from the city who lost their lives, Earl Beatty told the thousands attending that 'none of us are likely to forget the war which devastated the world so recently. None of us are likely to forget those gallant men who gave their lives for their King and country in that great struggle. But a time will come when the war will be but a feint echo down the path of time, and it is against that day that we erect enduring memorials in stone and bronze to replace those which are enshrined in our hearts.'

In a stirring speech reported in *The Western Morning News and Mercury*, he said: 'Those who pass this memorial a generation hence, and generations after that, will not be stirred with the sense of personal pride and sadness which we feel, but they will see in it a reminder of the virtues which preserved this empire of ours from destruction in time of great peril. It will serve as a reminder of the courage and the self-sacrifice of their fathers, and as an incentive to spur them to equal nobility of purpose and of action ... these men gave their lives for the future of England.'

Crediton's striking memorial – an oak shelter with a roof supported by eight huge oak pillars and a Portland stone centrepiece featuring the names of more than 130 men who died in the war – was unveiled on May 16, 1923 by Field Marshall Sir William Robertson, who served as the British Army's Chief of the Imperial General Staff between 1916 and 1918.

Sir William said it was a 'privilege to show honour to those men of Crediton who fell in the war'. He also hoped that no-one would forget the many who fought and survived. Many returned broken in health, maimed for life, perhaps blind, and many found great difficulty in obtaining a livelihood for themselves and their families, he told the watching crowds.

In a speech reported in *The Western Times*, he said the Devonshire Regiment served in all theatres of war, including Italy, Gallipoli, Mesopotamia, Palestine and India, and shared in most of the great battles – at Mons, the Aisne, Ypres, Neuve Chapelle, Vimy Ridge and Passchendaele. The regiment could 'fairly be said to be second to none'.

Relatives and friends of the men who lost their lives knew them from infancy, remembered them going to war, and how and when they left their home town and surrounding villages to fight overseas. Consequently, he was sure there were some 'sad memorials erected in the minds of many of those standing there that day'.

The seven grandsons of John Roberts who died in the war are remembered on memorials in the Devonshire villages of Rackenford, Cruwys Morchard, Witheridge and Oakford, and also in Tiverton, and in Dulverton, Somerset.

The village of Rackenford dedicated two memorials – a traditional granite monument, and a brass on black marble tablet at the parish church – in honour of eight local men who lost their lives, including brothers Samuel 'Sam' and John Francis 'Frank' Roberts, who were both killed in France in 1916.

The tablet was unveiled in November 1919 by Francis James Coleridge Boles, of Rackenford Manor. The ceremony was reported in *The Western Times* which said 'there was a good congregation and the service, led by the Rector, the Rev J A T L Beazor, was fully choral'. The Hallelujah Chorus was played and a 'muffled peal' was rung before the service.

The war memorial at the Church of the Holy Cross in Cruwys Morchard was unveiled in March 1920. Honouring eight local men who died in the war – including John 'Jack Roberts, who died from wounds sustained in action in France in 1915 – it was created out of polished white marble with a wreath and reproductions of the Union Jack and Flag of St George.

Described as a 'beautiful piece of work' in *The Devon and Exeter Gazette* of April 1 that year, it was inscribed with the following words: 'To the glory of God and in honoured memory of the following men from this parish who gave their lives in the Great War 1914–1919'. An oak tablet erected in the church porch was inscribed with the names of all from the parish who served during the war.

Witheridge remembered its fallen on a granite cross in the grounds of the Grade I listed Church of St John the Baptist. Honouring 17 men from the village – including Albert Roberts, who died from wounds sustained in action in France in 1915 – it was unveiled by local soldier Francis George Selley, who served as a sergeant in the 16th Devons.

It was an emotional moment for Francis, who was one of six sons of Witheridge butcher George Henry Selley to fight in the war. For among those listed on the memorial was his younger brother, Sidney Robert Selley, a corporal in the 8th Devons, who was killed in action in France on May 8, 1917, aged 23.

The Witheridge Historical Archive said the ceremony was surrounded in controversy when 'old Mrs Morrish', the mother-in-law of Military Medal holder Edward 'Ned' Stanley Ayre, who had been a sergeant in the 2nd Devons, stood on the steps of the memorial shouting that he should have been asked to carry out the unveiling.

Rifleman Sidney Roberts, who died of wounds in 1917, is remembered on two memorials, in Oakford, near Bampton, Devon and in Dulverton, Somerset. The Oakford memorial, a Dartmoor granite cross was dedicated on April 20, 1920 by the long serving Bishop of Zululand, the Rt Rev Wilmot Lushington Vyvyan.

A magnificent war memorial hall and library in Tiverton honouring the 281 men and women from the town who gave their lives in the war – including brothers William Henry and Walter Kingdom, who died in 1916 and 1918 respectively – was opened by the Lord Lieutenant of Devon, Lord Mildmay of Flete, on April 3, 1929.

According to a report in *The Devon and Exeter Gazette*, Lord Mildmay said Tiverton and its population of 10,000 had bravely borne its share of responsibility and sorrow and suffering in the war. Around 1,500 men and women from the town had served King and country during 1914–18, and one in five never returned.

With peace came 'the immense desire' for a permanent and worthy memorial, and it was rightly decided that it should be a benefit to the living as well as a tribute to the fallen. The building not only contained a library hall with room for 20,000 books, but also a fine assembly hall and rooms for social and recreational purposes.

In 1922, the Bishop of Exeter, Lord Rupert Ernest William Gascoyne-Cecil, dedicated an English oak screen in Tiverton's St Peter's Church in memory of those who died in the war. The screen, part of St Peter's War Memorial Chapel, was described in *The Western Times* as a 'beautiful piece of craftsmanship' that 'harmonised admirably with its surroundings'.

In unveiling the war memorial at Morchard Bishop on July 11, 1920 – honouring 24 local men, including Sergeant William James Roberts, John Roberts' great nephew, who was killed in action in 1914 – the 7th Earl of Portsmouth, John Fellowes Wallop, told the large gathering that, 'ten years ago no-one in that village would have thought the day would come when they would be unveiling and dedicating a memorial in that peaceful village, miles from business or manufacturing centres, to the services rendered by the parishioners in the greatest war the world had ever known'.

He said the people of the parish wished the monument, a Dartmoor granite cross, 'to be a link between the living and the dead, and of the fellowship that bound over 400 million people throughout the world', *The Western Times* reported. The memorial, 'if it was a sign of suffering, was also a sign of triumph, that the British Empire existed not for aggrandisement of individuals, but for the happiness and wellbeing of the world. It was also a memorial of love for those who had served, suffered and died for them.'

Thousands watched as a Devonshire granite cross remembering the 245 men of Barnstaple who didn't make it home, was unveiled at the entrance to the town's Rock Park by Earl Fortescue, Lord Lieutenant of Devon, in October 1922. Bideford's War Memorial Cross, at Chudleigh Fort East-the-Water, commemorating 21 men and women, was unveiled by the Mayor, councillor J U Fulford, in August 1921.

A pulpit believed to be the only one erected in Devon as a war memorial, was unveiled at Zeal Monachorum Parish Church in 1923. *The Devon and Exeter Gazette* said the pulpit was made from oak cut from a large tree in the parish and seasoned for 50 years. 'This tree was probably growing at the time of the Commonwealth; and young men of the parish called up at various epoch-making periods in our history had played as children under its branches. This tree has now been called to nobler service,' reported the newspaper.

ACKNOWLEDGEMENTS

This book would not have been possible without the chance finding of the old newspaper image of John Roberts. Its discovery, on the Witheridge Historical Archive, started the many years of research that resulted in the remarkable story of John and his grandsons being told here for the first time.

The contemporary illustration of John on the front cover – a new and brilliant piece of artwork by Tor Allen, who lives and works in the South Hams area of Devon – has been inspired by the old newspaper image and by pictures of my father Sydney George Roberts, who, like John, had impressive sideburns and a beard.

I would not have been able to piece together the lives of John's grandsons without the help and encouragement of descendants of John Roberts. Long chats with my father more than 40 years ago provided a wealth of information about his father, who was one of the 30 grandsons to serve King and country in the Great War.

The quest to trace and research the lives of John Roberts' grandsons involved help from many who can trace their ancestry back to the great man, notably Lynne Roberts, of Thorverton, Devon, grand-daughter of Private Archibald Roberts, of the 13th Hussars, and John and Margaret Chapman, of Norfolk.

The years of research involved perusing many thousands of newspaper pages, military records, Census returns and parish records, visits to the Devon Heritage Centre in Exeter, numerous museums, libraries, parish churches, churchyards, cemeteries, war memorials, and old family farms and smallholdings in Devon.

None of this could have been achieved without the unwavering love and support from my wife, Jenny, who inspired me to devote many hundreds of hours of my – and her time – to working on this seemingly endless project. It is of the greatest sadness to me that Jenny did not live long enough to see the publication of this book.

War diaries have provided a unique insight into the real-life, day-by-day experiences of John's grandsons on the front line. The diaries, kept by the National Archives in Kew Gardens, Richmond Surrey, and many of which are now digitised, have helped me to walk in the boots of those who served in France, Belgium, Mesopotamia, Egypt, Palestine and Gallipoli.

The British Newspaper Archive has provided a valuable source of information about those who died or were wounded in the war, the narrow escapes from death some had on the Western Front, tales of the bravery of those who fought in the trenches and the horrors many soldiers encountered in fighting for their King and country.

Newspapers on the Archive – notably *The Western Times, The Devon and Exeter Gazette, The North Devon Journal and The Western Morning News* – have provided a graphic insight into the tremendous sacrifices made by many of Devon's families in sending fathers, sons, brothers, uncles, cousins and friends to war.

They also helped to reveal how farmers and their sons found themselves at the centre of a recruitment war of words at home as many thousands of men were slaughtered on the front line in France and Flanders – and how Devon commemorated its fallen through unveiling hundreds of memorials across the county.

The wide range of military records – including medal cards, service honours, service and pension records, registers of soldiers' effects and Silver Badge records – and Census returns on Ancestry.co.uk, have been pivotal in helping me to confirm the deaths, war service and early lives of many of John's grandsons.

Burial, memorial and war cemetery records held by the Commonwealth War Graves Commission filled many gaps and provided invaluable leads. Parish records, particularly for Cruwys Morchard, Thelbridge, Witheridge, Sandford and Tiverton, held at the Devon Heritage Centres in Exeter and in Barnstaple, provided rich sources of information.

In the past five years, the incomparable Great War Forum has been crucial in answering many questions in tracing John's grandsons. Its members provided the key to numerous enquiries on battle, service, pension and medal records. They never failed to find a way forward when I was hitting so many brick walls.

The Long, Long Trail, the brilliant WWI website created as a labour of love by military historian Chris Baker, has helped immensely with my research, particularly with timelines for battles and offensives on the Western Front, the history and movements of regiments and battalions, casualties on the battlefield, and the introduction of conscription.

I have included extracts from and references to a number of excellent books which offer vivid accounts of battles and actions John's grandsons were involved in, notably:

- *The Devonshire Regiment 1914–1918*, compiled by C T Atkinson, originally published 1926. Naval and Military Press Ltd edition, 2002.

- *The 74th Yeomanry Division in Syria and France*, by Major C H Dudley Ward, originally published 1922. Naval and Military Press Ltd edition, 2004.

- *The War History of the 1st Battalion Queen's Westminster Rifles, 1914–18*, by Major J Q Henriques, originally published by the Medici Society, 1923. Naval and Military Press Ltd edition, 2003.

- *The Thirteenth Hussars in the Great War*, by the Rt Hon Sir Henry Mortimer Durand, originally published by William Blackwood and Sons, Edinburgh and London, 1921. Naval and Military Press Ltd edition, 2003.

- *The Coldstream Guards 1914–1918*, by Lt-Col Sir John Ross of Bladensburg, originally published 1928. Naval and Military Press Ltd edition, 2003.

- *From Bapaume to Passchendaele*, by Philip Gibbs, published by Echo Library, 2014.

- *The British Army in Mesopotamia in 1914–1918*, by Paul Knight, published by McFarland & Co, 2013.

- *A Small School in the Great War: The story of Sutton County School and its old boys in World War I*, written and published by Arthur Edward Jones, 1975.

A book by Martin Body – *The 2nd Devons War Diary: The 2nd Battalion Devonshire Regiment and its Lost Men 1914–1919*, published in 2012 by Pollinger in Print – has helped me to confirm deaths of two of John's grandsons who served in the battalion.

A Parish Patchwork by Daphne Munday, first published in 1985 and reprinted in 2000 and 2013 has provided a glimpse into the life of one of John Roberts' sons, Henry, a father of three sons who fought in and survived the war.

The following have also helped with my research:

- Gordon Smith, Naval-History.net
- *The London Gazette*
- Uboat.net
- Devon Family History Society
- Newton St Cyres History Group (who helped in researching George Burnett Roberts' life in the village)
- The Wartime Memories Project
- Exeter Memories
- Winkleigh on Line
- General Register Office (details of births, marriages and deaths)
- Vernon Rattenbury (researcher of the Uplyme Roll of Honour)
- Monica Pike, Tiverton

- Anita Kingdom
- Judith Binks, Washford Pyne
- Gov.uk (details of soldiers' wills)
- History Hub Ulster
- Chris Comber (researcher of *Salehurst Roll of Honour*)
- Haslingden War Heroes blog

The pictures

The pictures of graves of – and memorials to – the seven grandsons of John Roberts who died on the Western Front and in Mesopotamia have been kindly supplied by The War Graves Photographic Project. They have also allowed me to use pictures of the cemeteries in France and Belgium in which the graves and memorials are found – and of the Basra Memorial in Iraq where Corporal William Kingdom is remembered.

The War Graves Photographic Project (www.twgpp.org) have undertaken the immense task of recording, archiving and making available to descendants, images of the graves or memorial listings of every service casualty since the outbreak of the Great War. This task has been reliant solely on volunteers who have given freely of their time to visit, record and catalogue the many hundreds of thousands of graves and monuments scattered around the world.

Family pictures have been provided by relatives. The photograph of Archie Roberts, of the 13th Hussars, has been supplied by his grand-daughter, Lynne Roberts. Nicole Vallins has supplied the image of John Francis Bryant Roberts and his family, and Sarah Child has provided the picture of Sam Roberts, of the 8th Devons, when he was a pupil at Rackenford School.

The picture of Private Albert Roberts, published after his death in *The Western Times*, is the copyright of Trinity Mirror and appears on the British Newspaper Archive website. I am grateful that Trinity Mirror have allowed me to use the picture, along with extracts from five letters from the trenches and an article for which they hold the copyright.

SOURCES

Part one: John, his family and astonishing happenings at home

Primary sources

A. British Newspaper Archive (www.britishnewspaperarchive.co.uk) – *The Western Times, The Devon and Exeter Gazette, The Western Morning News, The North Devon Journal*

B. Ancestry.co.uk military records (www.ancestry.co.uk)

C. Commonwealth War Graves Commission (www.cwgc.org)

Chapter 1: An extraordinary find – a remarkable man

1. John Roberts – Witheridge Historical Archive (WI1086, photographic index, www.witheridge-historical-archive.com)
2. Third of Zeal Monachorum's population served in the war – Devon village record, *The Western Times*, Friday December 7, 1923, page 4. With thanks to The British Newspaper Archive
3. 160 families with four or more sons serving in the war – Devon's memorial, *The Western Times*, Tuesday June 10, 1919, page 2. With thanks to The British Newspaper Archive
4. Elizabeth Spratt – Twenty-seven grandsons in the Army, *North-Eastern Daily Gazette*, Middlesbrough, Monday October 5, 1914, page 2. With thanks to The British Newspaper Archive
5. Funeral card – with thanks to John and Margaret Chapman, Norfolk

Chapter 2: The magnificent seven

1. John Francis 'Frank' Roberts, killed while drinking tea in the trenches – News of the West: Rackenford, *The Western Times*, Friday October 6, 1916, page 10. With thanks to The British Newspaper Archive

Chapter 3: Patriotism – and great sacrifices

1. Susan Alford – Hard to beat: A Devon family's record of patriotism, *The Western Times*, Friday November 26, 1915, page 3. With thanks to The British Newspaper Archive

2. Pte and Mrs W Heard – Remarkable record, *The Western Times*, Friday November 2, 1917, Page 7. With thanks to The British Newspaper Archive

3. Arthur Cotton's 24 relatives – Patriotic Devon Families, *The Devon and Exeter Gazette*, Friday March 12, 1915, page 9. With thanks to The British Newspaper Archive

4. Mr and Mrs John Shaddick's 24 relatives – North Devon Family's Patriotism, *The Western Times*, Friday January 1, 1915, page 7. With thanks to The British Newspaper Archive

5. Hewett family's 17 relatives – Local and district news, *The Western Times*, Thursday March 11, 1915, page 3. With thanks to The British Newspaper Archive

6. Anderson-Morshead family – Patriotic Devon Families, *The Devon and Exeter Gazette*, Friday March 5, 1915, page 9. With thanks to The British Newspaper Archive

7. Mrs B Bourne's 19 relatives – Patriotic Devon Families, *The Devon and Exeter Gazette*, Friday March 12, 1915, page 9; District news: George Nympton, *The Devon and Exeter Gazette*, Friday August 2, 1918, page 3. With thanks to The British Newspaper Archive

8. Mrs Burton's 15 relatives – *The Western Times*, Friday March 31, 1916, page 11. With thanks to The British Newspaper Archive

9. Mr W H Carpenter's six sons – Proud Exeter record, *The Western Times*, Thursday June 29, 1916, page 2. With thanks to The British Newspaper Archive

10. Rodd family – Father and five sons in the Army, *The North Devon Journal*, Thursday November 4, 1915, page 5. With thanks to The British Newspaper Archive

11. George Pike and sons – Father and Sons from Uffculme, *The Western Times*, Friday June 22, 1917, page 7. With thanks to The British Newspaper Archive

12. John Newbery and sons – Father and Sons in the Army, *The Exeter and Plymouth Gazette*, Friday July 2, 1915, page 14. With thanks to The British Newspaper Archive

13. James Gilbert and sons – Father and Three Sons in the Forces, *The Devon and Exeter Gazette*, Friday September 22, 1916, page 9. With thanks to The British Newspaper Archive

14. Sealey family, Teignmouth – Teignmothian Makes the Great Sacrifice, *The Western Times*, Friday October 6, 1916, page 2. With thanks to The British Newspaper Archive

15. Mole family, Shaldon – Shaldon men killed and wounded, *The Western*

Morning News, Friday April 26, 1918, page 1. With thanks to The British Newspaper Archive

16. Davey family, Torquay – Local and district news, *The Western Times*, Wednesday December 8, 1915, page 3. With thanks to The British Newspaper Archive

17. William Bartlett, Heavitree – *The Devon and Exeter Gazette*, Friday December 22, 1916, page 6. With thanks to The British Newspaper Archive

18. Rawle family, Thorverton – Devon widow who has eight sons serving, *The Western Times*, Tuesday November 28, 1916, page 2. With thanks to The British Newspaper Archive

19. Stentiford family, Morchard Bishop – News of the West, *The Western Times*, Friday September 7, 1917, page 9. With thanks to The British Newspaper Archive

20. Turner family, North Tawton – *The Western Times*, Monday February 22, 1915, page 2. With thanks to The British Newspaper Archive

21. Publican Richard Ellis loses four sons – Devon family's record: royal sympathy for an Upton Pyne father, *The Western Times*, Friday May 10, 1918, page 7. With thanks to The British Newspaper Archive

22. Gratton family lose four sons – District News: Landkey, *The Devon and Exeter Gazette*, Friday December 22, 1916, page 5; Landkey soldier killed in action, *The North Devon Journal*, Thursday October 19, 1916, page 5. With thanks to The British Newspaper Archive

23. Two bishops lose five sons – with thanks to Exetermemories.co.uk (www.exetermemories.co.uk)

24. Knapman family, Thorverton – Gaps which the war has made in Devon homes, *The Western Times*, Friday November 17, 1916, page 7. With thanks to The British Newspaper Archive

25. Stephenson family, Barnstaple – Roll of Honour, *The North Devon Journal*, Thursday December 6, 1917, page 3. With thanks to The British Newspaper Archive

26. Clow family, Exeter – An Exeter family's sacrifice, *The Western Times*, Friday August 16, 1918, page 7. With thanks to The British Newspaper Archive

27. Bater family, Chulmleigh – Deaths, *The North Devon Journal*, Thursday September 5, 1918, page 8. With thanks to The British Newspaper Archive

28. Blight family, Filleigh – North Devon war items, *The North Devon Journal*, Thursday April 26, 1917, page 5; North Devon Roll of Honour for 1917, *The North Devon Journal*, Thursday January 10, 1918, page 2. With thanks to The British Newspaper Archive

29. Woodman family, Kilmington – The Kut advance: many men of the Devon Regiment fall fighting, *The Western Times*, Friday February 16, 1917, page 12; Patriotic Devon families, *The Devon and Exeter Gazette*,

Friday March 5, 1915, page 9; Roll of Honour, *The Devon and Exeter Gazette*, Tuesday November 16, 1915, page 5. With thanks to The British Newspaper Archive

30. Greenslade family, Bampton – Killed, *Sheffield Daily Telegraph*, Saturday September 18, 1915, page 7. With thanks to The British Newspaper Archive; Soldiers who died in the Great War, military records, Ancestry. co.uk

31. Greenslade family, Newport, Barnstaple – Killed in action: Barum family bereaved of a soldier son, *The Western Times*, Wednesday August 25, 1915, page 3; Barumite dies of wounds, *The North Devon Journal*, Thursday October 19, 1916, page 5. With thanks to The British Newspaper Archive; Soldiers who died in the Great War, military records, Ancestry.co.uk

32. Couldridge family, Bideford – Roll of Honour, *The Western Daily Press*, Saturday October 28, 1916, page 6; Well-known Bideford man dies of wounds, *The Western Times*, Thursday June 27, 1918, page 3. With thanks to The British Newspaper Archive; Soldiers who died in the Great War, military records, Ancestry.co.uk

33. Hamlyn family, Teignmouth – Roll of Honour, *The Western Times*, Friday September 28, 1917, page 8. With thanks to The British Newspaper Archive; Soldiers who died in the Great War, military records, Ancestry. co.uk

34. Paskey family, Barnstaple – News of the West: Barnstaple, *The Western Times*, Friday August 25, 1916, page 8; Death of a Barnstaple soldier, *The North Devon Journal*, Thursday October 10, 1918, page 5; Roll of Honour, *The Western Times*, Thursday October 31, 1918, page 3. With thanks to The British Newspaper Archive; Soldiers who died in the Great War, military records, Ancestry.co.uk

35. Stocker family, Uplyme – with thanks to Vernon Rattenbury, who has also researched all the names on his home town memorial (Lyme Regis), and those who served and returned; District news: Lyme Regis, *The Devon and Exeter Gazette*, Friday August 24, 1917, page 6. With thanks to The British Newspaper Archive

36. Burnell family, Dartmouth – Local and district news, *The Western Times*, Thursday February 24, 1916, page 3; News of the West: Dartmouth, *The Western Times*, Tuesday November 6, 1917, page 6. With thanks to The British Newspaper Archive; Soldiers who died in the Great War, military records, Ancestry.co.uk

37. Amy Beechey: Five soldier sons killed – *Lincolnshire Echo*, Tuesday April 9, 1918, page 3. With thanks to The British Newspaper Archive

38. Elizabeth Davies: *Hartlepool Northern Daily Mail*, Tuesday March 30, 1926, page 3. With thanks to The British Newspaper Archive

39. Cornish lady with six sons serving – A stricken Westcountry mother's patriotism, *The Western Times*, Saturday October 9, 1915, page 3. With thanks to The British Newspaper Archive

40. Father and five sons killed in action – *Coventry Evening Telegraph*, Tuesday, November 30, 1915, page 2. With thanks to The British Newspaper Archive

Chapter 4: Humble life of a history maker
1. Stickeridge Farm, Cruwys Morchard – 1841 Census return, Ancestry. co.uk
2. 1829: Geronimo – A noted Indian chief, *The Aberdeen Press and Journal*, Saturday February 20, 1909, Page 5; William Booth – General Booth lays down his sword, *The Western Times*, Friday August 23, 1912, page 6; Stephenson's 'Rocket' – Trial of locomotive carriages, *London Courier and Evening Gazette*, Thursday October 8, 1829, page 3; Metropolitan Police – *London Evening Standard*, Tuesday August 11, 1829, page 2; William Burke hanged – Execution of Burke, *The Western Times*, Saturday February 7, 1829, page 3; First Oxford-Cambridge Boat Race – *Woolmer's Exeter and Plymouth Gazette*, Saturday June 20, 1829, page 4. With thanks to The British Newspaper Archive
3. Agricultural workers 1851-1871 – researched from Census returns by Marjie Bloy, former Senior Research Fellow at the National University of Singapore
4. National Labourers Union meeting, Broadclyst – Farm labourers in Devonshire, *The Western Times*, Thursday October 22, 1874, page 3. With thanks to The British Newspaper Archive
5. Letter from 'a working man' – Labouring versus clerical poverty, *The Western Times*, Tuesday September 14, 1886, page 2. With thanks to The British Newspaper Archive
6. Emigration conference – The truth about emigration, *The East and South Devon Advertiser*, Saturday March 6, 1886, page 4. With thanks to The British Newspaper Archive
7. 'Plenty of work' in Queensland – The truth about emigration, *The North Devon Journal*, Thursday May 7, 1891, page 3. With thanks to The British Newspaper Archive
8. Henry Jordan letter – Bush-life in Queensland, *The North Devon Journal*, Thursday August 17, 1865, page 8. With thanks to The British Newspaper Archive
9. Worries over impact of emigration – Emigration: How it is draining Devon of men and money, *The Western Times*, Thursday March 20, 1913, page 9. With thanks to The British Newspaper Archive
10. John Roberts death – Witheridge news, *The Western Times*, Friday May 30, 1919, page 9. With thanks to The British Newspaper Archive
11. John Roberts funeral – Witheridge news, *The Devon and Exeter Gazette*, Friday May 30, 1919, page 5. With thanks to The British Newspaper Archive
12. John Roberts Jnr, orderly to Field Marshall Roberts – News of the West:

Rackenford, *The Western Times*, Friday October 1, 1915, page 14. With thanks to The British Newspaper Archive

13. Census returns for John Roberts for 1851, 1861, 1871, 1881, 1891, 1901, 1911 – Ancestry.co.uk

14. Funeral card for Mary Roberts – with thanks to John and Margaret Chapman, Norfolk

Chapter 5: Three brothers marry three sisters

1. Great War deaths – British Army statistics of the Great War, The Long, Long Trail (www.longlongtrail.co.uk)

2. 1911 Census returns – Ancestry.co.uk

3. Morrish sisters – with thanks to Monica Pike, Tiverton

Chapter 6: Devon farmers in recruitment 'war of words'

1. Farmers' sons: stumbling block to recruiting in North Devon – *The Western Times*, Thursday February 18, 1915, page 3. With thanks to The British Newspaper Archive

2. Gerald Reade poem – Fair Devon's sons, *The Western Times*, Saturday February 20, 1915, page 2. With thanks to The British Newspaper Archive

3. Daniel Arscott letter – *The Devon and Exeter Gazette*, Friday December 18, 1914, page 11. With thanks to The British Newspaper Archive

4. Tiverton branch of Devon Farmers' Union meeting – Protest against allegations of unpatriotism, *The Western Times*, Wednesday November 25, 1914, page 3. With thanks to The British Newspaper Archive

5. 'Unjust stigma' on farmers' sons – *The Western Times*, Wednesday January 13, 1915, page 3. With thanks to The British Newspaper Archive

6. 'Bad recruiting day for the Devons' – *The Western Times*, Friday February 19, 1915, page 5. With thanks to The British Newspaper Archive

7. 'Pushing the rake' – Straight talk … to the shirkers, *The Western Times*, Friday September 3, 1915, page 5. With thanks to The British Newspaper Archive

8. Military Service Act – The Long, Long Trail

9. The duty dodgers – *The Western Times*, Friday March 24, 1916, page 11. Letter © Trinity Mirror. Reproduced with permission of the British Newspaper Archive

10. Response to duty dodging accusations – Clerk replies to certain newspaper comments, *The Western Times*, Monday April 3, 1916, page 3. With thanks to The British Newspaper Archive

11. Crediton Tribunal exemptions – The farmers' difficulties, *The Western Times*, Wednesday February 9, 1916, page 2. With thanks to The British Newspaper Archive

12. Letter by 'Fair Play' of Sandford – Appointment of tribunals, *The Devon and Exeter Gazette*, Friday February 11, 1916, page 9. With thanks to The British Newspaper Archive

13. 'Slur' on Crediton Tribunal – Crediton Tribunal defended, *The Devon and Exeter Gazette*, Friday, February 11, 1916, page 9. With thanks to The British Newspaper Archive

14. Canon Boles' fears – Too lenient, *The Western Times*, Thursday March 2, 1916, page 2. With thanks to The British Newspaper Archive

Part two: The grandsons who did not come home

Chapter 7: The day death visited John and his family

1. Army B104-82 Form – How the next of kin were informed, The Long, Long Trail (www.longlongtrail.co.uk)

Chapter 8: Jack – baptism of fire on the Western Front ends in tragedy

Primary sources

A   War Diary for 2nd Battalion of the Devonshire Regiment – National Archives (www.nationalarchives.gov.uk)

B   *The Devonshire Regiment 1914–1918*, compiled by C T Atkinson, Naval and Military Press Ltd edition, 2002 (www.naval-military-press.com)

C   British Newspaper Archive (www.britishnewspaperarchive.co.uk) – *The Western Times, The North Devon Journal*

D   Parish records for Cruwys Morchard – The Church of the Holy Cross and Devon Heritage Centre

E   Ancestry.co.uk military records (soldiers who died in the Great War, Army registers of soldiers' effects, medal card, service awards) and Census returns for 1901 and 1911 (www.ancestry.co.uk)

1.   Chums to the end – *The Western Times*, Thursday May 20, 1915, page 2. Letter © Trinity Mirror. Reproduced with permission of the British Newspaper Archive

2.   Outcry over high explosive shortfalls – Alleged shells friction, *The Aberdeen Press and Journal*, Thursday May 20, 1915, page 5. With thanks to The British Newspaper Archive

3.   Sgt Eames letter – The Devons at Neuve Chapelle, *The North Devon Journal*, April 1, 1915, page 5. Letter © Trinity Mirror. Reproduced with permission of the British Newspaper Archive

4.   Sgt Gilliland letter – Experience told by an Exmouth soldier, *The Western Times*, April 27, 1915, page 6. Letter © Trinity Mirror. Reproduced with permission of the British Newspaper Archive

5.   Military funeral, Barnstaple – Another Barumite dies from his wounds, *The North Devon Journal*, Thursday April 1, 1915, page 5. With thanks to The British Newspaper Archive

6.   Aubers Ridge casualties – The Long, Long Trail (www.longlongtrail.co.uk)

7.   1894: Blackpool Tower opening – *The Liverpool Mercury*, Tuesday May 15, 1894, page 5; International Olympic Committee formed – The

new Olympiads, *Pall Mall Gazette*, Friday November 23, 1894, page 10; Gladstone resigns – Lord Rosebery appointed Prime Minister, *The Western Times*, Tuesday March 6, 1894, page 3; Birth of a royal prince – *The Totnes Times and Devon News*, Saturday June 30, 1894, page 8. With thanks to The British Newspaper Archive

8. Battle of Neuve Chapelle bombardment and casualties – Neuve Chapelle and the Boer War, *The Western Gazette*, Friday April 30, 1915, page 5. With thanks to The British Newspaper Archive

9. Pte John William Turner death – Two Barumites killed in action, *The North Devon Journal*, Thursday March 25, 1915, page 6. With thanks to The British Newspaper Archive

10. Jack's death – *The Western Times*, Monday June 14, 1915, page 2. With thanks to The British Newspaper Archive

11. Jack's will – Gov.uk (www.gov.uk/probate-search)

12. Boulogne Eastern Cemetery – Commonwealth War Graves Commission (www.cwgc.org)

Chapter 9: Albert – cut down at Battle of Loos
Primary sources

A War Diary for 8th (Service) Battalion of the Devonshire Regiment – National Archives (www.nationalarchives.gov.uk)

B *The Devonshire Regiment 1914–1918*, compiled by C T Atkinson, Naval and Military Press Ltd edition, 2002 (www.naval-military-press.com)

C British Newspaper Archive (www.britishnewspaperarchive.co.uk) – *The Western Times, The Devon and Exeter Gazette*

D Parish records for Witheridge – Devon Heritage Centre

E Ancestry.co.uk military records (soldiers who died in the Great War, Army registers of soldiers' effects, medal card, service awards) and Census returns for 1901 and 1911 (www.ancestry.co.uk)

1. 'Witheridge lad dies of wounds' – *The Western Times*, Friday October 22, 1915, page 11. With thanks to The British Newspaper Archive

2. Lt-Colonel Worrall lecture – The Devons: What they did in the Great War, *The Western Times*, Thursday November 25, 1920, page 2. With thanks to The British Newspaper Archive

3. 'P' Helmets – German threat of new poison gas, *The Scotsman*, Monday February 25, 1918, page 4. With thanks to The British Newspaper Archive

4. The Battle of Loos casualties – The Long, Long Trail (www. longlongtrail.co.uk)

5. Loos guns paraded through Exeter – Splendid story of heroism, *The Devon and Exeter Gazette*, Friday November 19, 1915, page 14. With thanks to The British Newspaper Archive

6. Memorable deeds of the 8th Devons – *The Western Times*, Tuesday April 8, 1919, page 2. With thanks to The British Newspaper Archive

7. Loos gun presented to Queensland – *Brisbane Courier*, October 20, 1916; *The Daily Standard*, Brisbane, August 20, 1917
8. 1895: W G Grace, 100 centuries – Honouring Dr Grace, *East and South Devon Advertiser*, Saturday June 29, 1895, page 2. With thanks to The British Newspaper Archive
9. Albert's will – Gov.uk (www.gov.uk/probate-search)
10. Wimereux Communal Cemetery – Commonwealth War Graves Commission (www.cwgc.org)

Chapter 10: Sam – killed on first day of Battle of the Somme
Primary sources
A   War Diaries for 8th (Service) and 2nd Battalions of the Devonshire Regiment – National Archives (www.nationalarchives.gov.uk)
B   *The Devonshire Regiment 1914-1918*, compiled by C T Atkinson, Naval and Military Press Ltd edition, 2002 (www.naval-military-press.com)
C   British Newspaper Archive (www.britishnewspaperarchive.co.uk) – *The Western Times, The Devon and Exeter Gazette, The Western Morning News and Mercury*
D   Rackenford parish records – Devon Heritage Centre
E   Ancestry.co.uk military records (soldiers who died in the Great War, Army registers of soldiers' effects, medal card, service awards) and Census returns for 1901 and 1911 (www.ancestry.co.uk)

1. Sam shot in the chest – News of the West, *The Western Times*, Friday October 1, 1915, page 14. With thanks to The British Newspaper Archive
2. July 1, 1916, a 'beautiful' and 'breathless blue morning' – Battle of the Somme, Sir Herbert Russell, *The Western Morning News and Mercury*, Thursday July 1, 1926, page 6. With thanks to The British Newspaper Archive
3. Bloodiest day in British military history – Sir Herbert Russell, *The Western Morning News and Mercury*, Thursday July 1, 1926, page 6. With thanks to The British Newspaper Archive
4. The attack on Mametz – The Long, Long Trail (www.longlongtrail.co.uk)
5. Copp brothers killed in action on July 1, 1916 – District news: Bradninch, *The Devon and Exeter Gazette*, Friday July 21, 1916, page 13 and Friday August 4, 1916, page 13. With thanks to the British Newspaper Archive; Commonwealth War Graves Commission, Thiepval Memorial records (www.cwgc.org)
6. Sam's burial, Devonshire Cemetery – Rackenford news, *The Western Times*, Friday July 28, 1916, page 9. With thanks to The British Newspaper Archive
7. Sam's memorial service – News of the West: Rackenford, *The Western Times*, Friday August 4, 1916, page 15. With thanks to The British Newspaper Archive

8. Devonshire Cemetery – Commonwealth War Graves Commission
9. A Letter from London – The Somme, *The Devon and Exeter Gazette*, Friday July 10, 1936, page 11. With thanks to The British Newspaper Archive
10. Remarkable chance meeting – Eleven years after, *The Western Morning News and Mercury*, Tuesday October 11, 1927, page 11. With thanks to The British Newspaper Archive.
11. *SS Osmanieh* sinking – uboat.net (www.uboat.net)
12. Sam's admission to St Mark's Hospital – Rackenford news, *The Western Times*, Friday January 8, 1915, page 10. With thanks to The British Newspaper Archive
13. St Mark's Hospital – The Wartime Memories Project (www.wartimememories.co.uk)
14. Sam promoted to lance-corporal – News of the West: Rackenford, *The Western Times*, Friday January 14, 1916, page 14. With thanks to The British Newspaper Archive
15. Captain Geoffrey Philip Tregelles – *The Devonshire Regiment 1914-1918*
16. Captain Tregelles Memorial – *The North Devon Journal*, Thursday January 11, 1917, page 5. With thanks to The British Newspaper Archive

Chapter 11: John Francis 'Frank' – shelled while enjoying a cup of tea
Primary sources
A   War Diary for 2nd Battalion of the Devonshire Regiment – National Archives (www.nationalarchives.gov.uk)
B   *The Devonshire Regiment 1914–1918*, compiled by C T Atkinson, Naval and Military Press Ltd edition, 2002 (www.naval-military-press.com)
C   British Newspaper Archive (www.britishnewspaperarchive.co.uk) – *The Western Times, The Devon and Exeter Gazette, The Western Morning News and Mercury*
D   Rackenford parish records – Devon Heritage Centre
E   Ancestry.co.uk military records (soldiers who died in the Great War, Army registers of soldiers' effects, medal card, service awards) and Census returns for 1901 and 1911 (www.ancestry.co.uk)

1. Body found 12 years later – Reported missing in 1916, *The Western Morning News and Mercury*, Friday March 9, 1928, page 11. With thanks to The British Newspaper Archive
2. 2nd Lt Eric Melville Gould – Killed in action, *The Western Times*, Saturday July 8, 1916, page 3; *The North Devon Journal*, Thursday July 13, 1916, page 5. With thanks to The British Newspaper Archive
3. Lance-Cpl William Cann – Thrilling escapes of a Thorverton lad, *The Western Times*, Friday August 4, 1916, page 8. With thanks to The British Newspaper Archive
4. Frank 'instantly killed'/memorial service – News of the West:

Rackenford, *The Western Times*, Friday October 6, 1916, page 10. With thanks to The British Newspaper Archive

5. Frank's death – News of the West: Rackenford, *The Western Times*, Friday September 22, 1916, page 9. With thanks to The British Newspaper Archive

6. Vermelles British Cemetery – Commonwealth War Graves Commission (www.cwgc.org)

7. 1891: Henry Tandey – On show, *The Midland Daily Telegraph*, Monday August 14, 1939, page 4. With thanks to The British Newspaper Archive

8. The Great Blizzard – The Blizzard, *Exeter Flying Post*, Saturday March 14, 1891, page 3; The gale and snowstorm, *The Western Times*, Thursday March 12, 1891, page 3 and Tuesday March 17, 1891, pages 2, 3 and 5. With thanks to The British Newspaper Archive

9. 2nd Devons in Malta – Inspection at Malta, *The Devon and Exeter Gazette*, Friday January 19, 1912, page 10. With thanks to The British Newspaper Archive

10. Frank's close shave at Neuve Chapelle – News of the West: Rackenford, *The Western Times*, Friday November 19, 1915, page 15. With thanks to The British Newspaper Archive

11. Comrades at school and in field of battle – News of the West: Rackenford, *The Western Times*, Friday July 28, 1916, page 9. With thanks to The British Newspaper Archive

12. Archie Snell taken prisoner – News of the West, Rackenford, *The Western Times*, Friday December 13, 1918, page 10. With thanks to The British Newspaper Archive

13. Captain James Allfrey Andrews memorial – Salehurst roll of honour, courtesy of Chris Comber (www.roll-of-honour.com)

14. Jago memorial chapel – War memorials, *The Western Morning News*, Monday December 22, 1919, page 7. With thanks to The British Newspaper Archive

Chapter 12: William Henry – struck down by heart disease in Mesopotamian desert

Primary sources

A   War Diary for 1/4th Battalion of the Devonshire Regiment – National Archives (www.nationalarchives.gov.uk)

B   *The Devonshire Regiment 1914–1918*, compiled by C T Atkinson, Naval and Military Press Ltd edition, 2002 (www.naval-military-press.com)

C   British Newspaper Archive (www.britishnewspaperarchive.co.uk) – *The Western Times, The Devon and Exeter Gazette, The North Devon Journal, The Western Daily Press*

D   Parish records for Tiverton – Devon Heritage Centre

E   Ancestry.co.uk military records (soldiers who died in the Great War, Army registers of soldiers' effects, medal card, service awards) and Census returns for 1901 and 1911 (www.ancestry.co.uk)

1. Siege of Kut – Commonwealth War Graves Commission (www.cwgc. org)
2. William's will – Gov.uk (www.gov.uk/probate-search)
3. Sheikh Sa'ad – *The British Army in Mesopotamia in 1914–1918*, by Paul Knight, published by McFarland & Co, 2013
4. Lt-General Lake despatch – recorded in *The Gazette* (*London Gazette*), issue 29823, November 14, 1916 (www.thegazette.co.uk)
5. Flies, sand heat: Plagues of Mesopotamia, Edmund Candler, *The Western Daily Press*, Friday July 14, 1916, page 7. With thanks to The British Newspaper Archive
6. Pte Thomas Green – Barumite's experiences in Mesopotamia, *The North Devon Journal*, Thursday July 20, 1916, page 5. With thanks to The British Newspaper Archive
7. William's death – News of the West: Tiverton, *The Western Times*, Friday June 30, 1916, page 10. With thanks to The British Newspaper Archive
8. Basra Memorial – Commonwealth War Graves Commission
9. Basra Memorial unveiling –*The Western Morning News and Mercury*, Thursday March 28, 1929, page 6. With thanks to The British Newspaper Archive
10. 1890: Forth Bridge opens – *The Western Times*, Wednesday March 5, 1890, page 4; Colliery explosion – *Exeter Flying Post*, Saturday February 8, 1890, page 7. With thanks to The British Newspaper Archive
11. 1/4th Devons in India – On duty in India, *The Western Times*, Monday December 6, 1915, page 2. With thanks to The British Newspaper Archive
12. The Kitchener Test – *The Western Times*, Tuesday February 22, 1916, page 3. With thanks to The British Newspaper Archive
13. 1/4th Devons leave India – Regrets and congratulations, *The Devon and Exeter Gazette*, Friday March 24, 1916, page 9. With thanks to The British Newspaper Archive
14. Rev Charles Arthur Vodden – *The North Devon Journal*, Thursday December 13, 1923, page 7. With thanks to The British Newspaper Archive
15. Pte Samuel Sanders – Roll of Honour, *The Western Times*, Thursday May 23, 1918, page 3. With thanks to The British Newspaper Archive
16. 2nd Lt Ricardio Sidney Rowse – Officer's sudden death, *The Western Times*, Tuesday September 7, 1915, page 3. With thanks to The British Newspaper Archive
17. Sgt George Kerswell – Braunton sergeant's experiences in Mesopotamia, *The North Devon Journal*, Thursday August 10, 1916, page 2. With thanks to The British Newspaper Archive
18. Major John Morth Woollcombe memorial – Ashbury Memorial, *The Devon and Exeter Gazette*, Wednesday February 2, 1921, page 3. With thanks to The British Newspaper Archive

19. Major Woollcombe memorial window – *The Western Times*, Thursday June 15, 1922, page 3. With thanks to The British Newspaper Archive
20. Lt-Colonel Acland Troyte memorial – 1/4th Devon memorial unveiled at Bampton Church, *The Western Times*, Friday June 20, 1924, page 8. With thanks to The British Newspaper Archive

Chapter 13: Walter – killed just 52 days before the war ends
Primary sources
A War Diaries for 1st Battalion Loyal North Lancashire Regiment and 8th (Service) Battalion of Border Regiment – National Archives (www.nationalarchives.gov.uk)
B British Newspaper Archive (www.britishnewspaperarchive.co.uk) – *The Western Times*
C Parish records for Tiverton – Devon Heritage Centre
D Ancestry.co.uk military records (soldiers who died in the Great War, Army registers of soldiers' effects, medal card, service awards) and Census returns for 1901 and 1911 (www.ancestry.co.uk)

1. Battle of Epehy – The Long, Long Trail (www.longlongtrail.co.uk)
2. Vis-en-Artois Memorial – Commonwealth War Graves Commission (www.cwgc.org)
3. Messines attack – Messines captured, *The Western Times*, Friday June 8, 1917, page 12. With thanks to The British Newspaper Archive
4. Battles of the Lys – The Long, Long Trail

Chapter 14: Sidney – fatally wounded in Battle of Langemarck
Primary sources
A War Diary for the 1st Battalion Queen's Westminster Rifles – National Archives (www.nationalarchives.gov.uk)
B *The War History of the 1st Battalion Queen's Westminster Rifles, 1914–18*, by Major J Q Henriques, Naval and Military Press Ltd edition, 2003 (www.naval-military-press.com)
C Ancestry.co.uk military records (soldiers who died in the Great War, Army registers of soldiers' effects, medal card, service awards) and Census returns for 1901 and 1911 (www.ancestry.co.uk)

1. The Battle of Langemarck – *From Bapaume to Passchendaele*, by Philip Gibbs, published by Echo Library, 2014 (ISBN: 978-1-40684-296-8), and can be ordered on Amazon or through any bookseller
2. Brandhoek New Military Cemetery No 3 – Commonwealth War Graves Commission (www.cwgc.org)
3. Rifleman Raymond Norrington – his story first appeared in *The Suttonian* Magazine and was republished in *A Small School in the Great War: The story of Sutton County School and its old boys in World War 1*, written and published by Arthur Edward Jones, 1975

4. 2/5th (Territorial) Battalion of the Royal West Kent Regiment – The Long, Long Trail (www.longlongtrail.co.uk)
5. Sidney's will – Gov.uk (www.gov.uk/probate-search)

Part three: The grandsons who survived

Chapter 15: Archie – survivor of two of the greatest ever cavalry charges
Primary sources

A   *The Thirteenth Hussars in the Great War*, by the Rt Hon Sir Henry Mortimer Durand, first published by William Blackwood and Sons, Edinburgh and London, 1921. Naval and Military Press Ltd edition, 2003 (www.naval-military-press.com)

B   13th Hussars' war diary – National Archives (www.nationalarchives.gov.uk)

C   Ancestry.co.uk military records (medal card, service awards, Silver Badge records) and Census returns for 1901 and 1911 (www.ancestry.co.uk)

D   Lynne Roberts, Thorverton, Archie's grand-daughter

1. The Fight at Lajj – *The Thirteenth Hussars in the Great War*
2. The Charge of the Light Brigade – National Archives
3. Capture of Baghdad – British in Baghdad, *The Western Times*, Wednesday March 14, 1917, page 2. With thanks to The British Newspaper Archive (www.britishnewspaperarchive.co.uk)
4. 13th Hussars' memorial – Hussar Memorial, *The Lichfield Mercury*, Friday August 6, 1920, page 7. With thanks to The British Newspaper Archive
5. Last survivor of Charge of the Light Brigade – Last of the 600, *Aberdeen Press and Journal*, Friday May 20, 1927, page 7. With thanks to The British Newspaper Archive

Chapter 16: Frank – shot in the head in fierce fighting in Palestine
Primary sources

A   War Diary for 16th (Royal 1st Devon and Royal North Devon Yeomanry) Battalion of the Devonshire Regiment – National Archives (www.nationalarchives.gov.uk)

B   *The Devonshire Regiment 1914–1918*, compiled by C T Atkinson, Naval and Military Press Ltd edition, 2002 (www.naval-military-press.com)

C   *The 74th Yeomanry Division in Syria and France*, by Major C H Dudley Ward, Naval and Military Press Ltd edition, 2004 (www.naval-military-press.com)

D   British Newspaper Archive (www.britishnewspaperarchive.co.uk) – *The Western Times*, *The Devon and Exeter Gazette*, *The Western Morning News*

C   Ancestry.co.uk military records (service and pension records, medal card, service awards, Silver Badge records) and Census returns for 1901 and 1911 (www.ancestry.co.uk)

1. Upper Beth-Horon – *The Bible* (First Book of Kings)
2. Joshua's cry for sun to 'stand still' – *The Bible* (Book of Joshua)
3. Jerusalem War Cemetery, Jerusalem Memorial, Ramleh War Cemetery, near Tel Aviv – Commonwealth War Graves Commission (www.cwgc.org)
4. Sgt Ernest J Ivey – From Turkish captivity, *The Western Times*, Friday December 27, 1918, page 5. With thanks to The British Newspaper Archive
5. General Allenby enters Jerusalem – Devoted guard over sacred places, *The Western Morning News*, Thursday December 13, 1917, page 5. With thanks to The British Newspaper Archive
6. 1892: Two Prime Ministers – *The Bideford Weekly Gazette*, Tuesday August 23, 1892, page 2; The Adventures of Sherlock Holmes – New publications, *The Western Times*, Friday December 16, 1892 page 2. With thanks to The British Newspaper Archive
7. Royal 1st Devon Yeomanry annual training – The Yeomanry camp at Rousdon, *The Devon and Exeter Gazette*, Tuesday May 7, 1912, page 4. With thanks to The British Newspaper Archive
8. The *Titanic* disaster – Liner collides with iceberg, *The Western Times*, April 16, 1912, page 8 and Tuesday April 23, 1912, page 8. With thanks to The British Newspaper Archive
9. *Britannic* sinking – Britannic mined or torpedoed, *The Western Morning News*, Thursday November 23, 1916, page 5. With thanks to The British Newspaper Archive
10. Royal 1st Devon Yeomanry in Gallipoli – with thanks to www.winkleighonline.com
11. Captain Edward Hain letter – Death of a Cornish officer, *The Western Times*, Thursday November 18, 1915, page 2. With thanks to The British Newspaper Archive
12. Private Grater letter – A glimpse at Devon lads nearing Jerusalem, *The Western Times*, February 22, 1918, page 10. With thanks to the British Newspaper Archive
13. *HMT Leasowe Castle* sinking – Sunk by submarine in the Mediterranean, *The Western Times*, Thursday May 30, 1918, page 4. With thanks to The British Newspaper Archive; uboat.net (www.uboat.net)
14. Pte John William Entwistle – with thanks to the Haslingden War Heroes blog (www.haslingdenwarheroes.blogspot.co.uk)
15. Lance-Cpl William Lock – News of the West: Parracombe, *The Western Times*, Friday September 13, 1918, page 9. With thanks to The British Newspaper Archive
16. Royal 1st Devon Yeomanry Memorial – Devon Yeomanry Memorial, *The Western Morning News*, Monday May 26, 1924, page 3. With thanks to The British Newspaper Archive

Chapter 17: John Francis Bryant – how he faced 70 days of hell on the Somme
Primary sources

A   War Diaries for 9th Battalion of the Devonshire Regiment and the 20th Infantry Brigade – National Archives (www.nationalarchives.gov.uk)

B   *The Devonshire Regiment 1914–1918*, compiled by C T Atkinson, Naval and Military Press Ltd edition, 2002 (www.naval-military-press.com)

C   British Newspaper Archive (www.britishnewspaperarchive.co.uk) – *The Western Times*

D   Ancestry.co.uk military records (medal card, service awards, Silver Badge records) and Census returns for 1891, 1901 and 1911 (www.ancestry.co.uk)

1.   Great achievement of the 9th Devons – Ginchy: village captured, *The Western Times*, Friday April 25, 1919, page 12. With thanks to The British Newspaper Archive

2.   1883: Douglas Fairbanks – *The Western Morning News*, Wednesday December 13, 1939, page 3; Victoria Hall tragedy – Terrible calamity at Sunderland, *The Exeter and Plymouth Gazette*, Friday June 22, 1883, page 2; Thomas Edison – Electric lighting in America, *Exeter Flying Post*, Wednesday January 10, 1883, page 6; Treasure Island – Just published, *The Exeter and Plymouth Gazette*, Friday December 14, 1883, page 8. With thanks to The British Newspaper Archive

3.   2nd Highland Field Company of the Royal Engineers – The Long, Long Trail (www.longlongtrail.co.uk)

4.   Royal Engineers' 112th Railway Construction Company – The Long, Long Trail

5.   Mills grenade – Famous inventor dies at Weston-Super-Mare: Sir William Mills, of hand-grenade renown, *The Western Daily Press*, Friday January 8, 1932, page 10. With thanks to The British Newspaper Archive

Chapter 18: George – artillery veteran of two wars
Primary sources

A   War diaries for 112 Brigade of the Royal Field Artillery and 26 Artillery Brigade – National Archives (www.nationalarchives.gov.uk)

B   British Newspaper Archive (www.britishnewspaperarchive.co.uk) – *The Western Times, The Devon and Exeter Gazette, The Western Morning News*

C   Ancestry.co.uk military records (service records, medal card, service awards) and Census returns for 1881, 1891, 1901 and 1911 (www.ancestry.co.uk)

1.   Vimy Ridge attack – *The Western Mail*, Thursday June 1, 1916, page 5. With thanks to the British Newspaper Archive.

2.   Royal Munster Fusiliers' at Mons and Etreux British Cemetery – Commonwealth War Graves Commission (www.cwgc.org)

3. Royal Artillery casualties – Royal Artillery Memorial, Hyde Park Corner, London
4. Lloyd George succeeds Asquith – News in a nutshell, *The Western Times*, Friday December 8, 1916, page 7. With thanks to The British Newspaper Archive
5. 'Golden age' of British Empire – National Archives
6. Devons in Boer War – Devon's tribute, *The Western Times*, Monday June 1, 1903, page 4. With thanks to The British Newspaper Archive
7. Battle of Wagon Hill – Devons' famous stand in Boer War, *The Western Morning News and Mercury*, Tuesday January 6, 1925, page 6. With thanks to The British Newspaper Archive

Chapter 19: William John – naval stoker who survived torpedo attack
Primary sources
A   *HMS King Alfred* Royal Navy log book – with thanks to the late Gordon Smith, creator of Naval History.net (www.naval-history.net)
B   British Newspaper Archive (www.britishnewspaperarchive.co.uk) – *The Western Times*
C   Ancestry.co.uk military records (Naval service records, service awards) and Census returns for 1901 and 1911 (www.ancestry.co.uk)
D   Uboat.net – with thanks to Gudmunder Helgason (www.uboat.net)

1. *HMS King Alfred* – Naval manoeuvres, *London Evening Standard*, Monday August 3, 1903, page 2. With thanks to The British Newspaper Archive
2. *HMS Bellona* – The Bellona's trials, *The Western Morning News*, Saturday November 13, 1909, page 8. With thanks to The British Newspaper Archive
3. Stoker deaths, Battle of Jutland – Naval History.net
4. Loss of British ships, Battle of Jutland – Naval-History.net
5. *HMS Drake torpedoed* – uboat.net; Naval-History.net
6. *HMS Cornwallis* torpedoed – uboat.net; Naval-History.net
7. *HMS Hawke* torpedoed – uboat.net; Naval-History.net; History Hub Ulster (www.historyhubulster.co.uk)
8. *HMS Albacore* explosion – Destroyer explosion, *The Western Times*, Tuesday April 7, 1914, page 8. With thanks to The British Newspaper Archive
9. French battleship explosion – *The Western Times*, Thursday January 9, 1914 page 5. With thanks to The British Newspaper Archive
10. *HMS Titania* stoker killed – Funeral of stoker, *The Western Times*, Tuesday December 28, 1915, page 3. With thanks to The British Newspaper Archive
11. *HMS Galatea* stoker thrown overboard – *The Western Times*, Tuesday March 25, 1919, page 6. With thanks to The British Newspaper Archive

12. Lynmouth Lifeboat launch – A difficult and arduous feat, *The West Somerset Free Press*, Saturday January 21, 1899, page 7. With thanks to The British Newspaper Archive

13. Tiverton County Sessions – *The Western Times*, Friday May 14, 1920, page 8. With thanks to The British Newspaper Archive

Chapter 20: Thomas – twice saved from fighting in the war
Primary sources

A *The Devonshire Regiment 1914–1918*, compiled by C T Atkinson, Naval and Military Press Ltd edition, 2002 (www.naval-military-press.com)

B British Newspaper Archive (www.britishnewspaperarchive.co.uk) – *The Western Times, The Western Morning News, The Devon and Exeter Gazette*

C Ancestry.co.uk military records (service records, medal card, service awards), Census returns for 1901 and 1911 and probate records (www.ancestry.co.uk)

1. Captain Wilfred Peek, High Sheriff of Devon 1912 – Passing of well-known Devon Baronet in Paris, *The Western Times*, Friday October 14, 1927, page 2. With thanks to The British Newspaper Archive

2. Re-examination of discharged men, House of Commons, June 1917 – Medical re-examination scandal, *The Western Times*, Friday June 22, 1917, page 12; Parliament and the medical boards, *The Western Morning News*, Friday June 22, 1917, page 4. With thanks to The British Newspaper Archive

3. Select Committee on Medical Re-examination hearing, July 1917 – Remarkable evidence, *The Devon and Exeter Gazette*, Wednesday July 11, 1917, page 3. With thanks to The British Newspaper Archive

4. Yelverton postmaster Leonard Stone – Heart disease in khaki, *The Western Morning News*, Tuesday July 4, 1916, page 7. With thanks to The British Newspaper Archive

5. Reginald Worth – Calstock case, *The Western Morning News*, Wednesday September 26, 1917, page 5. With thanks to The British Newspaper Archive

6. William Henry Chard – *The Western Times*, Tuesday March 14, 1916, page 3. With thanks to The British Newspaper Archive

7. 500 men a year invalided by valvular heart disease – *The Western Morning News and Mercury*, Friday September 28, 1923, page 6. With thanks to The British Newspaper Archive

8. Death of Heavitree wheelwright – Soldier's death, *The Western Times*, Wednesday November 30, 1921, page 2. With thanks to The British Newspaper Archive

9. Pte Fred Blackmore – *The Western Times*, Monday November 11, 1918, page 4. With thanks to The British Newspaper Archive

10. 2nd Lt P G Handford – *The Western Times*, Tuesday November 12, 1918, page 2. With thanks to The British Newspaper Archive

11. Lt George Raymond Dallas Moor – Death of Devon VC, *The Devon and Exeter Gazette*, Friday November 8, 1918, page 8. With thanks to The British Newspaper Archive

12. Rev G J Lester – *The Western Times*, Friday December 20, 1918, page 6. With thanks to The British Newspaper Archive

13. Pte Leslie Harold Stemson – *The Western Morning News*, Monday December 9, 1918, page 4. With thanks to The British Newspaper Archive

14. Harold Street – *The Western Times*, Friday February 14, 1919, page 7. With thanks to The British Newspaper Archive

Chapter 21: George Burnett – one of the great unsung heroes of the war
Primary sources

A   British Newspaper Archive (www.britishnewspaperarchive.co.uk) – *St Andrews Citizen, Derby Daily Telegraph, The Bedfordshire Times and Independent, The Hartland and West Country Chronicle, The Western Morning News, The Devon and Exeter Gazette*

B   Ancestry.co.uk military records (medal card, service awards), Census returns for 1901 and 1911 and probate records (www.ancestry.co.uk)

1. ASC losses 1914–1918 – RASC Memorial, Aldershot

2. ASC achievements 'closely allied to the miraculous' – The Army Service Corps, *The St Andrew's Citizen*, Saturday March 18, 1916, page 3. With thanks to The British Newspaper Archive

3. Ally Sloper's Cavalry – The Army Service Corps, *The St Andrew's Citizen*, Saturday March 18, 1916, page 3. With thanks to The British Newspaper Archive

4. Cpl J Hymers' article – Views of a disabled corporal, *Derby Daily Telegraph*, May 19, 1916, page 3. Article © Trinity Mirror. Reproduced with permission of the British Newspaper Archive.

5. Braemar Castle – The Army Service Corps, *The Bedfordshire Times and Independent*, Friday December 27, 1912, page 12. With thanks to The British Newspaper Archive

6. 'The Army Service Corps have never failed to meet the needs of our troops' – Field Marshall Sir Douglas Haig despatch, *The Gazette* (*London Gazette*), issue 30462, January 4, 1918 (www.thegazette.co.uk)

7. British First Army offensives – The Long, Long Trail (www.longlongtrail.co.uk)

8. ASC officers, warrant officers, NCOs and men – Proposed war memorial, *The Western Morning News*, Monday March 10, 1919, page 7. With thanks to The British Newspaper Archive

9. ASC becomes RASC – *The Devon and Exeter Gazette*, Saturday December 21, 1918, page 4. With thanks to The British Newspaper Archive

10. Tribute to ASC – *The Hartland and West Country Chronicle*, February 26, 1916, page 14. With thanks to The British Newspaper Archive

Chapter 22: Ben – the only one of three brothers to come home
Primary sources

A   British Newspaper Archive (www.britishnewspaperarchive.co.uk) – *The Western Times, The Western Morning News*

B   Ancestry.co.uk military records (medal card, service awards), Census returns for 1901 and 1911 and probate records (www.ancestry.co.uk)

C   Field Marshall Sir Douglas Haig despatches – *The London Gazette* (www. thegazette.co.uk)

1. Work of the Royal Engineers – The Long, Long Trail (www. longlongtrail.co.uk)
2. All branches of Royal Engineers praised – Field Marshall Sir Douglas Haig despatch, recorded in *The Gazette* (*London Gazette*) issue 31111, January 3, 1919
3. Bridging of the Somme at Brie – Field Marshall Sir Douglas Haig despatch, recorded in *The Gazette* (*London Gazette*), issue 30140, June 19, 1917
4. 'Peculiarly heavy burden' on the Royal Engineers – Field Marshall Sir Douglas Haig despatch, recorded in *The Gazette* (*London Gazette*), issue 30462, January 4, 1918
5. Tunnelling companies 'possess in the highest degree the qualities of courage, perseverance, and self-sacrifice' – Field Marshall Sir Douglas Haig despatch, recorded in *The Gazette* (*London Gazette*), issue 29599, May 26, 1916
6. 14,000 German mines and traps – Field Marshall Sir Douglas Haig despatch, recorded in *The Gazette* (*London Gazette*), issue 31111, January 3, 1919
7. Royal Engineers Memorial unveiling – Engineers' memorial, *The Western Morning News*, Thursday July 20, 1922, page 6. With thanks to The British Newspaper Archive
8. Ben joins Royal Engineers – News of the West: Rackenford, *The Western Times*, Friday October 1, 1915, page 14. With thanks to The British Newspaper Archive
9. Ben home from Flanders – News of the West: Rackenford, *The Western Times*, Friday February 8, 1918, page 9. With thanks to The British Newspaper Archive
10. Court injunction – Village vicar's action, *The Western Morning News*, Friday February 11, 1944, page 2. With thanks to The British Newspaper Archive
11. Acting Major Arnold Horace Santo Waters – Valour at canal crossing, *The Western Morning News*, Friday February 14, 1919, page 6. With thanks to The British Newspaper Archive

Chapter 23: Samuel and Sidney – new tragedy strikes 20 years after the war
Primary sources
A   British Newspaper Archive (www.britishnewspaperarchive.co.uk) – *The Western Times, The Devon and Exeter Gazette*
B   Ancestry.co.uk Census returns for 1901 and 1911 (www.ancestry.co.uk)

1.   Samuel's funeral – News of the West: Cruwys Morchard, *The Western Times*, Friday October 7, 1938, page 13. With thanks to The British Newspaper Archive
2.   United Services Fund – Distribution scheme explained in Exeter, *The Western Times*, Friday March 26, 1920, page 7. With thanks to The British Newspaper Archive
3.   Samuel Roberts Snr funeral – News of the West: Cruwys Morchard, *The Western Times*, Friday December 1, 1933, page 13. With thanks to The British Newspaper Archive

Chapter 24: Archie, Harry and Walter – the Sandford survivors
Primary sources
A   British Newspaper Archive (www.britishnewspaperarchive.co.uk) – *The Western Times, The Devon and Exeter Gazette*
B   Ancestry.co.uk Census returns for 1891, 1901 and 1911 and probate records (www.ancestry.co.uk)

1.   200 Sandford men in 'active service' – Sandford Parish Records, Devon Heritage Centre
2.   Henry Roberts, Sandford Mill – *A Parish Patchwork* by Daphne Munday – first printed in 1985 and reprinted in 2000 and 2013
3.   Archie 'gave promise of great usefulness' – News of the West: Sandford, *The Western Times*, Friday March 23, 1917, page 10. With thanks to The British Newspaper Archive
4.   Crediton Rural Tribunal – *The Western Times*, Tuesday February 20, 1917, page 3. With thanks to The British Newspaper Archive
5.   'Farewell message' – News of the West: Sandford, *The Western Times*, Friday May 25, 1917, page 9. With thanks to The British Newspaper Archive
6.   Funeral bearer – News of the West: Sandford, *The Western Times*, Friday April 25, 1919, page 9. With thanks to The British Newspaper Archive
7.   John Densem – Roll of Honour, *The Western Times*, Saturday September 7, 1918, page 3. With thanks to The British Newspaper Archive
8.   Walter, Crediton Rural Tribunal – *The Western Times*, Tuesday February 20, 1917, page 3. With thanks to The British Newspaper Archive
9.   Mary Roberts funeral – District news: Sandford, *The Devon and Exeter Gazette*, Friday January 20, 1933, page 5. With thanks to The British Newspaper Archive
10. John Roberts death – Copplestone resident widely mourned, *The Western*

Times, Friday September 22, 1939, page 8. With thanks to The British Newspaper Archive

Part four: The grandsons-in-law who survived – and a great nephew killed in action

Chapter 25: Wilfred Banting – wounded in courageous attack near Kut
Primary sources
A   War Diary for 1/4th Battalion of the Devonshire Regiment – National Archives (www.nationalarchives.gov.uk)
B   *The Devonshire Regiment 1914–1918*, compiled by C T Atkinson, Naval and Military Press Ltd edition, 2002 (www.naval-military-press.com)
C   British Newspaper Archive (www.britishnewspaperarchive.co.uk) – *The Western Times*
D   Ancestry.co.uk military records (medal card, service awards) and Census returns for 1901 and 1911. Service records for his brother, Albert (www.ancestry.co.uk)

1.   'Sight of a lifetime …' – *The Devonshire Regiment 1914–1918*
2.   Roll of honour – *The Western Times*, Tuesday March 20, 1917, page 4. With thanks to The British Newspaper Archive

Chapter 26: William Western – a blacksmith in huge ASC 'tin town'
Primary sources
A   British Newspaper Archive (www.britishnewspaperarchive.co.uk*)* – *The Western Daily Press*
B   Ancestry.co.uk military records (service records, medal card, service awards) and Census returns for 1901 and 1911 (www.ancestry.co.uk)

1.   'Tin town' – Scene at a remount depot, *The Western Daily Press*, Friday October 30, 1914, page 5. With thanks to The British Newspaper Archive
2.   Frontiersmen – Frontiersmen and horses, *The Western Daily Press*, Monday October 26, 1914, page 5; Breaking in Canadian horses, *The Western Daily Press*, Friday October 30, 1914, page 5. With thanks to The British Newspaper Archive
3.   Shirehampton statistics – Praise for Shirehampton, *The Western Daily Press*, Thursday April 3, 1919, page 5 and Thursday September 4, 1919, page 5. With thanks to The British Newspaper Archive
4.   Royal visit – Royal surprise visit to Bristol, *The Western Daily Press*, Wednesday September 8, 1915, page 5. With thanks to The British Newspaper Archive
5.   Ministry of Munitions Auction – *The Western Daily Press*, Saturday January 3, 1920, page 1 and Saturday January 24, 1920, page 7. With thanks to The British Newspaper Archive

6. Dismantling of depot – Shirehampton Remount Depot, *The Western Daily Press*, Monday February 2, 1920, page 4. With thanks to The British Newspaper Archive
7. Sale of equipment – *The Western Daily Press*, Saturday March 27, 1920, page 1. With thanks to The British Newspaper Archive
8. Depot 'gradually disappearing' – Dismantling the remount depot, *The Western Daily Press*, Monday May 10, 1920, page 5. With thanks to The British Newspaper Archive
9. Huts converted to bungalows – Some of Bristol's new dwellings, *The Western Daily Press*, Saturday January 1, 1921, page 3. With thanks to The British Newspaper Archive

Chapter 27: William James – killed in First Battle of Ypres
Primary sources

A War Diary for 1st Battalion of the Coldstream Guards – National Archives (www.nationalarchives.gov.uk)
B *The Coldstream Guards 1914–1918*, by Lt-Col Sir John Ross of Bladensburg, Naval and Military Press Ltd edition, 2003 (www.naval-military-press.com)
C British Newspaper Archive (www.britishnewspaperarchive.co.uk) – *The Devon and Exeter Gazette, The North Devon Journal*
D Ancestry.co.uk military records (medal card, service awards) and Census returns for 1901 and 1911 (www.ancestry.co.uk)

1. Battle of Langemarck – The Long, Long Trail (www.longlongtrail.co.uk)
2. Cpl Drew letter – Mons, Marne, Ypres, *The Devon and Exeter Gazette*, December 15, 1914, page 11. Letter © Trinity Mirror. Reproduced with permission of the British Newspaper Archive
3. Cpl A J Williams – Braunton soldier wounded by dum-dum bullet, *The North Devon Journal*, Thursday December 3, 1914, page 2. With thanks to The British Newspaper Archive
4. Ypres (Menin Gate) Memorial – Commonwealth War Graves Commission (www.cwgc.org)

Part five: Devon's tributes to its fallen heroes

Chapter 28: Memorial to thousands who died in the war
Primary source

A British Newspaper Archive (www.britishnewspaperarchive.co.uk) – *The Western Times, The Devon and Exeter Gazette, The Western Morning News*

1. Devon servicemen and women killed in Great War – 11,601 names, *The Western Times*, Tuesday May 17, 1921, page 5. With thanks to The British Newspaper Archive

2. 'The ceremony touched the souls of those present to their very depths' – County Memorial unveiled, *The Western Times*, Friday May 20, 1921, page 7. With thanks to The British Newspaper Archive
3. 'A wonderful picture of teeming humanity' – Sir Herbert Russell, Impressions of Exeter's great day, *The Western Morning News and Mercury*, Tuesday May 17, 1921, page 4. With thanks to The British Newspaper Archive
4. Sir Edwin Lutyens – County Memorial unveiled, *The Western Times*, Friday May 20, 1921, page 7. With thanks to The British Newspaper Archive
5. Prince unveils memorial – County Memorial unveiled, *The Western Times*, Friday May 20, 1921, page 7. With thanks to The British Newspaper Archive
6. Memorial service 1919 – Our warriors, *The Devon and Exeter Gazette*, Saturday June 7, 1919, page 4. With thanks to The British Newspaper Archive
7. Impressive service – *The Western Times*, Saturday June 7, 1919, page 4. With thanks to The British Newspaper Archive
8. 'The most representative united Devonshire service ever held in the Mother Church' – Devon heroes, *The Devon and Exeter Gazette*, Friday June 13, 1919, page 8. With thanks to The British Newspaper Archive

Chapter 29: How cities, towns and villages honoured their war dead
Primary source
A British Newspaper Archive (www.britishnewspaperarchive.co.uk*) – The Western Times, The Devon and Exeter Gazette, The Western Morning News and Mercury*

1. Fred Selby – Plymouth's gallant 2,000, *The Western Morning News and Mercury*, Monday May 21, 1923, page 3. With thanks to The British Newspaper Archive
2. Exeter Memorial, an 'exquisite work of art' – In proud and grateful memory, *The Western Times*, Friday July 27, 1923, page 3. With thanks to The British Newspaper Archive
3. Earl Beatty speech – Memorable scene, *The Western Morning News and Mercury*, Wednesday July 25, 1923, page 8. With thanks to The British Newspaper Archive
4. Crediton War Memorial unveiling – Crediton Memorial, *The Western Times*, Friday May 18, 1923, page 7. With thanks to The British Newspaper Archive
5. Rackenford War Memorial unveiling – District news: Rackenford, *The Devon and Exeter Gazette*, Friday November 7, 1919, page 13. With thanks to The British Newspaper Archive

6. Cruwys Morchard Memorial – District news, *The Devon and Exeter Gazette*, Thursday April 1, 1920, page 13. With thanks to The British Newspaper Archive

7. Witheridge War Memorial unveiling – Witheridge Historical Archive (memories of Mrs E Williams, www.witheridge-historical-archive.com)

8. Oakford memorial unveiling – News of the West: Oakford, *The Western Times*, Friday April 23, 1920, page 8. With thanks to The British Newspaper Archive

9. Tiverton Memorial Hall and Library opening – Lord Lieutenant opens Tiverton's new hall, *The Devon and Exeter Gazette*, Thursday April 4, 1929, page 7. With thanks to The British Newspaper Archive

10. Tiverton War Memorial, St Peter's Church – Chapel dedicated by the Bishop, *The Western Times*, Friday December 1, 1922, page 3. With thanks to The British Newspaper Archive

11. Morchard Bishop War Memorial unveiling – Morchard Bishop's testimony, *The Western Times*, Monday July 12, 1920, page 3. With thanks to The British Newspaper Archive

12. Barnstaple War Memorial unveiling – Impressive gathering, *The Western Times*, Friday October 20, 1922, page 3. With thanks to The British Newspaper Archive

13. Bideford War Memorial unveiling – Bideford Memorial, *The Western Times*, Friday August 26, 1921, page 10. With thanks to The British Newspaper Archive

14. Zeal Monachorum pulpit – Impressive service, *The Devon and Exeter Gazette*, Tuesday December 4, 1923, page 2. With thanks to The British Newspaper Archive